# DEVELOPING ACADEMIC THINKING SKILLS

## IN GRADES 6–12

A Handbook
of Multiple
Intelligence
Activities

JEFF ZWIERS

Menlo Park, California,
USA

INTERNATIONAL
Reading Association

800 BARKSDALE ROAD, PO BOX 8139
NEWARK, DE 19714-8139, USA
www.reading.org

The International Reading Association attempts, through its publications, to provide a forum for a wide spectrum of opinions on reading. This policy permits divergent viewpoints without implying the endorsement of the Association.

**Editorial Director, Books and Special Projects**   Matthew W. Baker
**Managing Editor**   Shannon T. Fortner
**Permissions Editor**   Janet S. Parrack
**Acquisitions and Communications Coordinator**   Corinne M. Mooney
**Associate Editor, Books**   Charlene M. Nichols
**Administrative Assistant**   Michele Jester
**Assistant Permissions Editor**   Tyanna L. Collins
**Production Department Manager**   Iona Muscella
**Supervisor, Electronic Publishing**   Anette Schütz
**Electronic Publishing Specialist**   R. Lynn Harrison
**Proofreader**   Elizabeth C. Hunt

**Project Editor**   Shannon T. Fortner

**Cover Design**   Linda Steere; cover image, Creatas

**Library of Congress Cataloging-in-Publication Data**
Zwiers, Jeff.
  Developing academic thinking skills in grades 6–12 : a handbook of multiple intelligence activities / Jeff Zwiers.
       p. cm.
Includes bibliographical references and index.
  ISBN 0-87207-557-5
  1. Thought and thinking—Study and teaching (Elementary)—Activity programs—Handbooks, manuals, etc. 2. Thought and thinking—Study and teaching (Secondary)—Activity programs—Handbooks, manuals, etc. 3. Cognitive learning. 4. Multiple intelligences. I. Title.
  LB1590.3.Z95 2004
  370.15'2—dc22
                                                                                               2004013771

# CONTENTS

# PREFACE

There I was, at a meeting working with teachers to develop reading and language activities in content area classrooms, and out of the blue, I started thinking about thinking.

I had been focusing on reading skills for several years when I began to notice that many classroom tasks and texts required additional cognitive skills beyond the 6 to 10 reading strategies usually described in the literature on content reading (including my own book, *Building Reading Comprehension Habits in Grades 6–12: A Toolkit of Classroom Activities*). I realized that students needed to be able to think in the academic ways in which authors or speakers expected them to think during reading and listening. I began to see that the more alignment of thinking existed between the information giver and the receiver, the clearer the receiver's understanding. So, I decided to research thinking processes to better understand the academic thinking skills that supported complex learning.

I started tallying the complex thinking demands that academic discussions, tasks, and tests placed on students. I noticed students struggling with types of thinking that teachers did not consider to be challenging at all; teachers seemed to assume that students could do them. I also developed an eye for the classroom activities that fostered academic thinking in the classroom—and for those that did not. As I shared these observations with teachers, they asked me for a resource that could get them started in designing more effective activities and assessments that cultivated thinking skills in addition to reading strategies. So I started a large binder of notes on thinking, a binder that would eventually become this handbook.

From the many terms used to describe the thinking processes used in teaching and learning, I chose the term *academic thinking skills*. Academic thinking skills, for the purposes of this book, are the mental processes that people use to organize and understand complex concepts. These skills fortify one another and overlap considerably as they work together to achieve their purpose of producing meaning and clarity inside the brain. There is a receptive and productive nature to these skills; we use them to organize information that we take in, which we then process and further organize in order to create new ideas and information to pass on to others.

After deciding to write this handbook, I was immediately confronted with two fundamental questions: (1) Which thinking skills should we teach? (2) How should we teach them? The answers to these questions vary widely. One might find hundreds of similar lists and taxonomies in the existing literature on academic thinking, with even more lists found posted on classroom walls.

## Which Skills to Teach?

To address the first question, then, I decided to first pore over the mountains of local, state, and national content standards. What I found were recurring mentions of thinking processes needed for success on such academic tasks as discussing current events, creating projects, reading articles, writing reports, taking tests, and so on. I then looked to see which thinking skills surfaced most often in the language of secondary-school textbooks and assessments. Finally, I analyzed the writings of the most prominent thinkers on educational thinking, such as Benjamin Bloom, Robert Sternberg, David Ausubel, Robert Marzano, Grant Wiggins, Hilda Taba, Arthur Costa, Barry Beyer, and others.

After cross-referencing and synthesizing all the information I had gathered, I still had a long list of thinking skills. I decided to focus on the types of thinking that (1) students seemed to struggle with the most, (2) were not frequently modeled or explicitly taught in school, (3) were required in order to comprehend the texts most students are asked to read and write, and (4) transferred well across content areas and into the "real" world. The 12 academic thinking skills that "made the cut" into this book are analyzing, comparing, categorizing and classifying, identifying cause and effect, problem solving, persuading, empathizing, synthesizing, interpreting, evaluating, communicating, and applying. These 12 skills combine in a variety of ways to help students understand most of the challenging content concepts taught in school.

# How to Teach Them?

Although I researched numerous books and articles that provided helpful descriptions of thinking skills, the literature lacked two important dimensions, in my opinion. The first dimension was practical suggestions for classroom activities to develop thinking skills within the context of content area teaching. The most common suggestions I found existing in the literature were activities full of questions. Questions, however, tend to limit learning experiences to the level of the student's verbal ability, also called verbal intelligence by Howard Gardner (1999). For many students, particularly the ones who struggle the most in school, using only verbal activities is not the best way to teach. Students often respond better to activities that incorporate other intelligences besides or in addition to the verbal.

Intelligences, as outlined by Gardner (1999), are the skills and abilities to solve problems, create effective products, or provide services that are valuable in one's culture. Verbal and math/logical intelligences are highly valued in the United States, as is evidenced by high-stakes tests. But teachers must also realize the power of using other intelligences in teaching and learning. Hence, one purpose of this book is to provide activities and "idea seedlings" that tap into students' multiple intelligences to develop academic thinking, especially in those students who struggle with the traditional teaching practices that focus on verbal and math/logical intelligences.

Of Gardner's (1999) eight main intelligences, I decided to emphasize four of them: interpersonal, visual, kinesthetic, and musical. I chose these four because of their prevalence and effectiveness in the research on high-quality teaching practices (Kolb, 1996; Marzano, 2000; Rivard & Bieske, 1993). I also chose them because I have seen activities based on these four intelligences work wonders for engaging students and for teaching academic language, thinking, and content in many secondary classrooms. The acronym GruViMoMaMu is used in this book to help readers remember to incorporate interpersonal, visual, kinesthetic, and musical intelligences: *Gru* is for group, *Vi* is for visual, *Mo* is for movement, *Ma* is for manipulatives, and *Mu* is for music. You will see these abbreviations throughout the activities.

The second dimension lacking in the thinking literature was the importance of academic language and classroom ideas for developing thinking. As I mulled over the conditions that cultivated thinking, I came to realize academic thinking's dependence on academic language. Of course, I was not the first to realize this. Lev Vygotsky described this dependence in 1962. His work has helped people to better understand how language allows them to establish and define a variety of relationships and concepts that make up academic thinking. We can visualize relationships between ideas or items to a certain extent, but soon we need to organize information with words in abstract ways, especially if we want to share our thoughts and information with other people. Thus, a working definition for *academic language* is the set of words and terms used to describe complex concepts and abstract relationships. This language is what we teachers want to hear and see from the mouths and pencils of our students. It is also the language most companies want to hear and see from their employees. Therefore, this book attempts to clarify and deepen teachers' understanding of the different types of academic language, and then to provide engaging ways to integrate its teaching into each lesson.

In grades 6–12, the standards for academic thinking and language increase in number and difficulty. Yet, unfortunately, these are also the grades in which teaching methods tend to become increasingly lecture based, increasingly textbook centered, and often less interesting to a large portion of students. This brings up the question of *how* to teach thinking skills, which is even more difficult than the first question of *which* skills to teach.

To research the most effective hows, I carried out numerous discussions with teachers and made numerous classroom visits, and I analyzed several well-known educational initiatives: backward planning for in-depth understanding (Wiggins & McTighe, 2000), dimensions of learning (Marzano, Pickering, & Arredondo, 1997), and the theory of multiple intelligences (Gardner, 1999). By building on these researchers' work, I set out to create a practical reference for content area teachers to help them tightly weave the teaching of thinking into their practice. This book strongly encourages the teaching of thinking skills in the context of teaching content. We teachers can use thinking activities to fortify content learning, and vice versa. I encourage teachers to approach the design of each lesson and activity with this question in mind: *Which enduring thinking skills and academic language can I build as I also teach the content standards?*

## About This Book

Some readers of this book might ask about the grade-level differences in academic thinking; grades 6–12 seem to cover quite a span on the cognitive spectrum. And yes, a 6th grader's use of persuasion or evaluation tends to be less developed than that of a 12th grader. The younger student tends to lack background knowledge and usually has had less practice with abstract relationships than the older student. Much of the difference, however, exists in the sophistication of the language used. For instance, I have seen my 6th-grade ELD (English Language Development) students come up with very effective arguments and counterarguments in persuasive assignments, along with insightful comments that showed empathy, interpretation, synthesis, and application. The messages were not eloquent, but many were clearer than those of older students. Regardless of grade level, we as teachers must strive to know our students' thinking strengths and weaknesses and then to help them stretch their thinking skills and language as much as possible during the school year. With enough scaffolding and modeling, any activity in this book can be used even in 6th grade; I leave it up to teachers to decide which ones are appropriate or adaptable to their particular settings.

The principal audience for this book is middle school and high school teachers "in the trenches," particularly teachers of content areas that require extensive reading, such as social studies, language arts, and science. (As I work mainly with these three content areas, I included fewer references to math in this book.) Preservice and intern teachers also will find this handbook useful. Teacher trainers who are most likely to benefit from using this book in their classes are those who teach courses in content literacy, academic language development, curriculum planning, and instructional methods. Other educators who might find this book handy are curriculum designers, resource teachers, and administrators who see the need for fortifying the curriculum with the teaching of thinking skills and academic language.

Part I of this book provides foundation and background information for teachers in using the methods. Chapter 1 describes academic thinking skills for teachers who desire a clear and concise foundation; offers a practical explanation of the importance of student background, language, and literacy in developing thinking; and describes the importance of academic language in driving the thinking skills. Chapter 2 discusses the key components of assessment and instruction as they relate to the development of thinking. It includes 10 teacher habits for effective instruction and assessment.

Part II contains the activities, grouped into chapters by thinking skills. Each skill (one skill per chapter) builds on the ones presented before it, so that the thinking skills become somewhat more complex throughout the book. These chapters (3–14) all have a similar format: First, there is a brief explanation of the thinking skill, followed by a list of academic language terms related to the skill and a paragraph frame (a skeleton paragraph to fill in) or two for using the academic language terms. Next come the teaching activities for building the thinking skill. Each teaching activity contains a brief synopsis and then gives the steps for implementing it. The activities follow the GruViMoMaMu sequence: Group activities are listed first, then visual activities, and so forth. (Note that some activities have elements of more than one modality, creating a wide variety of classroom possibilities.)

Part III contains reproducible blackline masters for the activities in chapters 3–14. Sample reproducible forms and worksheets for this book can also be found at the International Reading Association website, www.reading.org, in the Books area of the Publications section. Appendix A offers some additional activities based on the theory of multiple intelligences, Appendix B provides a list of essential questions and controversial issues, and Appendix C lists some familiar songs for use in designing music-based activities.

As a side note, if you also have *Building Reading Comprehension Habits in Grades 6–12*, you will notice that I have put a few of those same activities and graphics into this handbook. I did this because of the overlap that exists between the skills in this book and the habits taught in *Building Reading Comprehension Habits*, and because I realized that many people might not have both books.

The quote "I think, therefore I am" rings true for our students, who are becoming more independent individuals on what often seems to be an hourly basis. Whether it is thinking about a historical controversy or thinking about how the character in a novel relates to one's own life, thinking makes people who they are. We educators are privileged to play key roles in the development of thinking skills in young minds—minds that will grow and create a world more perceptive, forgiving, reflective, just, and wise than we can imagine.

# Acknowledgments

I am greatly indebted to the following people for their assistance, creativity, insights, and patience: Laura Pappakostas, Shannon Potts, Nadeen Ruíz, Kurt Kroesche, Steve Hammack, Nicky Ramos-Beban, Marisol Castillo, Rebecca Padnos-Altamirano, Kevin Krasnow, and Guy Roberts.

*JZ*

## Feedback

Please send comments and suggestions about this book. I would love to hear suggested modifications to these activities and success stories. Please also feel free to e-mail me with questions about specific situations that relate to older student literacy, language, and thinking. My e-mail is jazwiers@usfca.edu.

# MASTER LIST OF ACTIVITIES

## *Activities in Order of Appearance*

Gru = group, Vi = visual, Mo = movement, Ma = manipulatives, Mu = music

# PART I

# Foundation and Background

# Academic Thinking With Academic Language

Most people would probably agree that one of the primary purposes of school is to teach students to think. Yet people rarely take the time to explore what it really means to think.

Think about the different types of academic thinking that you use to teach. Some skills you probably use are those of interpreting, categorizing, classifying, synthesizing, problem solving, comparing, and analyzing. These thinking skills have, for most adults, become natural, automatic, fast little mental "subroutines" that organize, transform, and create the information needed for academic understanding. Students' academic thinking skills, however, can lack this automaticity, especially in school settings. This is where we teachers come in. We must be prepared to increase students' understanding of complex content concepts by developing their academic thinking skills and language.

The past two decades have offered numerous studies, articles, and books on thinking skills (see this book's References section). As pointed out in this book's Preface, these resources differ widely in their conclusions about thinking skills and how to teach them. Most, however, point to the general and arguably obvious conclusion that different thinking skills exist and that they should be developed in school.

For a bit of thinking background, one can start with Benjamin Bloom, one of the best-known researchers on thinking skills. His famous *Taxonomy of Educational Objectives* (Bloom, Engelhar, Furst, Hill, & Krathwhol, 1956) is a hierarchical list of six thinking skills that build on one another. The first (bottom) level is knowledge, which includes factual answers, recall, and recognition. The second is comprehension, which includes translating, interpreting, and extrapolating. The third is application of knowledge and comprehension to situations that are new, are unfamiliar, or have a new point of view. The fourth level is analysis, or breaking down a concept into its component parts. The fifth, synthesis, means combining elements into a pattern not clearly there before. The sixth and highest level is evaluation of a concept or idea according to some set of criteria and based on evidence. Bloom's set of thinking skills helped educators to see the ways in which thinking skills could be analyzed and the ways in which they could depend on one another.

As convenient as it would be to design instruction around Bloom's (or any other) linear model of thinking, we cannot effectively do this. Even Bloom and his coauthors admitted that academic thinking is much more recursive than linear. For example, Bloom et al. conceded that a person might use evaluation—the most difficult level of thinking according to their system—even before processing knowledge at a less difficult level. This suggests that humans' thoughts are more interconnected (i.e., more complex) than just a set of stages or steps that people follow. A person may not need to proceed through all the thinking stages in order to successfully synthesize or evaluate. And because of the nature of the brain, learning is more concurrent than sequential, implying that a lot happens all at once in the brain—a lot that is still not understood (Wolfe, 2001). In fact, we might call the brain "the greatest frontier."

Robert Marzano further advanced people's understanding of thinking by providing practical insights into how various thinking skills interrelate. He and his coauthors of *Dimensions of Learning* generated categories for thinking skills, such as focusing skills, remembering skills, organizing skills, and integrating skills (Marzano, Pickering, & Arredondo, 1997). Marzano's later research showed the importance of teaching students the skills of identifying similarities and differences, summarizing, and generating and testing hypotheses (Marzano, Pickering, & Pollock, 2001). Other researchers have taken from and added to the ever-evolving list of thinking skills and have created studies that showed the value of explicitly teaching the skills to students (Beyer, 1987; Chamot & O'Malley, 1993). One popular book that emphasizes academic thinking is *Understanding by Design*, by Grant Wiggins and Jay McTighe (2000). These scholars offer a framework comprising what they call six facets of understanding: explanation, interpretation, application, perspective, empathy, and self-knowledge.

Thinking, language, and content learning are symbiotic. They strengthen one another and depend on one another. Teaching thinking is therefore very effective when teaching engaging content matter—and teaching content matter is more effective when students are engaged in rich academic thinking. How often have you seen a typically nonengaged and unproductive student suddenly become engrossed in a project and outperform the rest of the class? When a topic is interesting or is taught in an engaging manner, students are more likely to put effort into actively thinking about the information—often without realizing that they are putting extra thought into the tasks (Stipek, 2001). Hence, if we can get our students "into" an activity to the point at which their sense of interest and motivation takes over, then their thinking skills and language develop in order to accomplish the academic task.

In contrast, the all-too-common use of worksheets, grammar-centered seatwork, and "answer 10 questions after reading" methods tends not to be active or engaging. Such passive "drill-and-kill" methods become boring and ineffective for many students long before they reach our classrooms. Students generally want to be challenged in their thinking, and they are ready to think more and more about the world and their roles in it. Most students desire to produce genuine products of learning beyond the required lab report and five-paragraph essay. Very few consider a multiple-choice test to be a motivating product of learning. Hence, the stronger the foundation of thinking skills that students have, developed in the context of authentic and engaging experiences, the more solid their understanding becomes of the many facts, concepts, and ideas they are supposed to learn in all classes.

Research abounds on the benefits of integrating the development of academic thinking skills into the curriculum (Ackerman & Perkins, 1989; Costa, 2001; Ivie, 1998; Marzano et al., 2001; Ruggiero, 2000). Most of the benefits appear in the form of increased motivation to learn and participate, as well as increased achievement on teacher-created and state-required assessments. Of course, as is the case with much educational research, one can never be completely certain whether the thinking skills interventions were the main causal factors or not. Nevertheless, in the vast majority of the studies listed above and throughout this book, the measured and perceived results were positive when a thinking skills program was integrated into content area teaching in the ways described here. (See chapter 2 for a discussion of the teacher habits and classroom conditions that help to maximize the teaching of thinking, content, and language at the same time.)

# "Academicizing" the Thinking Skills That Students Already Use

If we could ever truly measure them, we might be surprised to find out how often we use the 12 thinking skills in this book, especially when reading, listening, and talking every day. These skills are the workhorses of thinking that continually help people to put the pieces of understanding together in useful and lasting ways. They are constantly at work throughout the day, inside and outside of school. Inside the classroom, for example, a student may need to evaluate the impact of a war on foreign policy. To do this, he or she must also be able to analyze the events, determine causes and effects, establish value categories, and then evaluate the information according to certain criteria. Outside of school, the same student may need to evaluate the bad choices that his or her friends are making and decide whether being friends with them is worth the possible short-term and long-term consequences.

In order for us to build our instruction on what students bring to the classroom, it is important to remember that all students already use *all* the thinking skills in this book to varying degrees. They already use thinking skills for making sense of their world outside of school. It is even more important to remember that *all* students are capable of developing the skills to become better thinkers, readers, writers, and learners. We cannot let ourselves fall into the common trap of thinking that students cannot synthesize or are not ready for persuasion. They synthesize and persuade, etc., every day.

All humans use these skills for making their way through each day of life—for thinking about the world, their place in it, and how to solve life's problems. For example, many students already analyze and compare songs, evaluate the quality of a television show, persuade parents to let them go out, interpret the actions or words of a boyfriend or girlfriend, empathize with a friend, apply what they learned from the Internet to win a video game, and so on. Students simply need to transfer and extend the thinking skills they already use outside of school to the learning of academic concepts inside of school. In other words, they must learn to "academicize" their skills. This is where we come in. It is our job as teachers to create, model, and support experiences in which students can successfully do this in the academic arena.

Before reading the rest of this chapter, it is important to consider the automaticity of our own academic thinking skills. Most educators are fortunate to have had a wide array of rich and varied thinking experiences, many of which were facilitated by easy access to books, rich language experiences, educated parents, and good teachers. Academic thinking became automatic for us, and this automaticity can often prevent us from fully appreciating the thinking skills challenges of our students. One of our chief goals should be to help students build automaticity in their use of academic thinking skills, as opposed to just teaching students to use the skills when cued by certain school prompts or specific questions. When these skills become more automatic, the brain is freed up to do other things such as process the specific details, concepts, and abstract ideas of the content area.

# Thinking Skills in Content Areas

All content areas are not created equal. The thinking skills required for processing, reading, remembering, and applying principles in one discipline do not necessarily transfer to another discipline in equal measure. For example, the interpretive thinking needed for understanding a literary metaphor is more commonly used in language arts than in the other content areas. Problem solving is more commonly used in science and math than in other areas, and social studies employs more cause and effect thinking than English does.

Table 1 briefly presents some ways in which social studies, science, and language arts emphasize certain thinking skills. Following the table are two activities that are effective for developing academic thinking skills.

| Table 1. Thinking Skills in the Content Areas | | |
| --- | --- | --- |
| | **Many Tasks Ask Students To** | **Questions for Developing Content Area Thinking Skills** |
| **Science** | • Observe and analyze—Focus on the phenomenon you are observing, taking different perspectives and generating possible problems.<br>• Hypothesize—Make interpretations and predictions about the causes and effects of proposed solutions and explanations.<br>• Experiment—Compare treatments, interpret the data, and analyze the possible influence of extraneous variables.<br>• Reflect—Evaluate the strength of the data and synthesize them into a conclusion.<br>• Communicate—Express the conclusion in a clear way to other members of the community.<br>• Interpret new vocabulary and abstract meanings of familiar terms now assigned to science concepts. | • What is new in this text?<br>• What is the issue or problem?<br>• Are all possible solutions given or tried?<br>• What does this word mean in this text?<br>• Was the experiment effective?<br>• Were there extraneous variables that could have influenced the results?<br>• Is this important or practical?<br>• Does this need to be practical?<br>• How might this knowledge be applied?<br>• Is the conclusion reasonable?<br>• What is the main idea of the text?<br>• Is the author biased?<br>• Does he or she need money to fund the project?<br>• How does this relate to what we are learning in the course?<br>• What does the author want you to remember from this text? |
| **Social Studies and History** | • Analyze political, social, and historical processes; gather evidence by looking at documents and other physical records.<br>• Hypothesize what happened, why, and what people were thinking at the time. | • What is the purpose of this text?<br>• Who wrote it, and was he or she qualified?<br>• What bias is there?<br>• What evidence is given? |

*(continued)*

## Table 1.   Thinking Skills in the Content Areas (continued)

| | Many Tasks Ask Students To | Questions for Developing Content Area Thinking Skills |
|---|---|---|
| **Social Studies and History** (continued) | • Interpret inconsistencies or discrepancies of evidence with current theories and accepted ideas; examine biased ideas that influenced the writing of history.<br>• Synthesize ideas and interpretations from other observers of history and social studies.<br>• Identify causes and effects of historical and present events.<br>• Empathize with others (local and worldwide, present and past); strive to filter out narcissistic views of the world.<br>• Compare political systems, cultures, ideas, events, and perspectives. | • When was it written, and what other events were happening?<br>• What are the key points?<br>• What evidence do you know of that refutes this text?<br>• How does this have relevance or importance today?<br>• How does it relate to you?<br>• Have humans learned any lessons from this?<br>• How could this have turned out differently?<br>• What could have made it turn out differently?<br>• How would the world be today if this had turned out differently?<br>• Could the causes given here not be the real causes of the event/problem? |
| **Language Arts** | • Analyze literature for parallels to real life.<br>• Compare characters and works.<br>• Identify and infer causes and effects in a story.<br>• Empathize with characters and authors.<br>• Synthesize literary works and genres to come up with common themes.<br>• Interpret literary devices, themes, and figurative language.<br>• Evaluate the quality of a written text and the author's techniques.<br>• Communicate clearly one's own thoughts and feelings in writing. | • Where and when is this story set?<br>• What major events were going on?<br>• What is the culture of the characters?<br>• What is important to the people in this story?<br>• How are the characters related?<br>• What is the main problem?<br>• Does it take place in one period or skip to different time periods?<br>• What is the author trying to teach you through the use of this story and its characters?<br>• What are the characters' main traits?<br>• How do they change throughout the story?<br>• Why did the author put this part or character into the story?<br>• What type of figurative language is used?<br>• How is this similar to other stories you have read?<br>• What have you read or experienced that helps you visualize what is happening in the story?<br>• What will happen in the future to these characters? |

# ACADEMIC THINKING SIGNALS

One of the goals of this handbook is to explicitly teach students about thinking. We want to make often-invisible thinking processes more visible to them. Because thinking skills are quite abstract, it helps to use beyond-just-verbal ways to teach and learn these skills. Academic Thinking Signals is a movement (Mo) way to identify and recall thinking types. It also gives students a chance to interpret academic language and gives you a chance to check their comprehension in nonthreatening ways (i.e., ways that are less anxiety-producing than traditional grades).

## *Procedure*

**1.** Choose the relevant thinking skills from the following and practice the hand signals.

| Academic Thinking Skill | Hand Signals |
| --- | --- |
| Analyzing | • Make a chopping motion with one hand onto the other hand. |
| Comparing | • Use both thumbs and index fingers to make two "OK" symbols, then overlap the circles to make a Venn diagram in the air. |
| Identifying cause and effect | • Move one fist horizontally and make it bump the other fist in front of you. |
| Categorizing and classifying | • Make a large *C* with one hand, make the *C* horizontal, and then move that hand up and down to make columns in the air. <br> • Make a grid with straight and overlapping fingers. |
| Problem solving | • Solve a math problem (e.g., 64 × 8) in the air with your index finger. |
| Persuading | • Use both hands to motion an imaginary person to come toward you, nod head up and down. |
| Empathizing | • "Walk" your hands one in front of the other to symbolize walking in someone else's shoes. |
| Synthesizing | • Gather imaginary ideas from the air. |
| Interpreting | • Touch your index finger to your temple. |
| Evaluating | • Extend both arms out and act like a balance scale. |
| Communicating | • Hold an imaginary telephone to your ear. |
| Applying | • Hammer an imaginary nail. |

Explain to students what the skills mean, give examples, and then train students to do the hand signals. You can have students help you to create new hand signals if you and they so choose. This gives them some ownership in the process, too.

**2.** Show students some practice sentences or phrases that include the target academic language (e.g., "the difference between"). Have them guess which thinking skill is being used (e.g., compare) and then do the motion for it (e.g., making two overlapping circles in the air).

**3.** Think aloud in front of the students while doing a task or reading aloud.

**4.** Have students listen to your think-aloud, categorize the thoughts, and then do the appropriate signals without talking. This can show you which students understand the various thinking skills and which students need extra support. This step also has the advantage of being a quiet activity.

**5.** When appropriate, start a new phase in which you stop the task at a certain point and tell the students to do the hand signals matching *their* current thoughts. You can call on a student or two to elaborate. For example, "Lupe, I noticed from your hand motion that you made a comparison. What did you compare? Did anyone else make that comparison?"

**6.** Begin to stop at points during the reading and show students a hand signal to prompt them to think about the signaled skill. They can write their thoughts down and/or share them with the class. For example, while reading aloud, you might stop and do the hand signal for persuasion. Students would then write down how they think the author is persuading the reader or how they might use the information in the text to persuade another person to do something.

## PRO THINK-ALOUDS

Think-alouds are moments when you stop to describe your thinking process aloud to others while you are doing something (adapted from Davey, 1983; Farr, 2001). This is a powerful way for us as teachers to model thinking and academic language. We should stop and think aloud not only as we are reading aloud, but also when we are writing, filling in graphics, watching videos, doing labs, drawing, creating graphs, solving problems, and modeling any of the other activities in a lesson. Thinking aloud makes the invisible academic thinking skills visible to students.

This activity has the word *pro* in front of *think-alouds* in order to point out the importance of this method. Many teachers already think aloud and tend to think of a think-aloud as a fairly simple procedure. But this apparent simplicity can keep us from appreciating the complexity and power of thinking aloud. Bad think-alouds abound. They waste classroom time and sometimes confuse students. We must therefore strive to improve our understanding of thinking and language and must then try to improve our modeling of it each time we think aloud. This means that we must sharpen our own thinking (i.e., become pros at it) and then plan how best to share it with students, rather than just improvising. We must become adept at using the academic language we are trying to teach.

To think aloud like a pro, verbalize what you are doing whenever you do the following:

- Break a topic into categories and analyze them.
- Hypothesize causes and effects for actions and events.

- Question the validity and value of evidence in a text or speech.
- Craft a persuasive letter.
- Empathize with the main character in a novel or with people from history.
- Interpret figurative language; make analogies and modify the analogies; see where an analogy breaks down.
- Synthesize information from multiple sources and background knowledge.
- Connect to prior knowledge, readings, or experience and then prune away or discard those connections that are not helpful.
- Connect the current text or activity to the essential knowledge (or "big picture") of a unit or lesson.

## *Procedure*

**1.** Plan ahead. Use a wide variety of tasks and materials (stories, textbooks, essays, articles, graphs, pictures, etc.), and glance over them beforehand to prepare your thoughts. You can also bring in a text that is difficult for you (e.g., a college biology book) in order to give students a genuine sense of your thinking struggles and how you approach challenging tasks.

**2.** Let students know that you will be modeling your thinking and that they should compare their thoughts to yours during the process. Tell them to try to notice the academic language that you use.

**3.** Begin reading the text and stop at times to "step out" of the task and verbalize your academic thinking processes, such as analyzing, problem solving, persuading, and synthesizing. A few starter phrases are given here, and many more can be found in chapters 3–14. Also, point to any phrases that you use that might be shown on the classroom wall (e.g., as part of the Academic Language Bank activity). Some possible expressions to use are these:

- I think the character felt...
- This would fall under the category of...
- I wonder why...
- I need to see more evidence for...
- This character contrasts with...
- The real problem here is...
- The true cause seemed to be...
- The opposing side will probably argue that...
- This is a metaphor for...
- I have read other accounts that say that...

9

**4.** Optional: Have students keep track of your think-aloud comments and then categorize the thoughts. (See the charts on page 22.)

**5.** Now, give students a chance to think aloud. Try the 30–30–30 Scaffolding approach. Each 30 should *roughly* be a percentage of the total amount of work (reading, writing, and creating) done by the teacher or the students:

| | |
|---|---|
| First ~30% | Teacher reads and thinks aloud while students listen and take notes. Teacher may emphasize certain skills (e.g., analyzing, empathizing, etc.) that students will practice later on. |
| Middle ~30% | Teacher does the task in front of students and stops at points to prompt students to think aloud, either with the whole class or with partners (e.g., Think-Pair-Share, chapter 13). Examples of teacher prompts are "How might we break this down?" "How should we react to this argument?" "Turn to a partner and say what you think this analogy means." |
| Last ~30% | Students proceed independently and silently as they take notes on sticky notes, paper, computers, or graphic organizers in order to practice the emphasized think-aloud skills. |

**6.** Have students use tape recorders to practice. Use posters, bookmarks, and notecards with thought starters on them in order to spark ideas. Have students make clay figures, drawings, paintings, and projects for think-alouds. A good progression for practicing thinking aloud is describing thoughts while making a clay figure or a drawing, then while watching a video, then while reading and writing.

**7.** Optional: Have students take notes during partner think-alouds. One student does the task and thinks aloud, while the other listens and takes notes on a sticky note. The listener can also categorize each thought as one of the academic thinking skills. If students are reading a text or are writing, the student who did the task while thinking aloud can later put each sticky note at the spot on the page where he or she stopped to think aloud. The student can later categorize these on a sheet of binder paper in a notebook.

Following is sample think-aloud for composing a letter:

1. "First, I need to gather all the information from the articles and text to think about how I will organize my letter. I will start with the problem." (Synthesize)
2. "Now I need to define the problem and mention the possible solutions." (Problem Solve)
3. "This article says that production will taper off in 10 years. I interpret that to mean that there will be less demand. I wonder why. Maybe new technology will take its place." (Interpret Cause/Effect)
4. "Now I will address counterarguments and try to write how my proposed solution is the best, without showing that I am biased. In doing this, I will emphasize the evidence in this article by Stevens." (Persuade)

# Academic Language

As mentioned previously, academic thinking falls flat without academic language to support it. Academic language is the huge array of key words and phrases that help a student organize and process core knowledge and skills in school (Chamot & O'Malley, 1993). Academic language is important to consider because it is so pervasive across content areas. Yet the explicit and scaffolded teaching of it is often squeezed out by our focus on teaching content standards. Part of the challenge of teaching and learning academic language is that it is a moving target that often does not stand still long enough for us (or our students) to get a solid grasp. A helpful analogy (and also a form of academic language) is to see ourselves somewhat like fish, trying to describe water to a land animal. We teachers have been immersed in academic language and have used it for so long that it can be a struggle to see it well enough to explain it to others. For this reason, we must continue to cultivate our understanding of academic language so that we can equip our students to do the same. A brief overview of academic language follows, but many teachers will want to consult the sources given in this book's References section for more thorough discussions of the topic.

In a nutshell, language is what people use to communicate messages to others—and to themselves—as they think. Words are actually verbal symbols that carry a shared meaning between two people. Yet because we are all different, we do not always have absolute agreement on what each word and word combination means.

Perhaps one of the most salient and challenging features of academic language is that it describes concepts that people cannot easily act out or show with images. It is often used to describe abstract and intangible ideas, such as which invention was more influential, the reasons for a hypothesis, an interpretation of a character's actions, the contrast between two religions, etc. Academic language terms tend to carry abstract meanings that describe the relationships between ideas and concepts. For example, in the phrase "Nevertheless, the two men differed greatly in their views on slavery," the term *differed* refers not to physical differences, which can be seen, but instead to the views or ideas the men had about slavery. After reading this phrase, the reader would then expect an explanation of how the men's views differed. The reader must also know that *nevertheless* is a marker that defies expectations in a text, similar to the words *but*, *however*, and *yet*. These abstract connections are hard for many students to see, especially for English-language learners and struggling readers (Snow & Brinton, 1997). Notice that even the word *see* in the preceding sentence is an abstract term.

Academic language tends to do the following:

- Be context reduced, meaning that it describes ideas that are difficult to see, touch, or act out with movements (e.g., comparing a novel's character to a family member, evaluating the effects of the A-bomb, explaining cell mitosis).

- Use figurative expressions and terms, such as the use of concrete terms to describe abstract concepts. This also includes specialized meanings for familiar words in different disciplines (e.g., mouse, turncoat, catalyst, harbinger).

- Be like written language. Students who have not done extensive reading of academic texts are not accustomed to the longer and more complex language structures found in written texts (as compared with oral messages).

- Contain complex grammar such as multiple modifiers, subordinating conjunctions, parallelism, inversion, and passive voice (i.e., more impersonal).

As mentioned earlier, a major hurdle for us as teachers can be our own fluency and expertise at using academic language. We have been so immersed in academic terms that we can sometimes have trouble seeing them. This makes the terms hard to teach. Even when we do take notice of the terms, we tend to assume that students understand them because the terms appear to us to be common and straightforward, quietly mingling among the big and bolded content words that are better at grabbing textbook readers' attention. But, as most teachers have probably observed, not knowing a few of these terms can sabotage a student's comprehension. Therefore, one purpose of this book is to help us to look for ways of seeing, explaining, modeling, and highlighting academic terms.

A common question I hear as a language and literacy coach is, "What comes first, the thinking or the language?" My answer is, "Yes." The goal is to have both thinking and language develop as much as possible in the little time we have with our students. For some students, the thinking may precede the language; for others, the language terms may be introduced first, and the academic thinking may later develop in the context of using the terms in a group project or essay (Chamot & O'Malley, 1993). As students become engaged in a project or in the pursuit of an interesting and relevant goal, they will seek the tools (in this case, the terms of academic language) that best serve their needs. We need to make those tools available to students, somewhat like an assistant who hands tools to a surgeon during surgery.

## *Types of Academic Language*

When I teach students and train teachers, it helps me to separate academic language into four highly overlapping types: (1) content vocabulary, (2) academic thinking skill terms, (3) coherence and cohesion devices, and (4) classroom discussion terms. The first three types, in a sense, move from most noticeable to least noticeable, or from "big" to "small." The fourth type is the oral language used in classroom discussions. One helpful way to remember these types is by recreating the following diagram on the board or on an overhead projector and brainstorming, with the students' help, examples of the types of language that you use in your discipline. You can write this language outside each oval, as shown:

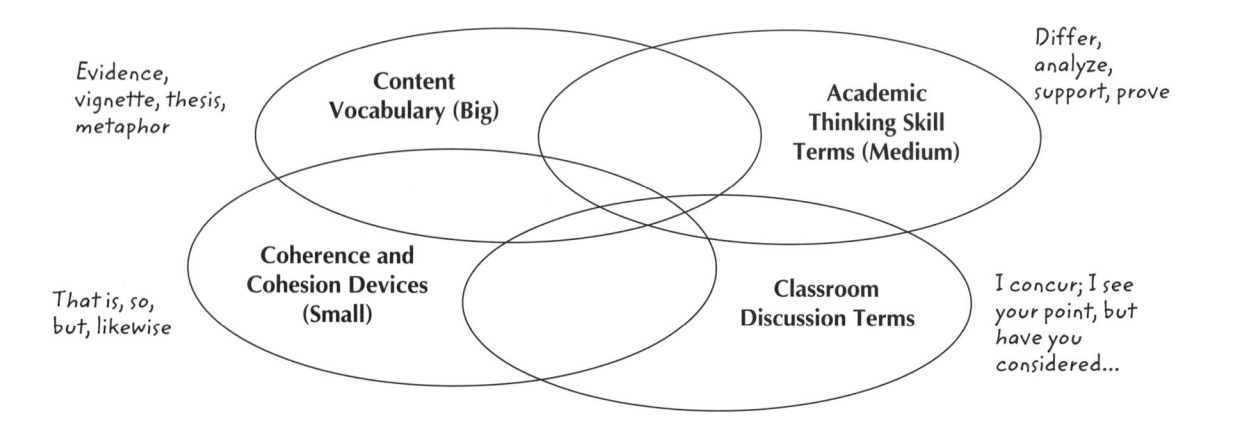

**Content Vocabulary.** The most visible type of academic language is the set of "big" content vocabulary words and terms, such as *photosynthesis*, *revolution*, *adaptation*, *internal conflict*, *denominator*, and *mitosis*. This type of academic language, even though the words tend to be long, is actually easier to teach and to learn than the other three. And because of their size and "boldness," these big words tend to be blamed for the struggles of many learners. Teachers often assume that if we simply drill students on these words, then students will learn them and their understanding will soar. Yet even a perfect memory of the big words' meanings does not alone suffice when one needs to combine them for understanding and discussing complex ideas.

**Academic Thinking Skill Terms.** The second (medium) type of academic language is the set of terms that describe and facilitate academic thinking. This is the language emphasized in this book. The terms in this category are subtle, yet pervasive. Some examples are *the difference between*, *the probability of it is higher than*, *it boils down to*, *it is similar to when*, *it falls under the category of*, *in this way*, *if...were...*, *because of*, and *yet from the point of view of....* Many of these terms are figurative and have abstract meanings that describe complex relationships among ideas in an academic context. Consider *boils down*, *higher*, *falls under*, and *point of view* from this list. These are all founded, in a sense, on more concrete meanings. In fact, even *concrete* is used here as a figurative term. We use these terms every day in our teaching and in our own thinking, yet we probably notice very few of them. Some terms are included in this book; it is up to you to find the ones most useful in your classroom.

One important area within this category that we need to scaffold for students is the language of task prompts, most often used to generate student writing. Following are some common task prompts and their meanings. You can create a similar table for your classroom to help your students discriminate between terms and to accurately do what each prompt says in order to succeed on writing tasks.

| Prompt | Means |
| --- | --- |
| *Discuss* | Depending on what follows the word *discuss*, this prompt usually requires the writer to do some or all of the following: analyze, explain, describe, and/or evaluate the various components and/or significance of a topic. |
| *Describe* | Communicate to the reader a complete and detailed "picture" of the object, events, process, or concept. Details often include time, place, people, actions, causes, effects, metaphoric language, etc. Description often requires analysis. Description is more visual than explanation. |
| *Explain* | Clarify a process or communicate the significance of a topic. Differs slightly from "Describe" above, in that it is less visual than description. |
| *Summarize* | Reduce the important information down into main ideas and supporting details that describe the key parts of the text or topic in paragraph form. |
| *Illustrate* | Use detailed examples to support a statement or side of an issue. |

| Trace | Describe or explain a subject in chronological order. This will often include interpretations of the significance of events, along with cause/effect inferences. |
|---|---|
| Respond (and reflect) | Communicate your reaction, opinion, or position after reading (or viewing) a text. Include examples and details from the text to support your response. The response may often include elements of application, reflection, interpretation, and critique. |
| Critique | Analyze and describe the positive and negative aspects of a topic. Make an overall recommendation for or against it. |
| Justify | Give clear and rational examples and details that support a decision, opinion, event, or statement. |

**Coherence and Cohesion Devices.** The third type of academic language overlaps with the second but is subtler. This is the set of words and phrases that creates coherence and cohesion in messages ("small" academic language). These are the transitions, conjunctions, pronoun referents, connectives, and prepositional terms that glue ideas together. Examples include words such as *such as, but, and, or, while, despite, although, yet, for instance, principal, key, this, that, given that.* A helpful illustration of this third type of academic language is the analogy of mortar and bricks (Dutro & Moran, 2003). These coherence and cohesion words are the mortar that holds together the bricks, which are the larger content vocabulary words and thinking skills terms.

Coherence and cohesion language plays a vital role in the creation—and, therefore, the comprehension—of expository text language. Authors of textbooks and articles often nominalize (turn verbs into nouns) and use structures such as the passive voice. Longer sentences might be used than those used in speech (notice the passive voice just used), and many sentences have multiple dependent and independent clauses, such as this one. This means that students need to be trained to keep more ideas in the brain while processing one sentence. Consider this example: "Despite many warnings by other resistance members, he was apprehended and taken to a maximum security prison, where he was interrogated and tortured for his role in the fighting." Did you notice the length of the sentence and the passive voice? Although we teachers, thanks to many years and pages of exposure to long sentences, may not be tripped up by them, our students are still training their brains to process such sentences all at once. One way to help students do this is to highlight coherence and cohesion language in sentences and to have students analyze their features.

**Classroom Discussion Terms.** The fourth type of academic language is the language used to cultivate, facilitate, and lubricate academic discussions in the classroom. It is also the oral language used, for the most part, in many professional settings such as business meetings, where the topics and concepts being discussed are more complex and abstract than those in most social conversations. For example, to affirm the ideas mentioned by other students in a discussion, a student might be trained to say, "My idea is related to ___'s idea," "I resonate with what she said," "You made a great point about...," "I hadn't thought about that," "My idea builds on ___'s idea," "I'd like to piggyback off that idea," or "Along those same lines, I feel that...." Or, to disagree, a student might say, "True, but I would like to point out that...," "However, we can't forget that...," "I found some conflicting evidence, though," "Then again, we shouldn't forget...," "I see it differently. Based on...," "That's a valid point, but I feel...," "I understand the idea of..., but I believe that...," "On the other hand,..." "I do agree with the part about..., but...," or "Yes, but what about...?" Responses such as these also must include the nonverbal responses and facial expressions that are appropriate for school and professional settings.

Classroom discussion language helps students learn to communicate for several purposes. One purpose is to express oneself clearly and effectively. Another purpose is to put one's thoughts into language that contributes to a team effort, working together toward a common goal of understanding. You have probably been to meetings or classes where there is a lot of talking that goes nowhere, where people's utterances are unconnected to previous utterances, and where the goal of the meeting or class is not met. For this reason, it behooves us to develop our discussion leading skills. We can model for students how to listen, respond, and stick to the topic of the discussion. I sometimes post the topic and the goal of the discussion in some prominent place in the classroom in order to remind the class—and myself—not to stray from them.

## Using the Academic Language Lists in Chapters 3–14

When it comes to student ownership of academic language, we need to make up for lost time for many students. We cannot sit back and expect them to absorb this language indirectly. We must explicitly teach it at times, not with worksheets and drills, but in the context of engaging learning tasks and content instruction. Chapters 3–14 of this book contain lists of academic language expressions and possible oral and writing prompts for developing each chapter's skill. Get to know the terms in each chapter, and notice when you and your students use them in discussions or written tasks. Try to keep a constant eye (and ear) out for this academic language. For example, in chapter 3 on analyzing, try to notice certain phrases that you and your students use when you break down complex concepts into understandable chunks. You can display these commonly used expressions on the wall in some format such as a poster or sign (see Figure 1 for a sample poster). Direct explicit attention to the terms that show academic thinking and that show learning of your content objectives, which should also be posted.

Highlight, praise, and validate the use of academic language by students. Positive reinforcement and feedback can encourage students to fortify their language arsenal with academic terms. Create and develop ways to build this language into classroom activities and assessments. Some teachers record student (and text) academic language on an overhead transparency, on a hand-held computer, or on notecards next to students' names, and then they share these quotes with the class. Also, you might want to categorize the students' expressions and prompts according to the four types of academic language described earlier.

The next chapter briefly discusses how to create checklists and rubrics for student learning tasks and activities. One of the best ways to use the academic language lists in chapters 3–14 is to put several of the terms into these rubrics or checklists for the process and products of a task. You might want to see and hear the language in conversation communication

Figure 1.    Sample Academic Language Poster

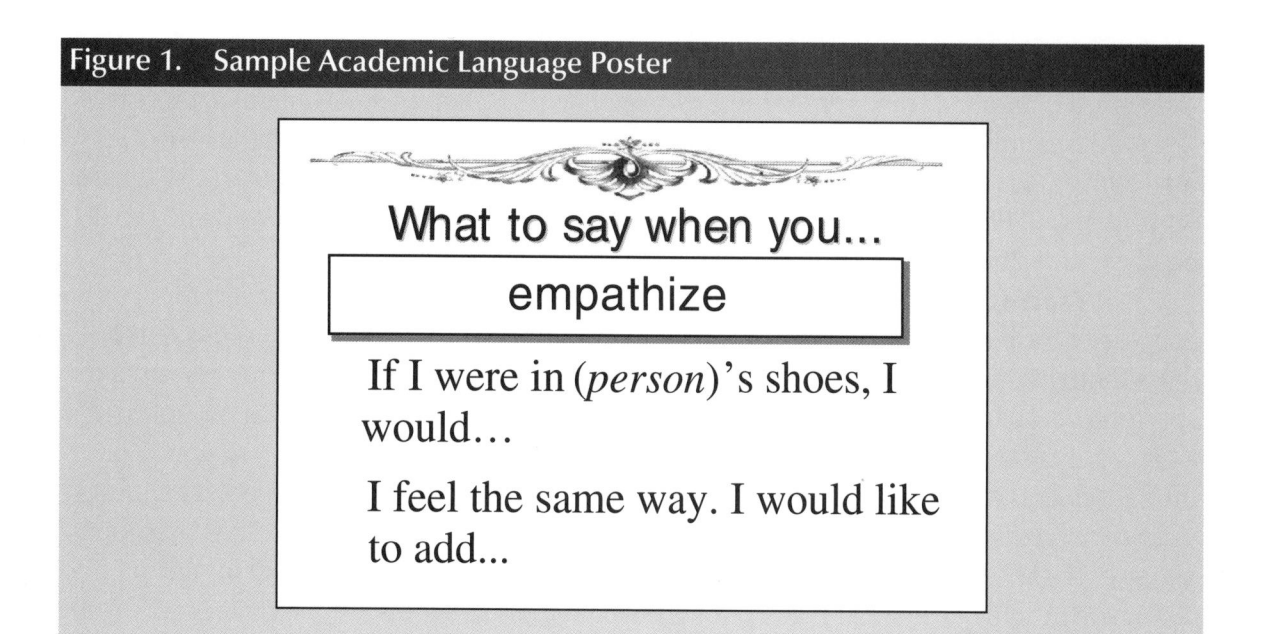

and presentation communication (spoken, written, visual, drama). For example, in the 3-D Balance Scale activity (chapter 12), you might want to hear terms such as *outweighs the advantage*, *granted*, *in spite of*, *long-term effects*, and *criterion*. Put these in a rubric, use them as you model the task, explicitly describe them, and highlight them in texts that you use in the activity. You can decide how you want to give points, extra credit, positive feedback, etc., when students correctly use the terms.

## Using the Paragraph Frames in Chapters 3–14

Writing is not usually considered a cooperative, kinesthetic, visual, or music-based method. However, it can be a very effective technique for building academic language and thinking skills. Lists, single paragraphs, letters, memos, reports, invitations, advertisements, essays, and filling in paragraph frames are types of writing that can be effective for building thinking and its expressions. This is because writing forces students to organize their thoughts well enough to express them academically, within a coherent piece of writing. Of course, it is vital to model the types of writing that you want your students to do, and to provide plenty of good samples for them to analyze (see Analyzing Writing Models, chapter 3).

A writing frame, like the ones found in chapters 3–14, is one way to nudge students into their linguistic zone of proximal development, the next step of learning beyond what one already knows (Vygotsky, 1980). Jerome Bruner (1985) used the term *verbal scaffolds* to refer to the types of support teachers give to students while they are in their zones of proximal development, particularly with respect to writing and reading. Writing and ideas for scaffolding it are integrated into many of the activities in this book to further strengthen students' language and thinking skills. In fact, the entire purpose of many of this book's activities is to scaffold writing and the thinking it requires.

Many teachers have asked me for ideas for scaffolding writing that concentrates on particular thinking skills. One effective practice is the use of writing frames. Although some might criticize the rigidity of these writing frames (like the ones found in chapters 3–14) I have seen many students, especially English learners and struggling readers, use these frames with success. Students gradually pick up the academic language and eventually use it to compose their own high-quality written products without help. The frames in chapters 3–14 are meant to get you started on creating your own subject- and student-specific frames. They are very generic, to allow you to fine-tune them (or you can even start from scratch). When creating your own frames, you can take some phrases out of the frames and refer to the lists of academic language expressions and prompts in each chapter. For additional writing activities that build thinking and language, see chapter 13.

Following are several activities for building academic thinking and language all day long in your classes. They can be used along with the activities found in chapters 3–14.

# ACADEMIC LANGUAGE BANK

The academic language bank is a way to organize, display, and validate the terms that you use in your class. In this activity, you devote sections of the classroom wall to the display and study of important academic terms (adapted from Cunningham, 1995). Academic language terms in the bank can serve as a constant and quick reference for reinforcing content and thinking. The bank concept is also a way to assign value to various terms that often do not get the attention they deserve. The bank can be an ever-evolving resource that you use as an anchor for the language in each unit that you teach. It also becomes a great visual resource of terms for students to use in oral and written classroom tasks.

In each of the thinking skill chapters (3–14), you will find a list of academic language terms related to that chapter's thinking skills. The Academic Language Bank is a very effective way to facilitate increasingly automatic use of the language by students. And for teachers, the terms posted in the bank are excellent reminders of the types of thinking and concept learning that we should observe and assess.

## *Procedure*

1. Create a large sign that says something like "ACADEMIC LANGUAGE BANK, INC." Put it over a space on the wall where you will put signs with the academic terms and phrases on them.

2. Cut some pieces of paper (e.g., 8½" × 14" sheets cut the long way to become 4¼" × 14") on which to write the terms (use green paper to look like dollar bills; you might even want to decorate the strips of paper to look like money). Get students started by putting a couple of sample academic language terms or phrases up in the bank. Each should be written as large as possible, and its meaning can be written in small letters below it. You can call these AL (academic language) bills.

**3.** Tell students that during the rest of the year, they will make one of the best investments ever: academic language. Tell them that the language they put into the bank—and that they learn—will enrich their thoughts and learning forever, guaranteed. You and they will gradually create the bank of terms on the wall, using language from classroom texts and from discussion.

**4.** Make the blank green signs available to students when they are doing tasks so that they can write down new terms to put into the bank. You might want to ask them to write at least one AL bill for each task. Tell students to watch out for terms that challenge their thinking, terms they have seen in different texts, and terms that seem to confuse them or complicate the reading. They can write these in pencil and then ask you if they are, in fact, academic language terms that are worthy of being in the bank. Or, you can post lists of this handbook's terms for different thinking skills. After students identify these terms in texts or in discussions (often from your speech during discussions), they can write the terms on AL bills and post them, as shown below.

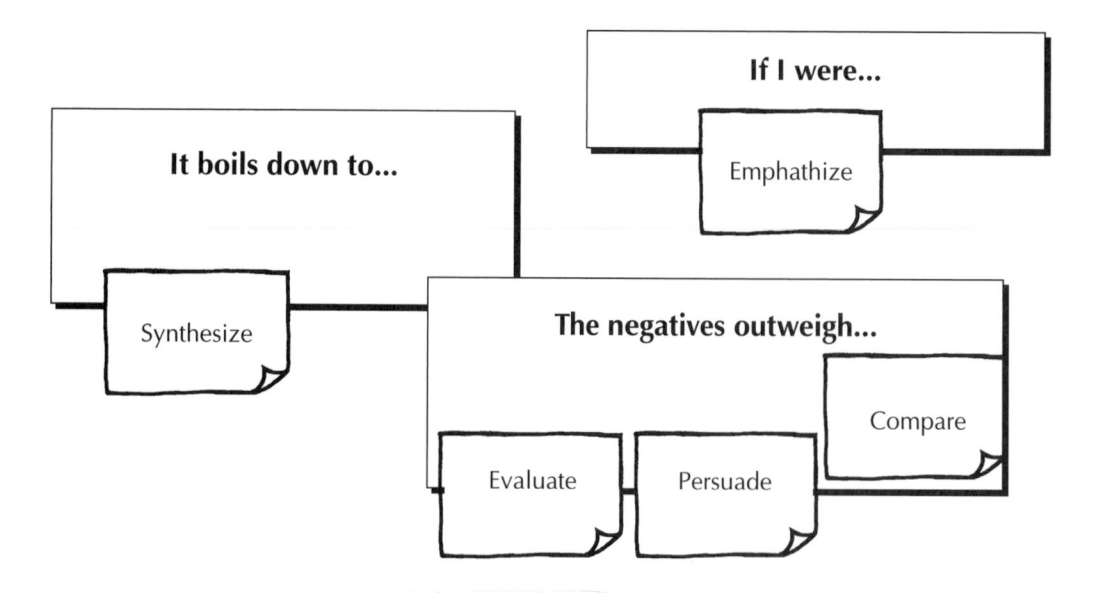

**5.** Optional: If you have taught students the names of some thinking skills, you might find this step to be productive. Give students a chance to match various thinking skills with the academic language that goes with them. They can put the name of a thinking skill on a sticky note and attach it to the appropriate AL bill, as shown above. Have students justify why they chose a certain skill and even give an example, if helpful.

**6.** Refer to the bank often to bring up and highlight the terms that show up in texts and discussions. Also, refer students to the bank when they are writing. For example, you might say, "It looks as though you want to describe your cause and effect hypotheses here. Is there any language that might be useful up there in the bank?"

**7.** Optional: Assign monetary values according to the relative importance of the bank terms. Students can argue for more value for certain words and less value for others. An example of the language they might use for this is, "This is an important term in this class because.... For example, I might say...."

**8.** A final option, once you have many AL bills posted in the bank, is to categorize the terms. This can be done by thinking skill, but you might have other categories, such as classroom discussion terms, common writing terms, transitions, idiomatic expressions, etc.

# ACADEMIC LANGUAGE ACTIONS

Similar to the previous Academic Thinking Signals activity, this activity focuses on academic language. Research abounds showing the success of using extraverbal ways to reinforce concepts (Druyan, 1997; Marzano, 2001). Movement can be a powerful way to learn challenging and abstract concepts, especially for students who struggle with verbal-based learning. This activity is a kinesthetic way to teach students the basic academic language devices in a text that preserve its cohesion and coherence (the third type of academic language mentioned previously in this chapter). These small but important pieces of language are similar to major direction markers on a trail: If you miss one, you can easily get lost. Hence, learning these devices can improve students' comprehension. For example, the better a student understands how the transition word *however* makes a reader expect a contradictory argument or example, the more quickly and effectively the student will maneuver through a text.

| Text Device | Hand Signals |
|---|---|
| *however, but, yet, on the other hand, nevertheless, on the contrary, then again, even though, despite* | • Move hand in one direction and then turn it 180 degrees.<br>• Walk one way and turn around.<br>• Look at one hand held out and then put out the other hand and look at it. |
| *and, furthermore, moreover, in addition* | • Hold up your two index fingers in the form of a plus sign. |
| *therefore, for this reason, because of this, thus, hence* | • Use one hand to make a rolling motion forward.<br>• Have one fist bump the other fist to get it moving. |
| *in conclusion, in essence* | • Hold up one hand with fingers spread, then close all fingers so the fingertips meet. |
| *granted, of course* | • Hold one hand out with palm up. |
| *for example, for instance, to illustrate, let's say* | • Put one finger down on palm of other hand. |
| *similarly, likewise, in the same way* | • Hold up both hands with interlinked fingers. |

## Procedure

1. Create a large, empty chart (poster or overhead) with two columns and "Text Device" and "Hand Signals" column headings as shown on the previous page. You will fill this in as you teach the actions.

2. Tell students that they will be helping you make this hand motion chart during the year to learn important academic language text markers. Find a text that has some of the terms shown in the chart on page 19 (you can bookmark this page for ideas or take some terms from chapters 4–14). As you read aloud, emphasize an appropriate term.

3. Read the term again in context, and ask students what they think it means. Ask them if they can think of a good hand motion to help them remember it. They will come up with some good ones, or you can use the ideas on the previous page.

4. Continue to build the chart, using other texts and using words from classroom discussions.

5. Have students use the terms in their writing. If they use one term too much, tell them to refer to the chart for other options.

6. Every so often, do a quick checkup: Say the words and see if students can do the motions. Then do the motions and see if they can say the words. They could also write down the words and share them with a partner or the class. Tell them to avoid looking at the chart (i.e., stand on the other side of the room).

# ACADEMIC LANGUAGE OBSERVATION AND FEEDBACK NOTES

Observing your students is vital in the assessment of learning. Much of what people can observe is shown to us through language. Language and thinking, in a sense, have a symbiotic relationship. Each needs and feeds the other. Academic Language Observation and Feedback Notes (adapted from Genesee & Upshur, 1996) helps teachers reinforce and validate students' use of academic language by noticing it in the classroom. Though teachers may tend to focus on content, there are times when a minilesson on academic language will provide a student with new ways of organizing and understanding the content.

## Procedure

1. Move around the classroom as students work, and write comments on a clipboard (on paper or a transparency), charts, note cards, or a hand-held computer.

2. Use this chart to provide specific and helpful feedback to students about their thinking during reading. For example, say, "Great, Silvia, you interpreted this analogy to help you understand this science concept!"

**3.** Use the following to interpret student comments as indicators of their thinking skills:

| Observed Academic Language | Thinking Skills Inferred |
| --- | --- |
| "There were three main aspects of this event that were important to the future. We need to look closely at their motives." | Analyzing |
| "This war was very different from the Korean War. First..." | Comparing |
| "These three should be in the same group because they...." "We should call this category...because...." | Categorizing and classifying |
| "I think the caste system in India prevents people from choosing what jobs they want to do." | Identifying cause and effect |
| "If the whales could find warm and protected waters, their calves would be safer." | Problem solving |
| "What is worse? An entire future without trees or a few years of creating new jobs that don't depend on trees?" | Persuading |
| "If I were a proton, I would be very positive, always looking on the bright side and hanging out next to my friends the neutrons, watching the wacky electrons circle around us like hummingbirds in very bad moods...very negative and sarcastic, those electrons." | Empathizing |
| "We need to remember what the other book said. And I remember what I saw in a movie about this." | Synthesizing |
| "I think it really means that she was tired of him. She was sad, so when she said she was thrilled, I think she was covering up her depression." | Interpreting |
| "The loss of the rain forest will be devastating to our future. How much is the extinction of one, two, 500 species worth? And think about the possible cures for diseases that are being lost." | Evaluating |
| "The best way to get this across is to use an analogy. I think they will understand it better if we use a drama, song, or poster." | Communicating |
| "What we learned about acceleration in math can help us here with this science experiment. We just need to use the numbers we found in our measurements." | Applying |

**4.** Add some of the more useful and common terms to academic language posters you might put up. Have students add the terms to their notebooks, if there is a section there for academic language. You can make a chart like the one that follows on which to record student comments and keep track of which skills are most evident and which are missing.

| Instructional Activity _____ | | |
| Date _____ | | |
|---|---|---|
| Student Name | Student Comments | Corresponding Thinking Skills |
| | | |
| | | |
| | | |

**5.** Share with the class language excerpts on the overhead projector or on a wall poster. You might even add some student comments to the Academic Language Bank on the wall, if you use that activity (see page 17).

**6.** Optional: Have students write a short paragraph that uses one or two of the academic language terms.

**7.** Another option is to have students keep track of their own language in a chart like the one below. (See the Think-Aloud Note Tables reproducible in Part III of this book, page 214.) During think-alouds, they can keep track of a partner's thoughts and then discuss the thinking skills that relate to those thoughts.

| Notes on Elisa's thoughts | Comparing | Problem Solving | Interpreting | Empathizing | Cause and Effect | Evaluating | Categorizing/Classifying |
|---|---|---|---|---|---|---|---|
| 1. It differs from the other story... | X | | | | | | |
| 2. It means that she wanted... | | | X | | | | |
| 3. One solution might be to look at... | | X | | | | | |
| 4. If I were her, I would have run... | | | | X | | | |

This chapter provided a look at how academic language and its development are crucial to academic thinking, and vice versa. The next chapter provides a look at several essential elements that make up effective instruction. Much of chapter 2 may be a review for many teachers, but a review is often useful.

# Teacher Habits for Developing Thinking, Language, and Content

Effective teaching requires that teachers continually look for ways to fortify current instruction and assessment of students' thinking, language, and content learning. Effective teaching means creating environments in which students are engaged, challenged, and saturated with various types of thinking—without being overwhelmed. Unfortunately, many students are either not engaged enough or are overwhelmed. Some classroom tasks, as mentioned in chapter 1, are simple "regurgitation" tasks, many of which are found on multiple-choice assessments. Other classroom tasks, especially in middle school and high school, require thinking skills and procedures that have not been taught or scaffolded sufficiently for many students. They have therefore either given up on learning or given in to the temptation of just getting by with the minimum effort.

To create and maintain a complex environment that is optimally conducive for learning for all students, we must have a well-developed set of routines, or teacher habits, that automatically kick in while we are preparing for, executing, and reflecting on each lesson. These habits often develop over many years of teaching. Ten of the most beneficial habits are discussed in this chapter. Although I realize that we need more than just 10 teacher habits, I chose these because they are especially powerful and necessary for successful teaching of academic language and thinking.

## Teacher Habit 1: Move From Standards to Assessment to Instruction

The best way to align standards, assessments, and instruction is to "backward plan." The method is called backward planning because you start with the final destination (learning goals) in mind, then create ways to know where students are along the way (assessments), and then design ways for them to get there (which is instruction) (Wiggins & McTighe, 2000). Following is a sample backward planning chart for GruViMoMaMu:

| Essential Question: | | | | | |
|---|---|---|---|---|---|
| | **Know**<br>Content Concepts and Vocabulary | **Do**<br>Skills and Tasks | **Think**<br>Academic Thinking Skills | **Say**<br>Academic Language |
| Standards and Objectives | | | | |
| Assessments (Traditional and GruViMoMaMu) | | | | |
| **Instructional Methods** Gru | | | | |
| Vi | | | | |
| Mo | | | | |
| Ma | | | | |
| Mu | | | | |

First, develop an essential question or theme that guides the learning. Essential questions help to promote academic thinking, and they provide a helpful anchor or framework for organizing a unit of study using multiple genres and activities. Such questions are revisited throughout the unit to encourage dialog and debate, which leads students to ask further deep content questions. Being able to answer these questions shows deep understanding of the content. Good essential questions have some basic criteria in common: They tend to be open-ended, thought provoking, controversial, and even counterintuitive at times. They require students to connect to background knowledge and experience. (See Appendix B for a list of essential questions.)

Next, think about what students need to learn in order to answer the essential question(s). Put these target learning objectives and standards in the four categories across the first line of the chart. The first column contains what you (and the state and district) want students to know. This will include the facts and concepts of your content area. Then put in what you want students to be able to do with the knowledge. This includes skills that you are teaching, such as writing, creating diagrams, making lab reports, and using the computer. Third, add academic thinking and comprehension skills that you want your students to use when they think about your content material and engage in the tasks that they perform. These will include many of the skills in this book, along with comprehension skills such as summarizing, inferring, questioning, predicting, and connecting to background knowledge.

Finally, ask yourself which academic language and expressions you would like students to use when they talk and write about concepts they are learning. Refer to chapter 1 for more ideas for this column.

As you fill in the objectives, think about ways in which students will show that they know them. These are the assessments that go in the next row of the chart. Assessment methods should generate *useful* information for both teacher and student in all stages of learning. Many teachers with whom I work have found that the most interesting tasks in the eyes of students can, at the same time, provide teachers with the most helpful information about their learning. For example, a teacher I know created several checklists for different stages of a science presentation on earthquakes. The checklists, in addition to being more interesting to students than typical tests, included thinking skills such as classifying and problem solving and were very useful to the teacher for assessment purposes.

We teachers should monitor student progress *while* students are thinking about learning, not just after. This helps us see students' strengths and weaknesses in using their skills while they learn (Genesee & Upshur, 1996). Many elementary teachers already do this informally in their minds; they usually know which students are struggling and in which areas. Yet in middle school and high school, with larger numbers of students and a focus on content, teachers are significantly more challenged to observe and keep track of their observations of student comprehension. With 150 or more students, this is understandable, but it is also rectifiable. The trick is to modify instructional activities so that they also serve as assessments. You can apply some of the suggestions found in this chapter to the activities in chapters 3–14 (see the list of steps on the next page).

Finally, start designing ways for students to learn the objectives well enough to succeed on the assessments. This is the instruction stage of planning. Notice how instruction comes last (Wiggins & McTighe, 2000) because this is a backward planning method. The table includes separate rows to emphasize the use of each of the GruViMoMaMu methods. These methods are described later in this chapter in more detail.

You should provide clear feedback to students with regard to their progress. Students want and need to know where they are strong and where they are weak. For example, a score of 79 on an essay or multiple-choice test provides little useful feedback. Useful feedback consists of specific, timely, and corrective comments that tell students where they stand in relation to a clear target of knowledge or skill (Marzano et al., 2001).

Assessments can provide useful feedback. Their usefulness—for both the teacher and the student—increases when the assessments are interesting and meaningful with clear criteria for success (Wiggins & McTighe 2000). Assessments that allow more choice, creativity of expression, and validation of original thought tend to be more successful.

Many very successful teachers tend to create nontraditional assessments, such as projects, graphic organizers, charts, checklists, matrices, and anecdotal records. These types of assessments tend to be more engaging—and more useful—to students than many question-based formats of assessment. In fact, every time I see a student with a set of questions to answer, I ask myself if there is any other way to get students to learn and process the target information: Is there a creative, more real-world way to show that they know it? People get very few "answer the questions" tasks to perform in the real world. Rather, they are asked to produce something by interpreting, analyzing, transforming, synthesizing, and communicating the information given to them. Moreover, the most informative assessments can sometimes be the ones that students do not realize are assessments.

One example of real-world activities that are effective for both learning and assessing is performance tasks. The G.R.A.S.P.S. process is based in the backward planning model of Wiggins and McTighe, outlined in *Understanding by Design* (2000). The G.R.A.S.P.S. acronym helps teachers remember the key components of creating performance tasks that deepen understanding and develop academic thinking. *G* stands for goals, mentioned above; *R* stands for real-world–type roles that students play in order to accomplish the task; *A* stands for audience (i.e., to whom they will present their performance); *S* stands for the situation, such as a conflict to be resolved, a challenge to be overcome, or a decision to be made; *P* stands for products and performances that show the learning and thinking; and *S* stands for the standards and criteria used to assess student understanding. In my experience (both in training other teachers and in my own teaching), I have noticed a large amount of focus on *P*, but not on the other five elements.

Every teaching activity can be a window into a student's thinking. Consider using the following steps to help you use teaching activities as assessments:

1. Know what objectives (thinking standards and content) you want to assess.

2. Figure out which academic language expressions best show the desired thinking. Refer to the academic language sections in chapters 3–14 for specific terms to look for.

3. Decide what type of evidence a student can provide to show his or her performance. The evidence could be information that students put into a graphic organizer, drawing, discussion, written text, presentation, etc.

4. Create a checklist (or rubric) that lists what is to be learned and how it is evidenced by the activity. These are also very helpful to inform students about what they are expected to know, do, say, and think. You can even include a section to take notes on the specific evidence for the skill. Following is an example:

| Identifying Cause and Effect | | | | | Evidence Notes |
|---|---|---|---|---|---|
| Infers causes | 1 | 2 | 3 | 4 | |
| Infers effects | 1 | 2 | 3 | 4 | |
| Uses evidence from text | 1 | 2 | 3 | 4 | |

5. One-on-one option: Pick one or two key aspects of academic thinking that will show up in the activity, and focus on them while discussing work with students and/or grading student work. For example, in the Purse of Persuasion activity (chapter 8), you might focus on the quality of evidence for the arguments and on how well the student addresses counterarguments. You would then focus your discussion with the

student or your written comments to him or her on these aspects. This can be time-consuming, but it can also be useful for the students who need the most help.

6. Share your observations and assessments with students, both as a whole class and on an individual basis. (Hand out the checklist/rubric *beforehand* so students know what is expected of them.)

## Teacher Habit 2: Offer Some Choice to Students

Most students are offered very little choice at school. Most state standards, for example, do not give a lot of either–or options for what students will learn. In fact, most grade-level content areas have more than a year's worth of standards to teach in just one year (not to mention the school days lost to testing). However, we can give students more choice in two areas: how they learn and how they show what they have learned. This is a big part of the differentiation movement that is growing across the United States—particularly in the lower grades, because their lower teacher–student ratio makes differentiation easier to implement (Benjamin, 2002). Differentiation is, however, catching on in middle school and high school classrooms as teachers increasingly realize the need to reach students in different ways. For example, in one district where I work, high school teachers are starting to use literature study groups in which each group studies a different book, rather than teaching one novel to the whole class at the same time. Likewise, the science teachers are providing choices for final projects to show concepts learned about cell biology. The advantage of choices such as these is that students feel more ownership of their learning (Stipek, 2001).

When you see that your students can learn the standards in more than one way, give them some choice in how they learn and how they are assessed. Granted, the classroom can be a little busier with more things going on, but more learning often results. One idea is a choice chart on which you (perhaps with students' help) can write multiple options for learning the unit. You can create a simpler grid of choices, but you can also embellish a bit, as shown in Figure 2. The top row can be the skills you want to build, and the left side can be the mediums of communication. The blank areas allow students to brainstorm and even come up with their own ideas.

## Teacher Habit 3: Connect the New to the Existing

This habit may be the first thing teachers are taught in teacher preparation courses. Experienced teachers get tired of hearing this, but we teachers all know that we could do a better job at it, particularly with struggling readers and English learners. We must remember that students are new to us each year, bringing with them a unique set of background experiences and knowledge. This year's Juan may have very different interests from last year's Juan; this year's Julie may have drastically different literacy needs than last year's Julie.

| | Compare and Contrast | Categorize and Classify | Persuade | Evaluate |
|---|---|---|---|---|
| **Poster** | | Create a poster that categorizes living conditions of three groups of people. | | Design a poster that evaluates the impact of industry on history. |
| **Letter** | Write a letter that compares rural life with city life. | | | |
| **Drama** | | | Create a drama that persuades factory owners to change working conditions. | |
| **Narrative** | Create a story that compares two families. | | | |
| **Webpage** | | Create a webpage that categorizes living conditions of three groups of people. | | Create a webpage that evaluates the benefits of industry. |
| **Essay** | | | Create an essay that persuades people to join together and fight the status quo. | |

Figure 2. Sample Choice Chart for Industrial Revolution Unit

Adapted from Heacox (2001)

We must therefore be creative in how we help students relate the concepts, habits, and strategies that we are teaching to what they already know and use. Chapter 1 mentioned the importance of helping students to build academic skills on their existing foundation of knowledge and skills. If we don't help students connect in this way, then they can quickly lose interest and/or become overwhelmed by too much disjointed information (Alvermann & Phelps, 2002). We can do several things to help students connect: (1) relate current learning to previous lessons, other classes, current events, school events, or life outside of school; (2) use familiar texts such as movies, songs, pictures, television shows, commercials, community issues, or controversial topics; (3) show students the similarities between thinking inside of school and outside of school by using a Venn diagram or T-chart; and (4) fill in the necessary background knowledge before the lesson or the reading session by using pictures, stories, gestures, and drama.

When students feel that they are not starting from scratch and that they already know something about a topic, then they will be more likely to be interested in learning a little more—especially if that "little more" relates to their lives in some way. Some topics do not seem to be all that relevant or interesting to many students; this is where our creativity as teachers comes in.

Remember to deliberately introduce students to each thinking skill, telling them that they already use it every day, both in and out of school. Point out that they have been using each skill for most of their lives. Then, if they ask why they are learning it now from you, tell them that it is a skill that can always use more work, a skill that people must continue to develop in order to understand more and more complex ideas over time. Tell them that we teachers are still developing these skills as well.

# Teacher Habit 4: Model

Modeling thinking is an important practice that makes the invisible thinking processes visible to students (Rosenshine & Meister, 1992). Many teachers of upper grades have probably not considered or might not know how to model academic thinking, and therefore they do not do it. They assume that students already know how to think academically or just need a little extra time to figure it out on their own. But remember that the invisible thinking processes (i.e., skills) that facilitate learning and comprehension often do not occur to students simply because the processes *are* invisible: Students have seldom seen or heard them. They have not had the chance to be an apprentice, so to speak, who naturally acquires the skills by being around a more expert model. Secondary students still need to observe another person modeling an academic task multiple times. We teachers are the best-qualified people to show students how to think academically about our subject area. We should model our thinking when reading challenging content texts and when performing tasks such as filling in graphic organizers, drawing mental images from a text, and creating written responses.

One effective way to model thinking is with think-alouds (Farr, 2001). These are effective ways to show students how teachers, as proficient learners, think about and mentally organize the many ideas that fill people's brains while people are reading and learning. By verbalizing our thoughts, we can "make visible" the hidden, complex skills and habits that help us comprehend. We can show how we also get stuck, figure out words, ask questions, solve problems, hypothesize, and analyze. Plenty of think-aloud suggestions can be found in the following chapters.

# Teacher Habit 5: Scaffold Language and Content Learning

Students need to be given opportunities to do what the teacher has modeled, but with teacher assistance that gradually diminishes as students acquire the skill or knowledge. Jerome Bruner (1985) introduced the metaphor of a scaffold to support learning. This term was related to Lev Vygotsky's zone of proximal development (ZPD), which describes learning that progresses just beyond what a student can do independently (1980). I simply prefer to think of scaffolding as "just enough help to get them to the next level of learning." Scaffolding is also explained as "gradually releasing responsibility" to the learner. This means that the teacher gradually turns over the responsibility for doing the task to the student, who does it more and more independently (Alvermann & Phelps, 2002).

To illustrate the scaffolding of learning, imagine a master artist with several apprentices. The master artist does not simply let her apprentices gather in the corner and create products on their own all day. She works with them, models various steps, voices her thought processes while she works, asks for comments, and provides clear feedback. She does not give a long lecture while the apprentices listen and take notes with the goal of passing an upcoming multiple-choice test on sculpture next Friday. (This latter method is the one used in many of today's teacher-centered formats, which tend to be too rigid and obscure—not to mention boring and irrelevant—for struggling learners.)

With the scaffolding method, the teacher does most of the task in the beginning, then uses scaffolding activities to build students' abilities to do the task. For example, you might start a lesson on interpreting figurative language with a popular song, and then show students how to fill in a chart that helps them to interpret figurative meanings. Gradually, you allow students to fill in the chart with less and less assistance, until eventually the chart is taken away and students can discuss figurative interpretations without the extra support.

Not surprisingly, research has shown that scaffolds can be very effective for building academic thinking (Rosenshine & Meister, 1992). Rosenshine and Meister synthesized the results of more than 50 studies and found significantly positive results from the scaffolding of cognitive strategies such as the thinking skills presented in this book. Thinking skills are abstract and difficult to see and are therefore difficult to teach; scaffolding allows students to break down thinking into more tangible components and to practice these with the support of the teacher. The skill of persuading, for example, entails various steps and incorporates other thinking skills. With a graphic organizer and even a chant of the steps, this rather complex thinking skill can be built gradually and in nonoverwhelming ways.

# Teacher Habit 6: Give Minilessons on Academic Thinking and Language

An important component of instruction is a minilesson. Minilessons are short and focused lessons that develop a particular thinking skill or strategy, given when teachers notice a need

(Mooney, Hoyt, & Parkes, 2003). Following are a few possible topics for minilessons, along with the thinking skills those minilessons would help to teach:

| Minilesson Topic | Academic Thinking Skill |
| --- | --- |
| Textbook prereading<br>Hierarchical organization | Analyzing |
| Using similes/metaphors<br>Different genres of literature | Comparing and contrasting |
| Determining importance<br>Summarizing | Categorizing and classifying |
| Inferences and predictions<br>Drawing conclusions | Identifying cause and effect |
| The scientific method<br>Using a textbook<br>Figuring out unknown words | Solving problems and hypothesizing |
| Addressing counterarguments<br>Finding and using evidence | Persuading |
| Personification<br>Multicultural perspectives and points of view<br>Using quotations | Empathizing |
| Under-the-surface questions<br>Using multiple sources<br>Internet searching<br>Taking notes | Synthesizing |
| Symbolism<br>Idiomatic expressions<br>Tone and voice<br>Using visuals | Interpreting |
| Credibility of sources<br>Opinions vs. facts<br>Author bias | Evaluating |
| Hooks and grabbers<br>Audience and purpose<br>Thesis statements<br>Transitions | Communicating |
| Writing a persuasive letter<br>Building a model of an efficient engine | Applying |

Minilessons can be done with the whole class or in small groups. For instance, you might notice three or four students who struggle in their interpretation of figurative language. During an appropriate time, you could take just those students aside to provide them with a minilesson on these skills. The steps for a minilesson are as follows:

1. **Introduction**—Let students know what they are about to learn. Connect the new concept to their prior knowledge and to the text being studied.
2. **Teacher modeling**—Show students how to use the strategy. Teacher think-aloud techniques are effective for this step. Explicitly use academic language, and highlight the academic language you are using.
3. **Student modeling and guided practice**—Let students gradually take charge of the strategy so that they require less support from you.
4. **Independent practice**—Give students opportunities to try the strategy in new situations and then to reflect on how it has been useful.

# Teacher Habit 7: Use Appropriate Teacher Language to Elicit and Cultivate Academic Thinking

What we say in class can have a significant impact on the development of students' thinking and language during each lesson. Class and group discussions are times when learning can be at its height, and we must do our best to model and facilitate rich talk. Following are a few suggestions for drawing students out to think about and share more of their thoughts on a topic. Many of the prompts are genuine questions for answers that the teacher does not already know. Encourage students to craft unique answers that are not merely for display of correct or incorrect knowledge, but that show complex academic thought. Try to get into the habit of using some of the following expressions:

- You are onto something important...keep going.
- I know you may not know, but if you knew, what might you say?
- You are on the right track.
- Can you think of a good example, perhaps from...?
- What did you notice about...?
- I noticed that you mentioned...tell me more about...?
- That's a good probable answer. How did you come to that answer?
- You may have forgotten, but tell me one thing you do remember about...?
- That's a great start. Keep thinking and I'll get back to you.
- There is no right answer, so what would be your best answer?
- What did you learn from this?
- Great thinking...keep going.

# Teacher Habit 8: Sharpen Lesson Transitions

Transitions create a bridge that helps students carry learning from one activity to the next. Transitions also help students to see the direction of learning, similar to stopping and looking at a map. Use the following ideas as "seedling" ideas from which you can create your own transitions.

- **Connect the activity to the objectives of the lesson**—"Which objective did the last activity help you learn? The next one will help us better understand...." For this, it helps to have the objectives visible in the room somewhere.

- **Summarize and bridge**—"Can anyone give me a synopsis of what we learned in the last activity? Write two sentences that summarize what happened in the last activity." "This next activity helps us learn more about...."

- **Connect to and build on background knowledge**—"OK, think silently about how the last activity might relate to your life or the world around us. Can you share some answers? Now we are going to dig a little deeper into what that means in this next activity."

- **Carry over and predict**—"We just learned some new terms and ideas that will help us with the next activity that we are about to do. Can anyone guess how they might help?"

- **Think-pair-connect**—"This next activity is a writing activity in which we need to think like scientists. Keep your notes in front of you, and think for a minute how you might use them for the next activity. Share your thoughts with a partner."

- **Ask a connecting question**—"We just read about.... Now, everyone think of a good summary sentence for what we just read..." (wait for responses). "Now, if we want to prove that plants need certain things, what might we do?" (This can lead into doing an experiment.)

- **LWS** (List, Want to Know, Still Need to Know)—"List what you have learned so far from the last activities. Now, list what you want to know and what you still need to know. Focus on the 'still need to know' list, and circle what you think will be covered in the next activity."

# Teacher Habit 9: Put More GruViMoMaMu Into Lessons

Unfortunately, the quantity and quality of engaging, beyond-just-verbal techniques used in schools seems to decrease in each grade from 1 to 12. In high school, many classes are seriously lacking in extraverbal teaching, which deprives many struggling students of optimal content and language learning conditions. Teaching methods that are based on multiple intelligences are especially helpful for reaching students who struggle with academic language processing and reading comprehension (Armstrong, 2003). Such methods offer students the extra support, entry points, relevance, and connections they need to reach deeper levels of understanding and more complex levels of thinking.

GruViMoMaMu is an abbreviation and reminder that helps to fortify lessons that meet the needs of all students. *Gru* stands for group, pair, and cooperative work; *Vi* for visuals and artistic representations; *Mo* for movement, kinesthetics, gestures, and hand motions; *Ma* for manipulatives and hands-on projects; and *Mu* for music, chants, rhymes, songs, and rhythm. GruViMoMaMus are the beyond-verbal, active methods that we can use in our teaching to fortify learning, especially for students who struggle with traditional, verbal-only formats of teaching. GruViMoMaMus reinforce content learning and make academic language more comprehensible. They tend to be more engaging than traditional formats in which students listen to a lecture and take notes or read a passage and answer questions.

These methods are based in part on the theory of multiple intelligences, a term coined by Howard Gardner (1999), who has written extensively on the subject. He has highlighted eight intelligences (see this book's Preface), with others being theorized each year. GruViMoMaMu develops and employs four of Gardner's eight intelligences: interpersonal, visual/spatial, kinesthetic, and musical. These are exciting teaching methods because they encourage the teacher to continually ask, "How can I *show* this thinking process? How can the students *act out* this concept? How can students *negotiate meaning* with other students and *create* a product that truly fortifies thinking?"

Some activities, such as hands-on science experiments, already use several GruViMoMaMu techniques. But you can always ask yourself if an additional beyond-just-verbal technique (e.g., a chant, an object from home, or a role-play) could be used to improve learning. The answer is often *yes*. Many students need to learn a concept through more than one intelligence, and it is often a nonverbal method that clarifies the verbal learning and allows the concept to stick in the student's brain. Picture a mountain with several roads to the top, one road for each of the GruViMoMaMu methods. The verbal road is often too steep for many students, who can still make it to the top of the mountain (which is the learning of standards) but need to do so by a different path. For this reason, the more standards there are to teach, the more GruViMoMaMu teaching techniques we should use. I often beg middle school and high school teachers to use these techniques more than they do now. Sadly, many teachers consider techniques such as chants and hand motions to be a waste of time or to be too juvenile for their students, and, therefore, many teachers do not even attempt them. Yet other teachers have come to me and said, "I thought my students would boo and hiss as if I were treating them like babies...but they loved it! And they still know the content after three months!"

## *Putting More Gru Into Lessons*

*Gru* stands for group work and cooperation. Gru methods are cooperative activities in which students must work together and communicate to achieve a common goal (Snow & Brinton, 1997). Many resources and studies (Hall, 1989; Johnson et al., 1981; Slavin, 1994) have extolled the benefits of cooperative learning. Such benefits include more in-depth understanding of content, more enduring learning, more engaged learning, better socialization, and better developed academic thinking and language.

In a properly designed Gru activity in a group setting, students must accomplish an interesting task together and use language as a bridge in the process. A student must take in academic language in order to understand what other students are thinking, and then that student must use academic language to express his or her own thoughts. If a clear understanding is not reached, the task cannot be accomplished. Students must therefore continue to negotiate meaning until understanding is clear enough to complete the task.

Teachers should model how to use academic language in carrying out tasks. For example, sit down in a "fish bowl" model group with three students, and model the language used for persuasion or evaluation. Have the rest of the class gather around, observe the sample group, and take notes. Devise ways for groups to keep track of instances when they notice themselves using academic language as they work. Perhaps one role in a group could be that of "Academic Language Gatherer." You can also put up wall posters showing the language that is needed for talking about the task and refer students to those posters.

A wide range of group activities exists, from pairs to quads to whole-class discussions. Teachers should be familiar with these techniques and not be reluctant to take the time needed to train students in them—and it does take time. For example, reciprocal teaching (Palincsar & Brown, 1984), a method commonly used for improving reading comprehension, takes several months of preparation and minilessons before it runs effectively. Some cooperative techniques are not right for every classroom. Pairs may work best in some classes, and larger groups in other classes.

Most of the activities in this book are very effective when adapted for pairs and groups. For example, one teacher was giving a lesson about *Lord of the Flies* (Golding, 1997) that used a character diagram. Though not on the agenda, the teacher had students write down several thoughts and share them with a partner on how Piggy might have been a scapegoat. If they hadn't been asked to share their ideas with a partner, many students would have just sat back and let the daily hand raisers answer. Instead, the brief Gru activity got more students engaged, and several quiet students felt that their answers, after being validated by partners, were good enough to share in whole-class time.

The act of communicating a concept to another person helps people to learn it better (Lyons & Pinnell, 2001). When people communicate, they are forced to organize and clarify their thoughts into coherent sentences before they speak. This process makes an imprint on the brain, creating ownership of the information and therefore facilitating more enduring learning. The process of discussing ideas with others also forces people to challenge their own preconceptions, to negotiate meaning, and to sharpen their thinking. Pair activities are particularly effective in the classroom because they can be constructed quickly (e.g., "Turn to a partner and...") and because anxiety is low: Only one other person is listening (see Think-Pair-Share in chapter 13). Groups of three to five students can also provide powerful learning experiences when done correctly. Students in these groups need to have their roles clearly defined. Initially, you should model what to say and how to say it by using minilessons and plenty of guidance during the process.

A few questions can help as you design cooperative activities:

• How can I get students to talk to one another about the key concepts I am teaching?

• What kind of language do I want to hear when I listen to groups?

• What roles should group members have?

## *Putting More Vi Into Lessons*

*Vi* stands for visuals, such as pictures, graphic organizers, diagrams, acronyms, and charts. All learners have varying degrees of what is sometimes called visual intelligence (Gardner, 1999). Visual intelligence is the mental skill of seeing and creating the images that a person uses to organize and process information. Most authors of narrative and expository texts expect, albeit unconsciously, their readers to visualize a large number of concrete and even abstract ideas while reading. We teachers must take stock of how much we visualize while we read in order to help students do the same. Then we must get into the habit of developing visual lesson components (many are given throughout chapters 3–14 of this book) that help students not only use, but also develop, their visual abilities as they learn.

Visuals tend to be summaries that show, rather than just tell, what the words of a text or concept mean. For English learners, visuals help make language "stand still" long enough for it to sink in and be understood. Visuals are helpful in all three stages of reading (pre-, during-, and post-). Image-based visuals include pictures, photos, videos, and maps. These help to show physical descriptions of a text's information and images.

For students who are still familiarizing themselves with the complexities (and inconsistencies) of English, the use of visuals to show the connections and structures of varying texts and concepts is especially helpful (Peregoy & Boyle, 2000). English learners, for example, "hit the wall" of frustration much sooner if spoken or written words are the only medium used in a lesson or text. Visual aids extend students' mental endurance and better communicate what the words truly mean in order to improve overall comprehension. This book contains many visual ways to organize information and to build the skills that diverse students can utilize to improve learning.

One fun and effective way to visually organize knowledge is with acronyms. An acronym provides a mnemonic, or what I call a visual–verbal reminder, that provides just enough of a frame to help a student (or adult) to remember key information or steps. I am always drawn to acronyms in complex texts because they help me to reduce information down to the essentials and then to remember it well after I am done reading or listening. If a speaker, for example, presents an acronym rather than six bullet points, I am much more likely to remember the concepts and even the details from the speech. Students benefit from these scaffolds as well. If an acronym is directly related to the task (e.g., Response to Literature Rap-Acronym in chapter 11 and PERSUADE Acronym Chant-Rap in chapter 8), then the student has a strong chance of producing the acronym and recalling its components. And, surprisingly, acronyms are fun and fairly easy to create. You might even want to give students the task of creating acronyms for you. This way, they do the work for you and they benefit from the extra problem-solving and language-processing exercises. You can tell them you would like an acronym to teach the concepts to future students.

Another, more visual way to organize information is with graphic organizers: drawings that use geometric shapes or tables to show connections between pieces of information (Hyerle, 1996). For many learners, seeing the relationships between concepts in a visually organized way helps them to better comprehend and remember. A semantic web, for example, teaches students how to conceptualize hierarchical relationships. Graphic organizers also make invisible, complex, and abstract thinking skills more visible, explicit, and tangible to students (Merkley & Jefferies, 2001). For example, a chart that categorizes rocks and minerals helps students to see the analyzing and comparing involved in organizing knowledge for practical purposes.

Perhaps the most important feature of graphic organizers is that they help a student to create a visual representation of what is being learned. This allows the student to clarify and better remember the relationships, sequences, and important concepts. Graphic organizers also demonstrate how different parts of the text or concept relate to one another, how the learning connects to the reader's life, and how to organize one's thinking about the concepts. Ultimately, the process of filling in, designing, and studying visual representations will develop into an automatic skill that no longer depends on the use of the actual graphic organizer. For example, I have used Venn diagrams so often that, now when I am reading a text that compares two concepts, I picture the two intersecting circles in my mind, which helps me organize and retain the information.

For students, the process of designing the graphic reinforces their understanding of the material by requiring them to reconstruct the information in their own words and to create connections that other students or the teacher may not have noticed. Students must mentally manipulate the information when they use and construct graphic organizers. This creative design process gives them more ownership of their learning and their interpretations of the text (Marzano et al., 2001). And when students see a task to be a relevant and fresh product of their own creation, they mind the extra thinking a little less. Moreover, most graphic organizers provide much-needed practice in identifying key elements of text and reducing them (i.e., synthesizing and summarizing) to fit in the spaces provided.

Students should be taught to design their own graphic organizers. I have noticed that many students who learn to make their own graphic organizers are better at remembering and understanding the information in a text than are students who are simply told to fill out a graphic organizer made up by the teacher. This makes sense: As students construct good graphic organizers from texts, they must put the information in their mental "hands" and shape it. They learn actively by doing something with the information rather than just answering questions (Hyerle, 1996). This promotes deeper learning. So as you develop your own expertise and insights as a graphic organizer builder, pass these tips on to your students. Provide a hefty supply of different models, and discuss why they are made the way they are. Ask students to think of other ways of graphically showing different types of information in addition to Venn diagrams and semantic webs. Their ways of thinking, interpreting, and organizing text information in graphic organizers often prove to be innovative and insightful.

**Using Graphic Organizers With Expository Texts.** Authors of expository texts, for the most part, are trying their best to communicate complex concepts and knowledge to their readers. As mentioned previously, many authors assume that their readers have already developed a certain level of academic thinking skills, active reading habits, and vocabulary that are needed to comprehend the text. Most textbooks, therefore, rely on challenging and specific vocabulary, along with numerous connections that students may not possess to previous content knowledge and readings.

*Work the graphic organizer.* I have seen many teachers put up a wonderful visual but only use it once. Remind yourself to use each visual to its maximum potential in all stages of the lesson. Refer back to it often. Add to it. Have students add to it and teach others from it. Use it as an anchor for the concepts in the lesson. Finally, use it to review key concepts before summative assessments.

*Assess with graphic organizers.* As discussed in the beginning of the chapter, graphic organizers can give teachers the chance to informally assess the ways in which students are understanding and organizing text information, and students' ways of thinking, interpreting, and organizing text information into graphic organizers often prove to be very innovative and insightful. Graphic organizers are great alternatives to tests and quizzes. You can assign point values to different areas of a graphic organizer, or you can create a rubric or checklist that covers what you want students to learn. You can use graphic organizers to assess how students do the following:

- Form main ideas and concepts
- Cling to incorrect or misguided assumptions about what has been read
- Organize information
- Form relationships between pieces of information
- Make connections to prior knowledge
- Use strategies to monitor comprehension
- Engage in higher-order thinking processes
- Visualize connections and frame the information for later retrieval

To more effectively use visuals, try asking yourself questions such as these:

- How can I show what I want students to learn in this unit?
- How can they visually show what they have learned?
- How can I use posters, photos, digital journals, Venn diagrams, semantic webs, flow charts, grids, and timelines?

## Putting More Mo Into Lessons

*Mo* stands for movement in teaching and learning, a concept that is also called kinesthetic learning. Mos are extraverbal methods that reinforce content learning and make language more comprehensible. Much of the recent research on the brain supports the use of active, kinesthetic experiences to improve learning (Wolfe, 2001). These techniques can be especially helpful when teaching new vocabulary and concepts (Marzano et al., 2001). Information, when combined with motor function and physical activity, becomes better "engraved" in the brain. Such facts "stick" better because more neural pathways are established than just the word-based path, which may not be as strong for many struggling students as the verbal pathways are in nonstruggling students. One teacher I know, for example, teaches the causes and effects of World War II along with hand motions for them, and she finds that students are much better at remembering the information when they write and take tests. This book includes three main types of Mo that we should be using in our teaching: (1) motions and gestures, (2) process simulations, and (3) dramas and role-plays.

**Hand Motions, Gestures, and Moving Around the Room.**  These are quick and easy ways to get students to act out or signal the important terms and concepts of the lesson. Even body movement can be powerful. *Voting with your feet* and *Take a stand* are common expressions in U.S. culture, and they can also be used to create activities in which students get up and go somewhere in the room in response to a controversial subject. For example, students who are in favor of the death penalty can be asked to stand on one side of the room, and students who are against the death penalty can stand on the other side. Students can then be asked to say why they feel as they do.

In order to effectively use hand motions, we as teachers must (1) decide if the concept or skill set is important enough to take the time for using movement and (2) create the most effective kinesthetic way to learn and remember the concepts. Students, of course, can be excellent helpers in coming up with good motions to use in teaching. One teacher I know wanted to use Mo methods for teaching the comparison of two ancient cultures. He asked for suggestions, and one student thought that a giant Venn diagram on the floor of the room might help. The teacher gave out cards listing important cultural traits. Each student then had to decide if the trait on his or her card was similar or different between the two cultures, and the students all had to be prepared to defend their answers. Students then placed themselves at the right spot on the Venn in the room. If their traits were very different, they stood at the outer edges, if only somewhat different, then toward the middle where the two cultures overlapped. Their movement in the activity helped them remember the facts, but, more important, the process of analyzing traits, comparing them, and evaluating them on a scale challenged them to think and speak academically.

One teacher I know has "Nonverbal Time" for 15 minutes each week, during which everyone in the room must communicate with only gestures, pantomime, charades, and visuals.

**Whole-Body Process Simulations.**  These are activities in which students act out parts or elements of a process and show how it works. For example, students might portray planets in the solar system, water molecules in the water cycle, minerals to be categorized in desk rows of the room, or variables of an equation. In a sense, students are making a diagram or equation come alive. This type of activity differs from role-playing in that, here, students are portraying objects that would not normally be animate.

**Experiential Exercises, Dramas, and Role-Plays.**  Some of the most powerful learning activities that we can give students are experiences that involve them as participants, rather than just observers. Experiential exercises, dramas, and role-plays allow the students to use intrapersonal and kinesthetic intelligences to simulate and recreate events and situations from history or a work of literature. In most experiential exercises, the classroom is transformed in some way to bring about the physical and psychological conditions you are trying to emulate. Students then put themselves into the shoes of those who might have actually been in that situation. Some examples include being in a trench in the Vietnam War, being on a jury in

*To Kill a Mockingbird* (Lee, 1960), being in a gang in *The Outsiders* (Hinton, 1967), being under the rule of a dictator, being in a meeting with President Abraham Lincoln, or working in a factory under oppressive conditions with low wages.

As you might well imagine, such experiences can demand a high amount of risk, creativity, planning, and time on your part. But the rewards are worth it: Students gain greater access to academic concepts, they tend to remember the ideas much more clearly, they have an anchor experience to which you can refer throughout the unit and year, and they enjoy it.

To create effective experiential learning activities, consider what types of experiences are feasible in the classroom and whether they are best learned by doing, rather than seeing or listening. Choose an event or situation that is key to the unit you are teaching (i.e., that is worth the extra time and energy in class) and that emphasizes people's thoughts, feelings, and actions in the scene. Think about how to use the desks as props in some way to develop the "stage." Consider the use of cards that tell students what is happening and that assign them their respective roles. (This, by the way, can be very powerful for developing oral language and improvisation skills.) Finally, create a plan for wrapping up the activity, sharing the process as a class, and connecting it to the key concepts of the unit.

Dramas and role-plays are usually done on a smaller scale than the experiential activities described previously. In dramas and role-plays, students act out a situation, event, concept, process, or story as if they were the real characters. Dramas usually require students to figure out the appropriate dialog and actions of the characters before they present the drama. The advantages of dramas and role-plays are that they force students to refer to the text for evidence, and they allow for lots of collaboration and language development opportunities.

A few guiding questions for using experiential activities and dramas include the following:

- How can some kind of movement, either with hands or the whole body, show this concept?

- Can students come up with their own motions?

- What kind of experience would help students understand the scene, the event, and the feelings of those involved?

### Putting More Ma Into Lessons

*Ma* stands for manipulatives, or the use of tactile learning, which is the most hands-on of the five GruViMoMaMu methods. Ma teaching means using anything that can be touched, held, or moved around during learning. This includes items such as cards, sticky notes, stamps, candy, sticks, dice, household items, rocks, machines, and clothes. Ma also includes project materials that allow students to create tangible products of learning beyond simple written compositions or tests.

One important reason that Ma is so valuable for learning is the way in which tangible objects help to make abstract ideas more concrete and memorable (Gregory & Chapman, 2002). I often hear teachers say, "That student is a tactile learner." In fact, most students (and teachers) with whom I have worked learn better through tactile methods. They thrive on tangible, touchable, manipulatable tools of learning, which can range from small sticky notes to homemade rockets. Ma teaching methods help to form a solid foundation for refining and reinforcing academic thinking with a written product. I have noticed repeatedly that students are more likely to write when they have just learned something through a hands-on experience than when they have simply read or listened to the information.

Another advantage is that Ma activities allow students to solve complex problems and process abstract concepts in concrete ways, often through a set of logical steps. This is because Ma overlaps with kinesthetic and visual learning: Students must look at objects that relate to the concepts being learned, and they must move the objects around as they learn. For example, before doing an experiment on sound waves, a student must visualize how the set-up will look, then put the pieces together, then manipulate them in order to test hypotheses and draw conclusions.

We need to reflect on how Ma methods can be integrated into many of the reading, writing, and problem-solving activities that we do. And we must make sure we encourage as much academic thinking as possible through the use of the manipulatives. I have seen the making of some projects (e.g., dioramas) use too much instructional time for the amount of thinking and learning that resulted. We must therefore be selective and strategic when designing Ma activities. We want the time that we spend, in and out of class, to be as productive as possible. Some questions that can help guide the design of effective Ma activities include these:

- How can I bring in or create objects or simulated objects that show concepts?
- What objects might be needed in simulations or dramas (in the Mo activities)?
- How can students manipulate things to show learning and remember concepts?
- Is there a problem that can be answered with experimentation?
- How can students record and then move information into categories?
- How can manipulatives be used to support other GruViMoMaMu activities?
- How can I use things such as clothes, sticks, clay, cardboard, index cards, sentence strips, posters, models, dice, instruments, tools, and hand-held computers?
- How much money and time are needed for materials and set-up for a particular Ma activity?

## *Putting More Mu Into Lessons*

Music can be a powerful learning tool. Today's students are listening to more kinds of music than ever, and they know many songs by heart. Their brains tend to grab onto the verses of songs and hold them for long periods of time. We teachers, innovators and adapters that we are, must tap into this brain trait of our students and use it to our advantage. You don't have to play guitar like Sting or sing like Pavarotti; you just have to take the "musical leap." Jump in and see what happens, even with some tapping and chanting. You will probably be pleasantly surprised. Music is interesting to many students, much more so than much of what they encounter during the school day. They usually appreciate attempts by a teacher to use music to help them learn, no matter what the quality of the music might be.

Chants and songs are great to use in the classroom for six reasons:

1. Music is effective for teaching and practicing academic language. If you or your students write a ditty with academic language in it, the song will be more deeply imprinted in the brain because of the repetition and rhythm. You can also highlight types of language as you analyze the song.

2. Music is great for teaching core vocabulary and concepts that you don't want students to forget (Readence, Bean, & Baldwin, 2001). For instance, I still have "The chro-mosome–is–the carrier–of the gene" in a cadence form stuck in my brain—from more than 20 years ago! Think about how many songs from way back when that you still have using up your brain cells and surfacing at odd moments.

3. Music helps people to learn and remember steps in a process. I was once talking with a science teacher who, during my workshop (while I was talking about the next topic), had started to write a quick chant about the steps of the scientific method. He used this chant with success in his classroom.

4. Music allows students to create songs about content concepts and to challenge themselves to reduce the concepts to the key points. Some teachers have even used student-created songs as prewriting scaffolds for essay writing.

5. Music helps students to interpret figurative language and develop their abstract reasoning abilities (Miller & Coen, 1994).

6. Music is fun for students. The fun factor can work wonders in amplifying learning, despite many secondary school teachers' perceptions that school must be serious all the time.

Following is a song or chant that I wrote to remind students of the many intelligences that we all have:

My name is Howie and I got eight kids
And they're all smart in different ways
I got mathematical intelligence
So, of course, I named them
One through Eight

Number One loves to hum at the top of her lungs
Number Two has a smelly aquarium
Number Three likes to sit in a tree and just think
Number Four always leaves his paints
clogging up the sink

Number Five waltzes 'round in pajamas all night
Number Six likes to count all the city lights
Number Seven's always gabbing with her 40 friends
Number Eight makes me read her stories
again and again

My name is Howie
And all I got to say...

Each of us is different,
And we're all smart in different ways.

Number One loves to drum on the garbage can
Number Two thinks it's cool to hold slugs in her hand
Number Three likes to ponder the meaning of life
Number Four makes Play-Doh cars—but they're all life-size

Number Five dances hip-hop while taking a bath
Number Six describes all of life with charts and graphs
Number Seven just told me she has 43 friends
Number Eight just wrote a book on different kinds
of intelligence

My name is Howie... (rest of chorus)

Finally, here are a few helpful questions that can help in the design of Mu activities:

- How can I or students create a song that embodies the learning that needs to happen?
- How can I incorporate the use of or the creation of a song, chant, poem, rap, or rhythm pattern in some way in this lesson or unit?
- Is there a song already out there that can serve our purposes?
- What vocabulary should be in the song?
- What instruments might be fun to use to play the song?

**Steps for Creating Charts and Songs.** Following are some steps for writing quick and effective songs with core content material:

1. Think about the key vocabulary and concepts that you really want students to know. Think of the concepts or vocabulary with which students struggle the most or the standards and ideas that students have not retained well over the years.

2. Jot down the ideas. Write short phrases or sentences that contain the meat of what you want your students to know and think about. Use academic language terms and content vocabulary. Choose words with transferable roots and affixes that you can teach in minilessons. Refer to course standards (I have even taken whole phrases directly from state standards), questions at the end of the appropriate textbook chapter, and chapter summaries.

3. Now think of a song that has lyrics or a theme that connects to the material you want to teach. It may be rare to find an existing song that works; however, I do have a friend who chose "Every Breath You Take" by the Police for teaching cellular respiration and "Break Down" by Tom Petty and the Heartbreakers for teaching the digestive system. Most likely, you will need to just pick a familiar tune that you know and that your students either know or would not mind learning. Start with a familiar tune, or let students bring one in that you can change (but do not let them bring in

songs with inappropriate lyrics). You can find a list of usable songs, some of which have simple rhyming patterns, in Appendix C.

4. Establish a rhyme pattern. Most songs will have a basic rhyme pattern, such as AABB or ABCB. In the second pattern, only two words have to rhyme, which means these songs will take less time to compose. Things do not have to rhyme exactly: *ten* can rhyme with *fan*, *all* can rhyme with *thaw*, or *ate* can rhyme with *clay*. The ending vowel sound is what should be emphasized. Yet even when a rhyme is not possible, using the song or chant will often be much better than not using music at all. Even a short four-liner works, to quickly start the class period or to fill in the last three minutes of class time when prelunch jitters are on the rise.

5. Ask students for their input. A song can be saved in draft form, and changed to fit your needs and as better ideas arise. I have been changing and using several songs for over eight years now.

6. Try it out. Get an mp3 drumbeat file, a drum, or an egg shaker to produce a beat—but take care not to let it become too loud, and do not put the instrument in the hands of a class clown. Have the whole class and parts of the class repeat verses so students can practice pronunciation.

7. Have students lead the chant when they feel comfortable doing so.

8. Give students bonus points for composing extra verses that fit into the song as you cover the unit. One teacher I know even gives students the option of composing a long song as a final synthesis of a quarter of physics teaching.

9. Reuse the song for minilessons on concepts, vocabulary, academic language, and even grammar. Put it on a poster in the classroom, and refer to it when related concepts arise in the lesson or textbook. If it the song teaches a sequence, put a big arrowhead next to the verse you are presently covering so students can focus on that main idea in the lesson.

# Teacher Habit 10: Keep an Evolving Collection of Best Practices

Each lesson should be composed of best practices. Best practices will differ across subjects, teachers, and classes; you need to figure out what works best for each group of students. We all must fill our lessons with the activities that maximize learning and the building of good academic skills. Best practices can be used all year long with a variety of subjects and texts. I often tell teachers who are reluctant to change teaching practices to start with one or two activities, keep doing those throughout the year, and add one more each month. By the end of the year, the best practices will replace most of the mediocre practices. (And one will enjoy teaching even more.)

Try creating a thinking binder (perhaps with reading, writing, and speaking sections, too) for quick reference while doing lesson planning. Table 2 shows a helpful organizer, filled in with some sample activities to show how it can be used. (Some sections are left blank in the GruViMoMaMu column because they do not happen to address any of those five modalities.)

You can also copy the Best Practices Collection Table reproducible (page 215). The main reason I like this format is that it forces me to think about the modeling and scaffolding I might need for each activity. I remember too many times when I have just dropped an activity onto students without modeling or scaffolding the needed thinking and skills. I also can forget what works best when and for whom until it is a day too late, and this chart helps me to access the information when I need it.

Another trick to remind me of these teacher habits is to go down the left margin of my lesson plans and workshop agendas and write shorthand notes to make sure I have included various components. I put little circles with *Model, Scaff, Gru, Vi, Mo, Ma, Mu,* and *OA* (ongoing assessment) in them. This way I can quickly notice if I am missing any of these components and quickly add it. For instance, recently I was about to present a workshop on differentiation and realized that I needed a kinesthetic component to wake my audience up. So I quickly came up with hand motions for GruViMoMaMu. Gru is two hands talking,

### Table 2. Best Practices Collection Table

| Lesson Stage | Activity<br>[Modeling and scaffolding reminders are in brackets] | GruViMoMaMu |
|---|---|---|
| Stage Setting and Concept Introduction | Teacher role-play<br>Video clip<br>Song<br>Using real objects in teaching | Mo<br>Vi<br>Mu<br>Ma |
| Practice | Start to fill in data table on overhead<br>Think-Pair-Share (chapter 13)<br>Jigsaw Groups (chapter 13) | Vi<br>Gru<br>Gru |
| Prereading | Teacher-guided improv role-play<br>Chant with hand gestures using vocabulary<br>Think-aloud | Mo<br>Mo, Mu |
| Reading | Model note-taking with sticky notes<br>Think-aloud<br>Academic Language Bank (chapter 1) | Gru<br><br>Vi |
| Prewriting | Semantic web—Start to fill in web<br>3-D Balance Scale (chapter 12)<br>[Minilesson on criteria—Model with large paper version] | Vi<br>Ma, Mo |
| Writing | PERSUADE Acronym Chant-Rap and Purse of Persuasion (chapter 8)<br>Persuasive letter<br>Color-Coded Writing (chapter 13) | Vi, Mu<br><br>Vi |
| Formative Assessment and Feedback | Minilesson on persuasive language<br>Two-minute conferences | <br>Gru |
| Summative Assessment | Persuasive poster [show samples]<br>Oral presentation [create a checklist for good presentations]<br>Student-made quiz [show possible questions] | Vi<br>Gru |

Vi is pointing to eyes, Mo is a running motion, Ma is grabbing something out of your hand, and Mu is holding an imaginary microphone. The audience may have thought me to be a little strange, but they woke up and they remembered the ideas.

These are just 10 of many habits we need to continue to develop in order to be effective teachers. Our students deserve the finest teaching we can provide, and I am convinced that the development of academic thinking skills is one of the most important gifts we can offer them. The next 12 chapters present 12 key academic thinking skills, the language that drives them, and some GruViMoMaMu activities that develop them in engaging ways. Please note that I have attempted to provide activities in each chapter that corresponded to Gru, Vi, Mo, Ma, and Mu. But education is not so neat and clean, and every chapter does not contain the same numbers or types of activities.

# PART II

# Twelve Academic Thinking Skills

# CHAPTER 3

# Analyzing

Analyzing means taking a closer look. It means breaking down a complex event, object, concept, or character into its component parts or attributes and then looking at each one in detail. Analyzing also entails recognizing how the parts relate to one another and recognizing the roles the parts play to form the complex whole (Beyer, 2001a). Similarly, it can involve finding patterns between components (Marzano, 1988). Other types of analysis involve looking at the main ideas, errors, feasibility, and validity of arguments. One basic example of analysis is the organization of this book. It breaks down academic thinking into 12 key thinking skills. Each skill has its own characteristics, language, and relationships to other skills.

I have put analyzing first among all the skills because so many other skills depend on it, especially the skills of comparing, categorizing, and classifying. These three Cs, interestingly, are needed for other skills such as problem solving, persuading, synthesizing, and evaluating.

The ability to analyze depends greatly on a person's previous experience and knowledge of how objects, ideas, or concepts can be broken down in the first place (Ruggiero, 2000). For example, an English teacher's knowledge of literary elements will likely allow him or her to break down a novel into more dimensions than a friend in the business world could break it into. The businessperson, however, will likely find many more ways of breaking down the process of running a successful business than would the teacher. The more immersion, challenge, and practice one has in the thinking practices of a given discipline, the better one will be at analyzing within that discipline. This supports the argument that students need to see and hear—explicitly—analysis in action within each content area.

Analyzing is at the core of most academic tasks. Textbooks break down their subjects into as many parts as possible in order to provide students with an in-depth understanding. Assessments, in a similar way, break down large areas of learning into smaller parts. Many tests use short multiple-choice questions to assess the skills and knowledge associated with the various components of math, history, literature, and more. The expression "The better we understand the parts, the better we understand the whole" sums up much of what we do in schools and the workplace. In other words, we analyze.

The ability to analyze texts is a vital skill to develop in the upper grades, especially for students who struggle with reading comprehension (van den Broek & Kremer, 2000). Text analysis is the ability to break up long sentences into component clauses in order to cut the information into understandable chunks. Analysis also involves clarifying pronoun references and referring to previous parts in a text or discourse to access needed information. One helpful type of text analysis is breaking down text into various components such as author's purpose, text structure, visuals, questions, subheadings, and key words.

A more critical type of analysis is the ability to determine ambiguity or lack of information in a message. This relates to the ability to question the relevance of details in an argument and the ability to evaluate (see chapter 12) the validity of supporting information. Students who are good at critical analysis of texts tend to ask many of the following questions:

- What is the purpose of the text? Does it inform, persuade, entertain, or narrate?

- Is the author qualified to write on the topic? Does she or he have a bias that might affect the writing? Will the author gain, monetarily or otherwise, from writing this text?

- Does the author state opinions, stereotype, or generalize? Does he or she use overly strong words such as *ridiculous, crazy, insane, worthless, pathetic, ideal, obvious,* or *clearly*?

- Does the author present and then address counteropinions?

- Are credible supporting facts given? Are their sources provided?

- Are the conclusions supported by the facts? Could there be other factors or variables that influenced the outcome?

Our goal as teachers should be to have our students automatically ask these analytical questions as they read and then actively strive to answer them.

# Academic Language, Prompts, and Frames

The following expressions, prompts, and frame are for use with the skill of analyzing. Get to know these terms, and point them out when you and your students use them in discussions or written tasks. Refer to chapter 1 for ideas on how to use academic language expressions, oral and writing prompts, and paragraph frames to develop academic thinking skills and academic language.

Some common expressions used when analyzing include the following:

- When we break it down into the components of..., we can see that...

- The elements (parts) are related in the following ways:

- There seems to be a hierarchical relationship between these components...

- Let's see how the pieces fit together to make...

- Each component plays a key role. First...

- We can describe it as...; its important traits are...

- The function of...is...

- Can we break down this component even further? How about...?

- We need to identify the....

- This is related to, extraneous to, or not applicable because...

- The least (most) essential statements are...

- I think it is more helpful to break it into these categories…
- This finding is inconsistent with this one because…
- The relationship between…and…is…
- There is a pattern that emerges when we look at…
- When you take a close look at this part, you see that…

Following are some prompts that encourage students to analyze when speaking or writing:

- Debate the following issue/statement:
- Explain the justification of…
- Describe the process of…
- Identify the most important traits of…
- Imagine you are a…and describe…
- Make a detailed description of…
- Analyze the contributions of…to…
- Investigate the events surrounding…
- Create a personality profile of…
- Write a dialog for two persons with opposing points of view.

Frames like the one below help students to gradually pick up academic language and eventually use it to compose their own high-quality written products without help. One frame is given here to get you started on your own subject- and student-specific frames. This one is very generic, to allow you to fine-tune it or even to start from scratch. When creating your own frames, be sure to refer to the lists of expressions and prompts given above.

### Paragraph Frame for Scaffolding Analyzing

_____ consists of several important components (facets/elements/traits). The first component is _____. It plays the key role of _____. The second component is the _____ _____, which influences how _____. The third and final component of _____ is its _____. It is important because it _____. These components form _____.

Remember to start with student background knowledge when introducing activities that build this skill. You can create a starter board of background knowledge topics such as friendship, family, school, music, advertising, culture, sports, television shows, movies, famous people, wars, or recent units you have studied in class.

# Activities for Developing the Skill of Analyzing

## ANALYZING WRITING MODELS
### (Gru, Vi)

This activity is the "immersion and analysis" stage of teaching writing. It is most often used with a genre of writing such as persuasive, narrative, or response to literature. It is powerful because it is inductive. It hands the reins of thinking and analysis over to students, who then see what to do when they write. In this activity, rather than being told to come up with a number of writing elements, students figure out much of it on their own. They look at both good and bad writing samples. They generate a list of qualities and components to include when they write their own pieces. This is the first step of teaching different genres of writing. As an added bonus, students tend to learn the content and style of the writings they analyze.

## *Procedure*

**1.** Choose a writing genre that you want to teach, and find several model papers from your own writing or from books, former students, or the Internet. By the way, writing your own essays can reinforce previously learned content and give you keen insights into the challenges of doing what you ask students to do.

**2.** Put students into pairs or groups, and give each group two or three writing models (e.g., two or three essay responses to literature).

**3.** Depending on the grade level and genre, give students the task of finding certain attributes of the genre. Before they start, work with them to create a checklist of what elements they predict they will find in the essay. They might come up with items such as introduction, thesis statement, and conclusion. Add and explain any others that they might not mention. Use the overhead projector to show students how to color-code or otherwise mark these attributes.

**4.** Have groups read the papers, discuss the attributes (Gru), and then mark them. Then have students take notes in a chart (Vi) such as the one shown here, on which they can mark which traits are necessary, helpful, or best avoided in this type of writing.

| Necessary Elements | Helpful Elements | Elements to Be Avoided |
|---|---|---|
| Transitions | Hook, because it grabs the reader's attention | Clichés |
| Conclusion | Quotation | Passive voice, because it's dry and gets readers confused about subject |
| Thesis | | |

**5.** From this chart, you can then create a class chart or rubric that will help students to create their own compositions.

**6.** Optional: Try using symbols or visuals to accompany the writing elements. These help the students who are better at remembering pictures and their associations as they concurrently think about their compositions. Possible symbols and visuals for writing include

- A fishing hook for the opening hook
- A table with the thesis in the top and pieces of evidence in the legs
- Bridges for transitions
- Dialog bubbles for quotations
- A funnel for the conclusion

**7.** Continue with any needed minilessons on the attributes with which students struggle the most.

## SEMANTIC ORGANIZERS (Gru, Vi)

Semantic webs and other visual organizers have long been used effectively for organizing information hierarchically. Many are actually text outlines arranged in visual form. Semantic organizers tend to have a central concept, surrounded by key supporting concepts that increase in detail as you move away from the central concept. For the purposes of reading comprehension, the central concept is usually a main idea or author's purpose. The next outward spaces contain main headings and key supporting concepts, then subheadings, with related details written on the periphery.

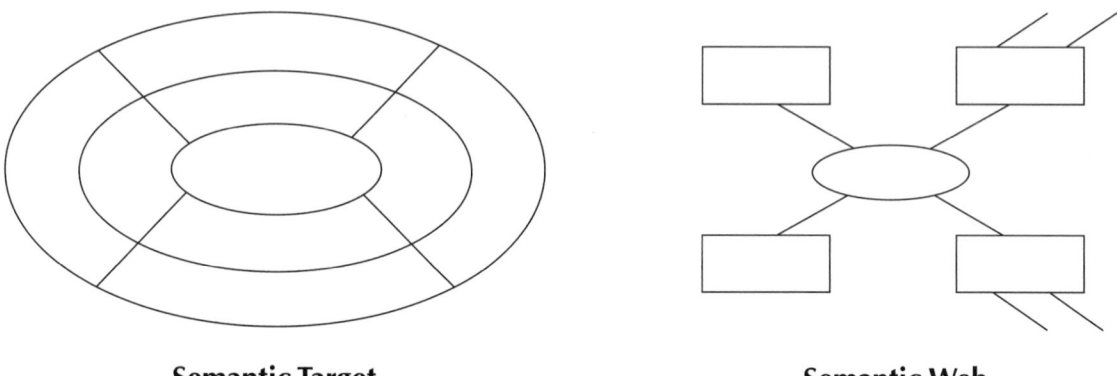

**Semantic Target**          **Semantic Web**

### Procedure

**1.** Choose or design a semantic organizer that will help students organize information hierarchically (Vi), and choose a text to use with the exercise. Remember that most knowledge is organized hierarchically into categories; discrete pieces of information fall into these categories according to their characteristics. Therefore, texts that compare, persuade, analyze, describe, classify, and interpret all lend themselves well to use with semantic organizers.

2. For prereading, write a topic or a predictive question(s) on the board that relates to the text's key ideas, and write some key vocabulary from the text. Draw a simple web on the board or on a separate poster sheet. Ask students the following questions: "What is the name of the group?" "In which group does this belong?" The answers will be the categories that will go in the web's boxes. Eventually, students will fill in the boxes themselves, working in groups or independently.

3. After filling in the main categories, students will have a general idea of the text. Have them summarize (perhaps in a Think-Pair-Share) what they expect the text to cover.

4. During reading, have students read silently as they fill out their own copies of the web. For some groups, you can read the first part of the text aloud and model the filling in of the web on the board. Emphasize the use of key concepts and phrases that are expressed in the words of the reader, rather than using sentences copied from the text. Students can also draw symbols or images in the spaces to help them better remember the information.

5. Using the semantic web as an aid, have the students retell (to a partner or group, for a Gru activity) the important points of the text. The listeners can then remind the teller of any important information not included. Putting the pieces of the text back together in their own words helps students take ownership of the information, which solidifies it in their minds. The semantic web helps the brain build visually based connections (Vi).

6. Semantic organizers also provide an excellent framework for writing that is based on the text. The boxes (or other shapes) on the organizer can help a student get ideas for possible paragraph separations. You can give students a list of transition and connector words to use that are appropriate to the style of the writing they are doing.

# NOTE-TAKING WITH THINKING CODES (Vi)

One way to analyze a written text is to take notes directly on the text. This is active interaction with the text. The remaining chapters of this book cover a broad range of thinking skills that authors use to communicate their messages; it is helpful for students to generate symbols for these thinking skills in order to internalize the skills and use them in their own learning and writing. This activity is adapted from ideas by Knight (1990) and Lyman (1987), who generated various sets of codes for note-taking, both for teachers and for students. Note that you can use this method for any activities in this book, and even for other vital reading and writing behaviors, such as summarizing, questioning, predicting, inferring, figuring out word meanings, connecting to background knowledge, reading ahead, and rereading.

## Procedure

1. Generate a rough idea of a code (or symbol) for thinking, reading, or writing behavior that you want to emphasize. (Perhaps hand motions, too.)

2. Introduce the behavior and its elements to the class. For example, you might want to teach the skill of using criteria to evaluate in a current unit you are teaching on heroes and their contributions. Students should already know some basic ideas about evaluating, but for more, you can refer to chapter 12 of this book. You can introduce the skill of using criteria to evaluate, and then come up with a code for the skill (Vi), ideally with the help of the rest of the class. You can also use some of the following ideas:

| Reading or Writing Behavior | Code | Language Clues for the Behavior |
|---|---|---|
| Comparing | ⌒⌒ (overlapping circles) | similar, analogy, like, same, similar to, not only...but also |
| Contrasting | ●● (overlapping filled circles) | distinction, different, distinguish, differentiate, differs from, by contrast, unlike, although, yet, however, on the other hand |
| Identifying cause and effect | C → E | a consequence of, outcome, impetus, influence, factors, so that, because of, as a result of, since, in order to, this led to |
| Analyzing | ⚲ (magnifying glass) | break down, components, elements, factors, aspects, dimensions, parts, close look |
| Defining a problem | DEF | issue, boils down to, challenge, obstacle |
| Hypothesizing | HYP? | possible solution, might, hypothetical, maybe, chances, probability, likely |
| Stating opinions | OPIN | I believe that, it seems to us that, we should, it is foolish to, I feel strongly that, in our opinion, might, probably, could have, maybe, possibly |
| Stating a main idea, thesis, or purpose of text | MI | it boils down to, the main issue is, therefore, in essence, the heart of the matter |
| Using strong or weak examples or evidence | EX. (Strong) (ex.) (Weak) | for example, for instance, one case, to illustrate this, one form of this, a manifestation of this is, you can see this in |
| Empathizing or appealing to emotion | ♡ | feel, inside, moral, heart of the matter, realize inside |
| Using criteria to evaluate | EVAL | rate, judge, ethical, moral, weigh, right, wrong, consider, dilemma, two sides, value, importance |

| Synthesizing | | bring together, gather, integrate, to conclude, summarize |
|---|---|---|
| Classifying and categorizing | | an example of, is described as, belongs in the category of, is in the group because it... |
| Interpreting | INT | infer, can be seen as, this implies that, we assume that...because |
| Presenting counterarguments | ←<br>→<br>← | on the other hand, then again, however, opponents say, problems with this are |

**3.** Put a written text (e.g., a page from a textbook or novel) on the overhead projector, and model the process of finding a section of text that corresponds with the behavior. Model for students how to put codes next to a spot where you think, "This is what the author is doing here" or "This is what I am doing in my head at this point."

**4.** Have students follow along in their own texts and then code the text themselves in groups or pairs, when ready to do so.

**5.** Have students take notes with codes and then share the most interesting parts of their notes with partners.

# CHARACTER BIO CARDS (Mo, Ma)

Character Bio Cards is an analysis of a person in a fictional, biographical, or narrative account. The activity is most often used in language arts, but it can be effective in other disciplines as well. Students, with the help of the cards, focus in on various elements of a person's life. They can even use elements in their own lives. The graphic is useful before, during, and after reading, and it is also a useful organizer for writing biographies. The Mo portion is also a fun variation that gets students to put their actions where their words are.

| **Plans**<br><br>Kill the whale | **Thoughts**<br><br>Revenge | **Feelings**<br><br>Fear<br>Rage | **Personality**<br><br>Crazy<br>Obsessed<br>because he risked<br>so much |
|---|---|---|---|
| **Strengths**<br><br>Persistence<br>because never<br>stopped | **Actions**<br><br>Risked others'<br>lives | **Words**<br><br>Call me<br>Ishmael | **Weaknesses**<br><br>Obsessed<br>with revenge<br>Physical |

## Procedure

**1.** Ask students why it can be helpful to study the life of a person. Answers might include to be more like that person; to study the times in which he or she lived; to understand his or her work; or to reflect on how to live a meaningful life with actions, thoughts, and words.

**2.** By thinking aloud, model the process of looking for key information in a text or video about a character. Some traits to analyze might be thoughts, future plans, personality, feelings, childhood, strengths, weaknesses, words, or actions. Choose which traits you want to use, and write each trait on a blank piece of paper or an overhead transparency. If possible, try to color code the cards. Some teachers have even cut them into different shapes.

**3.** Fill in the cards and include evidence to support the claims made about the person. For example, if a person's strength is persistence, put the reason you think this on the card as well. Let students participate and help you. Ask them for solid evidence for their answers.

**4.** Let students read text or watch the entire video and fill in all the cards. Students can add to answers and even create new categories for cards (Ma), if they wish.

**5.** Encourage students to include symbols and little drawings to help them remember the answers on the cards.

**6.** Have students mingle among themselves and compare their cards (Mo). This is the time when they can share answers with other students and discuss any ideas that conflict.

**7.** You can tally the responses on a master chart on the board, if you have time. It is interesting to see what comes up and to hear the evidence used.

**8.** Optional: Have students in pairs pick a card or two and then create a gesture or action that teaches it. For instance, if a character's strength was compassion, a student could extend his or her hands out; if a character's plan was to escape, the student could bend imaginary bars and sneak through them.

**9.** Writing option: Model how to use the information from the cards to create an outline, and then from the outline, to create a written product. Model the thinking you go through as you do this: "I know that he was a stubborn man. But I'll bet his stubbornness led him to go on in the face of so many challenges. Now, how should I write that? I should start with a thesis statement...."

# STORY MAP TABLEAU (Mo, Gru, Vi)

A story map is a tried and true way to show the important elements of narrative text (Buehl, 2001; Johns & Berglund, 2001). The Story Map Tableau is a kinesthetic–dramatic version of this graphic organizer. It can also be used with history texts as an outline of important events, with supporting events shown leading up to the climax (e.g., a war). Science teachers have even used it with success for processes such as volcanic eruptions and for discussing solutions to environmental problems.

## Procedure

1. Model on the overhead or on a poster sheet how to fill in the story map (Vi) for various narratives and accounts, such as short stories, songs, fables, television shows, movies, and novels. (You can find a Story Map blackline master in Part III of this book, page 216.)

2. First, fill in the character names around the oval. You can add doodles or notes, such as *protagonist/antagonist* labels, next to the names.

3. Fill in place and time. Discuss why the author might have chosen this setting.

4. Write the main problem or conflict in the large diagonal box. If you are filling in the map during reading, emphasize the use of pencil, as the conflict may change as you read.

5. On the left-hand lines, put the important events that lead up to the final climax/resolution of the problem. This is great practice for summarizing, because the lines don't allow much space for writing.

6. Summarize the climax/resolution in the banner box at the top.

7. Put the final events on the "ending events" lines to the right.

8. Discuss the message or lesson that the author might have intended when writing the text. Consider historical, moral, social, political, and entertainment purposes.

9. After the graphic is filled in and discussed, have the whole class share and agree on the important events that you put on the board or on the overhead.

10. Divide the class into groups of four to eight students (Gru). Then give each group two or three story events from the Story Map to present. Ask each group to create a tableau (Mo) for each of their assigned events (tell them that a tableau is a silent, frozen group of students acting out an event up in front of the room, usually with a narrator). Alternately, they could act out the events.

11. Have groups do each tableau in the order in which each appears in the story or event.

12. Optional: Make a new, modified version of the story map graphic organizer to match the particular story/event you are using before filling it in. For example, some stories have an early resolution and a large number of events in the "falling action" (the lines along the right side).

# SEMANTIC RACECAR (Ma, Vi)

The semantic racecar is a kinesthetic and visual way to break down a concept. It is a visual organizer that can be adapted to teach a large number of concepts. This activity works better if there is a person being studied, such as a historical figure, a character from a novel, a scientist, or the student. The wheels and other parts of the car become the elements or attributes that students will analyze, as shown:

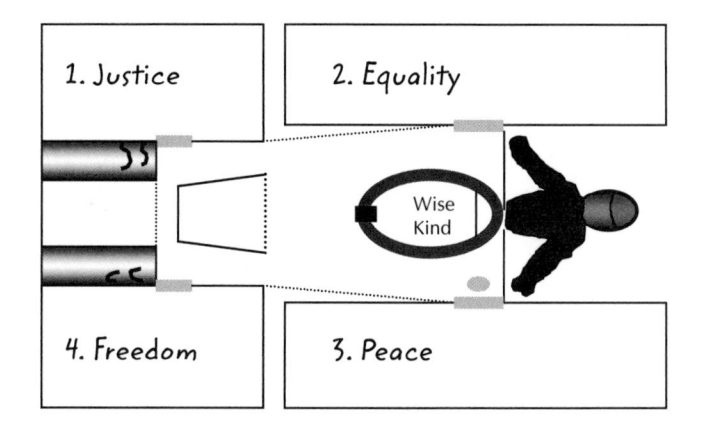

## *Procedure*

**1.** Give students the graphic (Vi) (see the full-size blackline master in Part III of this book, page 217), individually or in pairs, and have students research a person. They should come up with several important qualities that the person had. These should be written in the driver's seat, next to the steering wheel.

**2.** Have students find four main stages or ideas in the person's life or in the event in which the person played a role. These four are written on the wheels.

**3.** Have students find two key accomplishments or two key supporting people in the person's life. Have them write these on the engine (under the hood).

**4.** Ask students to figure out what powered or fueled the person. What passion did the person have? This information should go next to the fuel tank.

**5.** Now, have students cut their papers along the solid, thin black lines. Have them fold along the dotted lines. They must fold the arms up to move the driver underneath and up through the slot so that he or she is in the driver's seat. Then have students fold the engine tubes so that they are facing downward, then fold along the dotted line so the engine tubes are now underneath the hood and facing up. Students should be able to lift the hood and see them (Ma).

**6.** Have students curl the wheels around to make circles and tape them together. To prevent sag, they can tape the thin strips together underneath the car.

**7.** Have students share the components of their cars with other students in groups or pairs.

**8.** Optional: Have students put the cars away and write a quick paragraph on what they remember about the person. They can even write expressions such as "She was fueled by the passion to...."

# ANALYZING CHANTS (Mu)

This is a chant frame that you can use and adapt to help students break down a concept, idea, character, or event. The frame is meant to start you off, but you and your students will ideally modify it or create a completely different chant about the topic of study. Refer to chapter 2 for more specifics on how to create effective chants and how to get students to create them as well.

## Procedure

**1.** Consider the topic of study, and pull out key target learning concepts that you want to analyze. These will help you start off the chant. Students can help in this process as well.

**2.** Create the chant on the overhead projector and have students follow along on their own paper, copying down the words as you go along.

**3.** Fill in the first line with an appropriate entry in order to model how to begin.

**4.** Have students share possible lines as you continue to fill in the chant. When you think they can do some on their own, let them try to finish the chant.

**5.** Call attention to the different types of academic language in the verses. Feel free to change them if you want.

**6.** Once the chant is finished, let different groups or pairs perform it for the class. Let them rehearse, if needed. Have instruments or downloaded mp3 drumbeats to help with the beat.

> **Chant Frame for Analyzing**
>
> I'm not here to sing to you about love
> There's enough of those songs, no doubt
> I'll sing about _____
> It's complex so we gotta break it down.
>
> The _____
> Is the first part we'll analyze
> It's important because it _____
> And it _____
> (size, eyes, why, flies, tries)
>
> Then there is _____
> An important component, too
> It _____
> Without it, what would we do?
>
> We can't forget the _____
> It plays an important role
> It _____
> In case you wondered, well, now you know

## Variation

Encourage students to come up with their own chants and songs. They can adapt popular songs or make up songs that go with a basic beat. They can even make up hand motions to certain parts, as shown in the following Cell Mitosis Chant by Kevin Krasnow and Jeff Zwiers (hand motions are shown in parentheses). This can be rapped or chanted.

> Now here's a simple story I like to tell
> Of the reproduction skills of a cell
>
> Before the little cell's life comes to an end
> It's got to procreate to continue the trend.

In the very middle there's a ring, let's say (fingers make a circle)
It's called a nucleus and houses DNA

DNA is stuff we mustn't underestimate
It makes up genes that pass on the cell's traits

The DNA coils up good and tight,
To make a chromosome; it's quite a spiral sight (hands in fists together)

Yet the chromosome doesn't have just one side
It's made of two chromatids that just can't hide (hold fists separately)

The chromatids are bound nicely together
By a centromere through good and bad weather (one fist grabs other thumb)

Then it's time for the chromatids to say goodbye
Spindle fibers separate them, but they don't cry (fists pulled apart)

For they are on their way to make a brand new cell
That has all the parts and pieces to turn out well

With a pinch around the center, the cell splits in two
Now you can't tell which is which and who is who

Most commonly seen under a microscope, it's
The making of twin cells by the process of mitosis

# CHAPTER 4

# Comparing

Comparing (which includes contrasting) means finding similarities and differences between two or more things. Most of the things we compare in school are objects, ideas, events, processes, or living things. Research has shown that the improved ability to compare correlates well to increased success in academic tasks (Marzano et al., 2001).

Individuals compare all the time, often in order to choose one thing over another, make other decisions, and organize knowledge. As people go through life, they compare ingredients, prices, books, movies, vacation spots, employees, employers, schools, politicians, friends, lesson ideas, and so on. Comparing is a powerful way for people to understand a complex subject or person because they see the subject's characteristics "lined up" next to the characteristics of a similar subject.

Often, we don't know a thing well until we find out what it is not. For example, we may understand a zebra better by comparing it to a horse: The zebra has stripes, is smaller, and lives in large herds in Africa. We remember that it is like a horse but different in key ways. Uncovering the similarities and differences helps us better define, understand, and remember what we are learning.

Comparing is heavily dependent on the ability to analyze, which was covered in chapter 3. Students must break down the concepts they are studying into component parts and then see if those parts are similar or different. This is not as difficult with animals, minerals, and vegetables, but when dealing with historical events, cultures, people, literature, and scientific processes, it is a bit more involved. The components students must analyze for academic tasks are harder to grasp and, therefore, harder to compare. One person might find more similarities than another person would, based on their ways of analyzing it. And they might both find fewer similarities than an expert on the subject.

As an example, try comparing two wars. You first need to break down the wars into "usable" components. Each way of breaking down the accounts depends, of course, on a person's knowledge of the possible ways in which events can be analyzed. A science teacher might look at the two wars, for example, from a more technological perspective. An English teacher might look at the wars from a social perspective. For two wars, some of the possible components to emphasize and compare might be separate battles, social and political causes and effects, details included and excluded in various accounts, technology, points of view, and primary text excerpts, to name a few. Other good academic topics to compare (besides wars) include different experiments with the same conclusion, the same experiment with different conclusions, two opposing persuasive articles, different ways of solving a math problem, two stories by the same author, or two versions of the same story from different authors or countries.

# Academic Language, Prompts, and Frames

The following expressions, prompts, and frame are for use with the skill of comparing. Get to know these terms, and point them out when you and your students use them in discussions or written tasks. Refer to chapter 1 for ideas on how to use academic language expressions, oral and writing prompts, and paragraph frames to develop academic thinking skills and academic language.

Some common expressions used when comparing include the following:

- When we break it down into the components of...
- They are similar because...
- The two differ because one...while the other...
- If we look closely at...we will see that...is different from...
- This is much like when...
- Notice how the two compare.
- Let's consider the opposite case of...
- It is like a...but differs in that...
- On the other hand...
- In contrast to what (person) says, I...
- Despite these similarities, the two are very different in that...
- These are similar in the following ways:
- It is important to distinguish between...
- Yet there is an important difference...
- This is related to (extraneous to, not applicable) because...
- The least (most) essential statements are...
- I think it is more helpful to break it into these categories:
- This finding is inconsistent with that one because...
- The relationship between...and...
- There is a pattern that emerges when we look at...

Following are some prompts that encourage students to compare when speaking or writing:

- Compare your experiences to the experiences found in the text (e.g., stories, textbook excerpts, poems, biographies, pictures, articles, movies).
- Compare characters to other characters in the same story, to themselves at different points in the story, or to characters in other stories or related expository texts.
- Compare the themes, authors' purposes, or main ideas of two different narratives.
- Create two historical accounts of the same event through different viewpoints.

- Compare the event as described by this primary source document to that of the textbook.
- Compare and contrast these two people.
- Compare the contributions of...
- Write a dialog for two persons with opposing points of view.
- Distinguish between...

Frames like the one below help students to gradually pick up academic language and eventually use it to compose their own high-quality written products without help. One frame is given here to get you started on your own subject- and student-specific frames. This one is very generic, to allow you to fine-tune it or even to start from scratch. When creating your own frames, be sure to refer to the lists of expressions and prompts given above.

### Paragraph Frame for Scaffolding Comparing

_____ and _____ are similar in several ways. They both _____. They also _____. Furthermore, each _____. Because of these similarities, we can _____. However, _____ and _____ differ in some key areas. First, _____ , whereas _____. In addition, _____. In contrast, _____. These differences help us to see _____.

Remember to start with student background knowledge when introducing activities that build this skill. You can create a starter board of background knowledge topics such as friendship, family, school, music, advertising, culture, sports, television shows, movies, famous people, wars, or recent units you have studied in class.

# Activities for Developing the Skill of Comparing

## TRIAD COMPARE SHARES
### (Gru, Vi, Mo)

This is a group and kinesthetic–visual activity that also builds academic language for comparing. It has obvious GruViMo elements and even some Ma and Mu, if you want. This is effective because students are working together toward a goal and are given some creative allowance with respect to how they will present the concepts. (As usual, model this activity before asking students to do it on their own.)

### Procedure

**1.** Choose the two concepts the students will compare.

**2.** Put students in triads. Tell them to think about the parts of the two concepts that are the same and those that are different. They can make a Venn diagram if they want. For more variety among the presentations, you might have each student group compare a different set of things, such as different characters, events, processes, etc.

**3.** Have students then choose two differences and two similarities. Student A will be the one to act out or show the two differences, student B will act out or show the two similarities, and student C will be the main speaker and will present. To present the similarities, students A and B can stand next to each other and hold up the same sign between them or do the same action while student C is speaking behind them.

**4.** Have all students think about how they want to present their components, either with hand motions (Mo), drama (Mo), or visuals (Vi). Each action or presentation of a visual should be quick.

**5.** Have students prepare their presentations on a 3" × 5" card. This part of the activity is when the academic language is developed: Students should write their cards using language like the following sample (without the italic comments). Student C will present the information on the card, ideally without reading it.

> Student C: We compared the French Revolution with the American Revolution. We found several differences. On one hand... *(student C points to student A)*
>
> Student A: The French Revolution began with people who... *(student A speaks, and/or acts out what student C is saying)*
>
> Student C: The American Revolution, on the other hand... *(student C points to student B, who starts presenting)*
>
> Student B: started with people who.... The tactics and weapons also differed. The French tended to fight with.... However, the Americans usually fought in...
>
> Student C: We also found some important similarities. First, both revolutions involved.... *(students A and B act out similarity)* In addition, both...

# COMPARISON ROAD (Vi)

The Comparison Road (adapted from Zwiers, 2004) helps students build the vital skill of seeing both sides of a concept or issue. In this activity, which is similar to a semantic web, a reader taps into background knowledge to create a possible "map" for progressing through a text and gathering important information along the way.

## *Procedure*

**1.** Make a transparency from the Comparison Road reproducible in Part III of this book (page 218). Put the transparency on the overhead projector and write the issue or problem to be solved in the oval and clarify it for students. The issue can come from a book or from the standards to be taught in the unit. The activity works well if the issue in the oval is a controversial topic in some respect.

**2.** Have students offer ideas to fill in the signs so that they show the key opposing points on opposite sides of the road (Vi). (Some teachers have used this activity as a scaffold for persuasive essay writing.) The signs will contain major clues, headings, and ideas that help readers make their way to the destination (issue). The students can add more signs, if needed. The signs can be done before, while, and/or after reading about the issue.

**3.** Around each sign, write supporting details and paraphrases that describe the importance of the sign's heading. Have students offer ideas for what to write here.

**4.** Tell students to continue to revise the signs and their surrounding supports if the text or discussion changes their initial impressions for them.

# VENN VARIATIONS (Vi, Gru)

The Venn diagram is the classic graphic used for showing the similarities and differences between two or more subjects. Similarities go in the middle where the shapes overlap, and differences go in the nonoverlapping sections. I have seen teachers use a host of Venn variations with powerful results. Here are a few examples:

**Thoughts**  **Feelings**  **Actions**

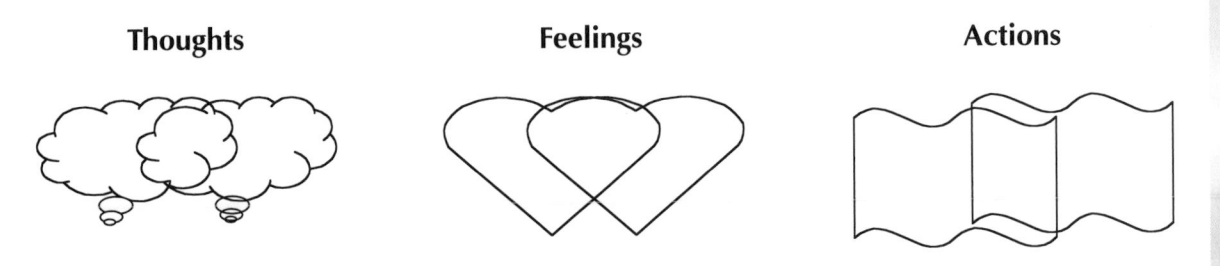

Following is an example of a Venn diagram for comparing four concepts:

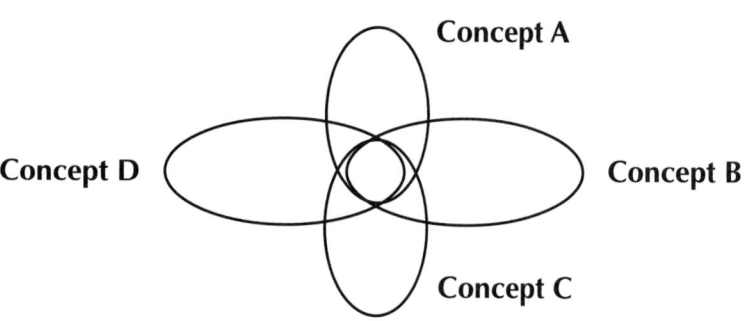

## Procedure

1. Consider what you want students to compare. Remember, comparison is a great way to get students to analyze two or more areas or concepts. Students might be more motivated to compare two things than to simply learn one thing. So, you get "two for the price of less than one," in a sense.

2. Now come up with some kind of clever diagram (Vi) with overlapping shapes that relate to the topics you are studying. If it is thoughts, you might use two thought bubbles, and if it is feelings, you might use two hearts, as shown previously; goals might have two soccer balls; explorers might have ships; etc. Bring students into the process, and ask them to help you come up with some interesting shapes. If they help design the diagram, they will be more invested in using it.

3. Have students draw the shapes on a piece of paper or the board. Label each shape with the name of one of the items you are comparing.

4. Put students in pairs and ask them to discuss which components or attributes they will analyze for the two subjects being compared. Next, have them decide whether the two subjects have those components in common. If a component is shared by both subjects, it goes in the middle of the diagram. If a component or attribute is only possessed by one subject, it goes on the side to which it belongs. It is very important for students to be able to defend their choices. For example, if students say that two historical figures were both insane, they should have evidence to support this.

5. Share the results with the whole class.

# WHOLE-CLASS KINESVENNIC
## (Mo, Gru)

This is a kinesthetic activity based on the Venn diagram. It allows students to move around according to the comparisons they make. In this way, they can interact and "compare their comparisons." They remember the experience and the content better because the whole body is involved. After the students gain a decent grasp of how to use a Venn diagram on paper, let them show their knowledge in a bigger way using this activity.

## Procedure

**1.** Put tape or rope on the floor in an overlapping pattern as shown in the following example. You are turning the entire classroom into a Venn diagram (Vi).

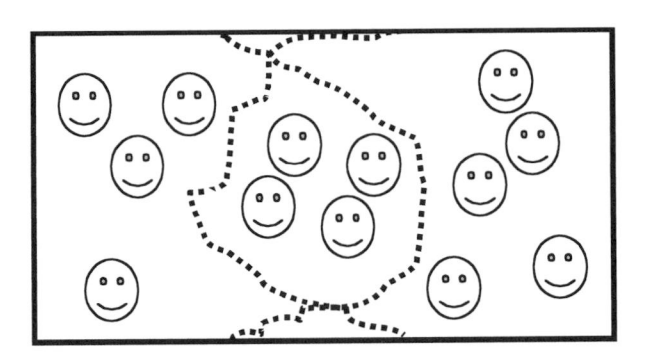

**2.** Decide on two different concepts to compare, such as two wars, two people, two events, two governments, etc. Display these two titles in some way on different sides of the room.

**3.** Have students help you analyze the two main concepts and generate elements to compare and contrast about them. Write these elements on large notecards that will be visible from any part of the room. There should be enough cards for most of the students to have one card each. The students who do not have cards will be note-takers and will critique the evidence.

**4.** Give out the cards and tell students to look at what is written on their cards and take a minute in silence to decide where they will go in the room. They can then discuss it with one other person if they want.

**5.** Say, "Go," and let students move (Mo) to stand where they think their cards belong.

**6.** Ask each student to defend his or her position with solid evidence.

**7.** Critiquers should ask students for clarification of their evidence and take notes during the process. Have them write their notes on paper Venns that correspond with the one on the floor. A good ongoing question to tell critiquers to ask is, "Why do you think these things were different (or the same)?"

# COMPARISON STICKY
# NOTE GRID (Ma, Gru)

A grid (or table) is an easy way to break down a topic and compare each component. You can supply some or all of the categories, if needed. The grid allows students to organize various categories of information according to variables that are placed in columns and rows. A grid is also an effective way to get students to analyze ideas, reduce information in order to compare it, and then describe it in their own words. For many expository descriptive texts, particularly in science and social studies, a grid is an effective way to compare important chunks of information. Grids help students to analyze characters, solutions to problems, symbols, wars, policies, and time periods. More than just a "data entry" tool, grids and matrices can be used as a springboard for discussing, drawing conclusions, and inspiring further research.

## *Procedure*

**1.** Draw a grid on an overhead transparency or a poster sheet. Examine the text and choose the categories you would like to use. Put these in the left-hand column of the grid. Then decide which variables to put across the top row. (You might not have categories in the left-hand column if studying only one concept.) Have students copy down the information on their own papers as you go.

**2.** Think aloud to the class while filling out sticky notes during reading (Ma); fill in the sticky notes with specific information from the grid (see above). Put them directly on the grid in the appropriate cells. Show students how to generate their own questions as they read. Questions should be based on the grid, such as "What does the membrane do?"

**3.** Show students how to find evidence from the text to support each of your entries. Write this information on the back of each sticky note.

**4.** Have students finish the grid in groups.

**5.** Have students then discuss the grid in pairs (Gru), and have them move their sticky notes around the grid as they discuss the grid with their partners. Each pair should end up with one "joint" grid that was better than either individual one.

**6.** Circulate through the room, and have students give evidence for some of their answers. Have them refer to the text for evidence if needed.

**7.** When students are finished, have them analyze the table for patterns and relationships. With these patterns and relationships, students can generate hypotheses for discussion or research.

**8.** Have students write a final conclusion based on the information on the grid. They can then take the sticky notes off the grid and organize them for writing in a linear outline or semantic web. (You may want to model this the first few times.)

**9.** Optional: A powerful way to build academic language with a grid is to use academic language column-toppers—to place the terms above the columns where you will use them. This provides an excellent scaffold for writing complete sentence descriptions. The following grid was created for a science lesson.

| Academic Terms | What It Is (looks like, contains, is made of, is composed of) | Where It Is (is located, is found, surrounds, covers, is inside) | What It Does (function, job, purpose, role, allows, protects) |
|---|---|---|---|
| Organelles | | | |
| Membrane | | | |
| Nucleus | | | |

## SONG COMPARISON CHART (Mu, Vi)

This engaging activity allows students to analyze and compare songs that you or they bring into the class. The process of looking at a song for its strengths and weaknesses is a complex process that can transfer to other academic areas, especially literary analysis.

### *Procedure*

**1.** Bring in two recorded songs (Mu), or have students bring in songs with age-appropriate lyrics and choose two of their songs. The songs will ideally relate to the topic of study, but even if not, students will learn how to use the chart and compare abstract concepts in the process. You can find songs that are applicable to issues being covered in various content areas: nuclear arms, Vietnam, drugs, love, heroism, and so on. Write out the song lyrics and photocopy them.

**2.** Have students listen to both songs and write notes as they listen. Have them write down images and feelings that come up.

**3.** Have students listen to the songs again, this time thinking about the topic, figurative language, and how well the words match with the music. Model how to notice if there are two levels—the surface and a deeper meaning—in the songs.

**4.** Hand out the printed song lyrics and have students fill in a chart (Vi) like the one below. Model this on the overhead projector or a poster sheet as you think aloud. The first row is for the topic. Ask students, Do both songs have the same topic (if so, write the topic in the A & B column), or do they differ? How do they differ? They might both be about peace, but song A may mention Vietnam and song B may be about Iraq. In this case, all three columns would have entries.

**5.** For the Purpose row, ask students what the composer's purpose was for writing this song. To make money? To change the world? To persuade people to think a certain way? To vent some emotions? Students can discuss this in pairs, if needed.

**6.** For the Metaphor row, ask students what type of figurative language there is. Are there any common metaphors? What do they mean?

**7.** For the Real? row, write students' impressions of how realistic the song is. Is it historically accurate? Does it exaggerate human emotions too much? Does it apply to real life today?

**8.** For the Appeal? row, ask why the song would appeal to some people? Which lyrics are the most powerful? Why might it not appeal to some people?

**9.** Finally, for the Music column, decide how well the music fits the lyrics. Could there have been better melody or instruments used to improve the song? Why did the composer or singer create it that way?

**10.** Have pairs of students then share their entries with one another and then with the whole class.

**11.** You can then choose to compare other pairs of songs brought in by students.

|          | Song A | Songs A & B | Song B |
|----------|--------|-------------|--------|
| Topic    |        |             |        |
| Purpose  |        |             |        |
| Metaphor |        |             |        |
| Real?    |        |             |        |
| Appeal?  |        |             |        |
| Music    |        |             |        |

# COMPARISON CHANTS (Mu)

This is a response chant that encourages students to remember the similarities of and differences between two or three concepts. The frame is meant to start you off, but you and your students will ideally modify it or create a completely different chant about the topic of study. Refer to chapter 2 for more specifics on how to create effective chants and how to get students to create them as well.

## Procedure

**1.** Consider the topic of study, and pull out key target learning concepts that you want to compare. These will help you start the chant. Students can help in this process as well.

**2.** Write the chant on the overhead and have students copy it down on their own paper as you go along.

**3.** Fill in the first line with an appropriate entry in order to model how to begin.

**4.** Have students share possible lines as you continue to fill in the chant (Mu). When you think they can do some on their own, let them try to finish the chant in groups or pairs.

**5.** Call attention to the different types of academic language in the verses. Feel free to change them if you want.

**6.** Once the chant is finished within different groups or pairs, have students share their versions with the class. Let them rehearse, if needed. Have instruments or downloaded mp3 drumbeats to help with the beat.

---

### Chant Frame for Comparison

Excuuuuuse me, I was wondering something
Can you help me compare the following things
One is _____ you see
And the other is _____ I believe

Tell me, what are the characteristics they share?
It's time to break them down and compare

They both _____
And they _____
Furthermore, they _____
And they share _____

Tell me, how can I distinguish one from the other?
Like the contrast of two different brothers?

Well, the _____
While the _____
The _____
Yet the _____

---

# Categorizing and Classifying

As soon as we begin to learn the names of things, we begin to compare them. Then we categorize and classify them. For example, many young children consider any four-legged animal to be a "dog." Gradually, though, children learn other categories for animals and more complex pieces of knowledge. Categorizing and classifying are key skills for organizing academic information into logical and usable groups (Marzano et al., 2001). These key skills are especially helpful for separating important from unimportant information, which is one of the main components of effective learning and reading comprehension (Baumann, 1986).

## Categorizing

Categorizing happens when a person already has a category name, such as a title, heading, main idea, group label, or summary. The person then finds information to fit under this category name. Finding information to fit under a category involves looking for facts, traits, and examples that have the commonality described by the category title. This type of organization (i.e., this thinking process) is very common in textbooks—but it does not help much if students do not notice or think about the textbook's headings or subheadings and how they connect to the text that follows.

Categorizing is heavily dependent on a person's ability to analyze, because it is through analysis that one breaks down the concept to see if it has the traits or conditions required to fit under the category in question. In other words, categorizing is a form of deductive reasoning. One starts with a generalized principle or heading (e.g., an obvious topic sentence) and then proceeds to mentally put subordinate ideas and concepts underneath.

The mental process of categorizing while reading may look something like this:

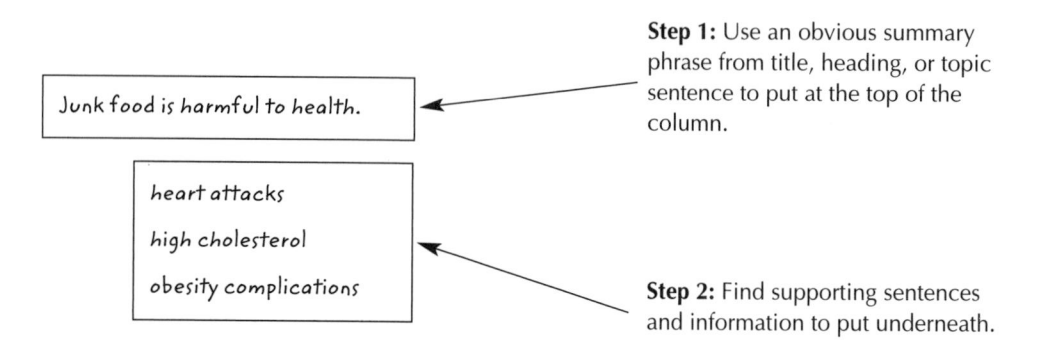

**Step 1:** Use an obvious summary phrase from title, heading, or topic sentence to put at the top of the column.

Junk food is harmful to health.

heart attacks

high cholesterol

obesity complications

**Step 2:** Find supporting sentences and information to put underneath.

# Classifying

Classifying is very useful for academic tasks such as summarizing, comparing, and outlining. As Jaworski and Coupland (1999) say,

> Academic study, but in fact all aspects of experience, are based on acts of classification, and the building of knowledge and interpretations is very largely a process of defining boundaries between conceptual classes, and of labeling those classes and the relationships between them. (p. 4)

Classifying is more inductive than categorizing and therefore the more challenging skill for struggling students to develop. It is inductive because a student must infer unstated generalizations and principles based on observation and analysis. The generalizations and principles become, so to speak, category headings, or "classes."

To classify information from a text (or speech) that does not offer convenient headings for every section or paragraph (many texts are like this), the student must analyze the details, such as words, sentences, or paragraphs, and then look for what they have in common. The student then groups the facts and concepts by their possible commonalities, according to the importance of the commonalities. The student must keep the author's or speaker's overall purpose in mind while doing this, in order not to group information by less useful criteria. For example, a young student may group animals by color, a less important commonality, rather than by number of legs, skeletal structure, or skin and fur characteristics. Often the reader will need to generate a rough category name for his or her group that describes why they are together (e.g., "These sentences all describe how atoms attract to make molecules."). This category name becomes the "summary" under which the reader continues to classify other sentences—or modify, as the message dictates.

When people use the skill of classifying, they have to come up with a class or category name *during or after* figuring out how to group the items.

The mental process for classifying looks somewhat like this:

| Summary Phrase |
| --- |
| • Title of text<br>• Sentence 3<br>• Phrase from sentence 4<br>• Picture 1 |

**Step 1:** Fill in the column with sentences and other pieces of information that seem to be important to overall text meaning and seem to belong in a group because of similarities.

**Step 2:** Use your analysis of similarities and differences to establish a topic phrase. This becomes the category name, or main idea, of those sentences.

In each activity in this chapter, start with the ways in which students already use this skill in nonacademic contexts. Start with the concrete and familiar; then move to the more abstract and academic. For example, in the Desk Category Columns activity you can start with common texts from movies, television shows, posters, or songs. Point out to students how easily they generate main ideas and summaries when dealing with familiar texts. Then transition the activity into the topic or text of the lesson you want them to study.

# Academic Language, Prompts, and Frames

The following expressions, prompts, and frames are for use with the skill of categorizing and classifying. Get to know these terms, and point them out when you and your students use them in discussions or written tasks. Refer to chapter 1 for ideas on how to use academic language expressions, oral and writing prompts, and paragraph frames to develop academic thinking skills and academic language.

Some common expressions used when categorizing and classifying include the following:

- It is important because...
- It is not that important because...
- It belongs in the category of...
- We should put this in the...group because...
- I would call this a type of...
- It fits in this (column, file, genre, etc.) because...
- I don't think it fits anywhere; it needs a new category that we could call...
- These have in common the...
- The fact that it...distinguishes it from this.
- This is a very relevant point because...
- These traits make it belong in the...category.
- The elements are related in the following ways...
- This is related to (extraneous to, not applicable) because...
- The least (most) essential statements are...
- This is an important quote because...
- There is a pattern that emerges when we look at...

Following are some prompts that encourage students to categorize and classify when speaking or writing:

- Create a table that categorizes these.
- Categorize the following traits.
- Find the most relevant statements and quotes about...
- Find the main idea of this paragraph, speech, movie, etc.
- Classify the following group of...

Frames like the following help students to gradually pick up academic language and eventually use it to compose their own high-quality written products without help. Two frames are given here to get you started on your own subject- and student-specific frames. These two are very generic, to allow you to fine-tune them or even to start from scratch.

When creating your own frames, be sure to refer to the lists of expressions and prompts given previously.

## Paragraph Frames for Scaffolding Categorizing and Classifying

1. It is helpful to place the _____, _____, and _____ in the same group. They have important commonalities such as _____ and _____. Likewise, the _____ and _____ belong together because they _____. However, the _____ is distinct because it _____. We need to create a new category for it, such as _____.

2. We believe that the most important aspect of _____ is its _____. It is vital because _____ _____. Another important aspect is _____ because it _____. Then again, some minor details, such as _____ and _____, are hardly worth mentioning.

Remember to start with student background knowledge when introducing activities that build this skill. You can create a starter board of background knowledge topics such as friendship, family, school, music, advertising, culture, sports, television shows, movies, famous people, wars, or recent units you have studied in class.

# Activities for Developing the Skill
# of Categorizing and Classifying

## DESK CATEGORY COLUMNS
### (Gru, Mo)

This is a kinesthetic activity that gets students moving around as they think about categories and classes. You can use it throughout the year for any kind of categorizing. I have seen it used in various content area classes in different grade levels.

### Procedure

**1.** Put the students' desks in rows that will become the columns under which students will categorize their chunks of information.

**2.** Generate enough pieces of information so that every student gets a card or paper with a piece of information on it. (You can also devise other ways to assign information chunks to each student.) These are the chunks that students will categorize and classify.

**3.** Tell students to work together (Gru) as a class to discuss how they are going to group their chunks of information. Give them an example, such as sports: sports with round balls might be in a group, team sports might be in another, outdoor sports in another, and so on.

**4.** Allow time for students to move around (Mo) and sit in the correct rows.

**5.** Have each group create a large sign that labels their category. This label should show the reason these particular students are in the group. (This is also the process of classifying.)

**6.** On the back of the students' information cards, have each student write a justification for being in his or her particular row.

**7.** Have students share their group titles and say why they created the groups.

**8.** You can continue the activity by coming up with other labels or classes for groups and seeing how fast students can rearrange into new category columns.

## SENTENCE CATS AND CLASSES (Vi)

This activity provides practice in categorizing and classifying at the sentence level. For many students, this is where comprehension problems lie: They assign equal importance to all the sentences in a text, and then they try to memorize them all. Rather, they need to learn to quickly chunk information into a main gist and move on. They need to compress the text into a few words so that the information will fit (e.g., "This paragraph was about..."). The activity has three different forms.

## *Procedures*

### Sentence CLASSifying

**1.** List the sentences of a paragraph in order, with numbers. Remove the topic sentence if it is obvious. You can also use sentence strips that allow students to hold the sentences (Ma).

**2.** Have students work in pairs to find common features and to create a class or category above the list of sentences (Vi).

**3.** Have students write the category as a main idea—no longer than a simple sentence, but more than one or two words. Be sure to model this many times before asking students to do it.

### Sentence CATegorizing

**1.** In a longer text, remove the topic sentences from the paragraphs or generate a paragraph main idea sentence for those paragraphs without topic sentences.

**2.** List these topic sentences out of order somewhere else on the page or on the front chalkboard.

**3.** Have students read the list and then the text to find the paragraphs that correspond to each topic sentence or main idea. Be sure to model this many times before asking students to do it.

### Oddball Sentences

**1.** Create and add an anomalous sentence to each paragraph in a text.

**2.** Ask students to find and cross out the oddball sentence and to explain (in writing or in a group setting) why it does not fit.

**3.** Students can then write summaries of paragraphs or of the entire text. Be sure to model this many times before asking students to do it.

**4.** Teach students what to do with odd sentences in real texts.

**5.** Optional: Have students add oddball sentences to a text. Or, you add an entire oddball paragraph to a text, then have students find it and cross it out.

Following is a sample paragraph for Oddball Sentences. The oddball sentence is shown in italics.

### Sharks Dying of Good Ratings

The public fear perpetuated by the media has led to the slaughter of millions of sharks each year. Virtually all of these innocent creatures have never even seen a human being. The media have succeeded in leading many people to believe that all sharks are waiting to eat every swimmer who ventures beyond knee-deep water in the ocean. *The ocean has many areas with shallow water.* News programs often devote long segments to shark attacks (which are seldom fatal) and omit the statistics of how many hundreds of people died on the highways in traffic accidents that same day. The more we learn the truth about how sharks live, eat, and behave, the more we will respect them and their role in their ocean domain.

# MAIN IDEA MEMORY STORAGE (Ma, Vi)

Main Idea Memory Storage (Zwiers, 2004) is a visual and kinesthetic simplification of the active thinking we use to comprehend. It is based on research related to semantic organizers and their positive effect on comprehension and retention (Marzano et al., 2001). This activity gives a student practice in keeping one "mental hand" on the main idea and the other "mental hand" on the summary chunks of information that relate to the main idea. This can be done alone or in pairs, silently, or out loud as a think-aloud. As always, you should sufficiently model the activity before asking students to take over and do it on their own.

## Procedure

1. Make a transparency from the Main Idea Memory Storage reproducible from Part III of this book (page 219). Place the transparency on the overhead projector. Begin reading a challenging text and think aloud about the process of using initial clues to form a rough main idea (i.e., class) for the text. Write your rough main idea on a sticky note (use clear ones for the overhead) and place it in the top box on the page (Vi). Then explain to students that you will modify the main idea while you read. If you like, you can tell them that you are assigning your left hand only to the main idea and say that the summaries can only be touched by your right hand.

2. Read aloud and stop at an appropriate point to summarize. Create a summary note (a different color from the main idea note, ideally) and place it in one of the six boxes in the middle of the page. Discuss with students whether the summary requires you to change your main idea note or not. If so, write a new main idea note and replace the old one. The old one can stay underneath or go down on the lower right side of the page. Repeat this several times.

3. When the six supporting idea boxes are full, explain how to shuffle them around (Ma) based on importance, the upper three being more important than the lower three, and how to consolidate two or more notes into one (i.e., categorizing and classifying).

4. As you read the text, continue to use sticky notes to modify the main idea and move around the important information found in the text.

5. When a revised main idea forms, move the old main idea to the space at the lower right.

6. When students understand what to do, give them a photocopy of the sheet and have them go through the process in pairs as you circulate through the room and support them. They can then share their diagrams with others and defend their choices.

# CATEGORIZING–CLASSIFYING CHANTS (Mu)

This is a chant frame that students can fill in and then sing or chant in order to remember it. It helps students to think about how to categorize and classify information and also to consider reasons for doing so. The frame is meant to start you off, but you and your students will ideally modify it or create a completely different chant about the topic of study. Refer to chapter 2 for more specifics on how to create effective chants and how to get students to create them as well.

## Procedure

1. Analyze the topic and pull out key elements. These will help you start off the chant. Students can help in this process as well.

2. Put the chant on the overhead projector and have students copy it down on their own paper as you go along.

3. Fill in the first line with an appropriate entry in order to model how to begin.

4. Have students offer possible lines as you continue to fill in the chant. When you think they can do some on their own, let them try to finish the chant (Mu).

5. Call attention to the different types of academic language used for classifying and comparing in the verses. Feel free to change it if you want.

6. Have students work on finishing the chant in groups or pairs, and have them share their results with the class. Let them rehearse, if needed. Have instruments or downloaded mp3 drumbeats to help with the beat.

---

**Categorizing–Classifying Chant for** _____

I think the _____, _____,
and _____
Belong in the _____ group
Because they all share _____
That's what I think. How 'bout you?

You see the _____, _____,
_____, and _____
The _____ and the _____, too
All have in common _____
So they belong in the _____ group

But the _____ because it _____
belongs in its very own class
Let's give it the heading _____
Now I'm done, I need the bathroom pass

---

Following is a sample categorizing–classifying chant on the topic of geological changes:

I think the _____*sun*_____ , _____*the rain*_____ , and _____*the wind*_____

Belong in the _____*weather*_____ group

Because they all share _____*the skill of eroding mountains*_____

That's what I think. Now, how 'bout you?

Well, the _____*steam*_____ , _____*lava*_____ , _____*magma*_____ , and _____*ash*_____

The _____*cone*_____ and _____*eruption*_____ , too

All have in common _____*volcanic transformation*_____

So they belong in the _____*volcano*_____ group

But the _____*meteorite*_____ because it _____*didn't come from Earth*_____

belongs in its very own class

Let's give it the heading _____*"extra-terrestrial objects"*_____

Now I'm done, I need the bathroom pass

CHAPTER

# Identifying Cause and Effect

The skill of thinking about cause and effect is important for several reasons. First, it is an excellent jumping-off point for asking deeper questions about content material. Second, it trains students to produce logical hypotheses based on evidence and logic. Third, it is found throughout the science and social science standards. Fourth, and perhaps most important, cause and effect thinking tends to inject more interest into the study of science, social studies, and English. Students, in considering possible causes and effects, get to think about possibilities rather than just memorizing the answers to fact-based questions. Exploring causes and effects develops in students the skill of analyzing the concepts of a discipline and hypothesizing the relationships between those concepts.

Cause and effect thinking tends to revolve around two core questions that provide a starting point for more questions and connections: (1) What caused this to happen? and (2) What happened as a result of this? Of course, these questions breed even more interesting ones such as, What caused the cause? What would have happened if...? and What would happen if...? The beauty of these offspring questions is that they require additional thinking skills such as hypothesizing, interpreting, and problem solving.

To identify a cause, we must first have a solid understanding of the effect in question. Then we must possess background knowledge about the possible relationships between this effect and its possible causes. Likewise, to clarify effects, we must also understand the cause in question and understand its relationships to possible effects. This means that we must know certain principles of cause and effect in the discipline. This requires some basic conceptual knowledge.

For example, I read an article about the Industrial Revolution that had a statistic on decreased life expectancy. I inferred that the cause was poor conditions in factories and unhealthy living quarters. I think I had seen pictures or a movie relating to that period. I also already knew that unhealthy living conditions could cause more disease and death. Likewise, when an earthquake happened, I used my knowledge of plate tectonics to infer its cause. These examples help show that we cannot teach cause and effect in a vacuum. Students need to have an adequate understanding of the social, political, physical, and psychological principles that bring about—and result from—change in the world.

Each content area will have different emphases for understanding cause and effect. As you are the expert in your content area, it is up to you to model and scaffold the type of thinking you want students to acquire. You must develop your activities with such skills in mind, and you must encourage students to come up with creative responses—based on evidence and solid reasoning, of course.

Following are general strategies for teaching cause and effect that can apply to all classes:

1. Model the cause and effect questions that you ask yourself as you think about the concepts you are teaching. Why did Attila the Hun not attack Rome? What were the effects of the mixing of these two compounds? Why did Romeo kill himself?

2. Model the thinking process of hypothesizing possible causes and effects to answer the questions above. Model the language (and write it down somewhere for students to see) that you use to process your answers. In literature, most causes involve psychological processes. In science, the causes typically fall under physical, biological, chemical, geological, and subatomic laws. In social studies, most causes in history fall under the categories of

   - fear
   - racism
   - religion
   - compassion
   - desire for fame
   - desire for knowledge
   - desire for freedom
   - desire for truth
   - desire for wealth
   - desire for power
   - natural events

3. Scaffold the process of figuring out cause and effect with activities that support content and language learning. Some ideas for activities can be found in this chapter. Remember to gradually release responsibility for performance to the students, and support them as they develop independence in a task. For example, if you give them a Cause and Effect Timeline (page 87), allow them to work in pairs and meet with them to encourage multiple ways of connecting causes to effects in the timeline.

# Academic Language, Prompts, and Frames

The following expressions, prompts, and frames are for use with the skill of identifying cause and effect. Get to know these terms, and point them out when you and your students use them in discussions or written tasks. Refer to chapter 1 for ideas on how to use academic language expressions, oral and writing prompts, and paragraph frames to develop academic thinking skills and academic language.

Some common expressions used when identifying cause and effect include the following:

- I think...was caused by...
- That wasn't caused by...because...
- Just because it happened after...doesn't mean it was caused by...
- The main cause was probably...
- I hypothesize that...caused...
- The most likely cause was...
- The...led to..., which led to...
- He was motivated by...
- The effects of...were...
- The reason...
- That wasn't caused by...because...

- It was more than mere coincidence in this case because...
- Even though many people thought the cause was..., I believe it was...
- The relationship was more correlational than causal. That is...
- Each...played a key role. First...
- The function of...was to...
- The relationship between...and...was causal.
- There is a pattern that emerges when we look at...

Following are some prompts that encourage students to identify causes and effects when speaking or writing:

- Argue that there was a causal relationship between...
- Describe the causes and effects of...
- Investigate the events surrounding...
- What motive did she have for...?
- If you were...would you have...?
- Create a poster with evidence that supports two possible causes (or effects) of...
- Write an alternate ending or outcome for this event.

Frames like those shown below help students to gradually pick up academic language and eventually use it to compose their own high-quality written products without help. Two frames are given here to get you started on your own subject- and student-specific frames. These two are very generic, to allow you to fine-tune them or even to start from scratch. When creating your own frames, be sure to refer to the lists of expressions and prompts given above.

### Paragraph Frames for Scaffolding Identifying Cause and Effect

1. The cause of _____ is not obvious as we are led to think. Even though many people think the cause was _____ , I believe that the main cause was _____. First, _____. Second, _____. Therefore, if I am correct, then we must _____.

2. The effects of _____ are significant because _____ _____. First, we have the _____. Though some people think this is just a coincidence, I believe it is more. For example, consider _____. In addition, _____. Because of these arguments, we should at least begin to _____.

Remember to start with student background knowledge when introducing activities that build this skill. You can create a starter board of background knowledge topics such as friendship, family, school, music, advertising, culture, sports, television shows, movies, famous people, wars, or recent units you have studied in class.

# Activities for Developing the Skill of Identifying Cause and Effect

## CAUSE AND EFFECT DIAGRAM (Vi)

This activity allows students to systematically think about the multiple causes and effects of an event or condition in question. It then lets students ponder how much influence the cause might have had and then consider how much influence the event or condition had on its effects. I have found this activity to be a good way to spark interesting discussions about science, literature, and history concepts.

### *Procedure*

**1.** Distribute copies of the Cause and Effect Diagram (see blackline master in Part III, page 220) to each student or each pair of students.

**2.** Model how to analyze a fairly easy event or condition such as having the flu, the ring's heaviness around Frodo's neck in *The Lord of the Rings*, getting a poor grade, or breaking up with a boyfriend or girlfriend.

**3.** Move on to more challenging events or conditions, such as the Boston Tea Party, the Black Plague, the Vietnam War (see sample below), tidal movement, sunburn, the workings of electric lights, Ahab's desire to kill the whale, Dally's demise, and so on.

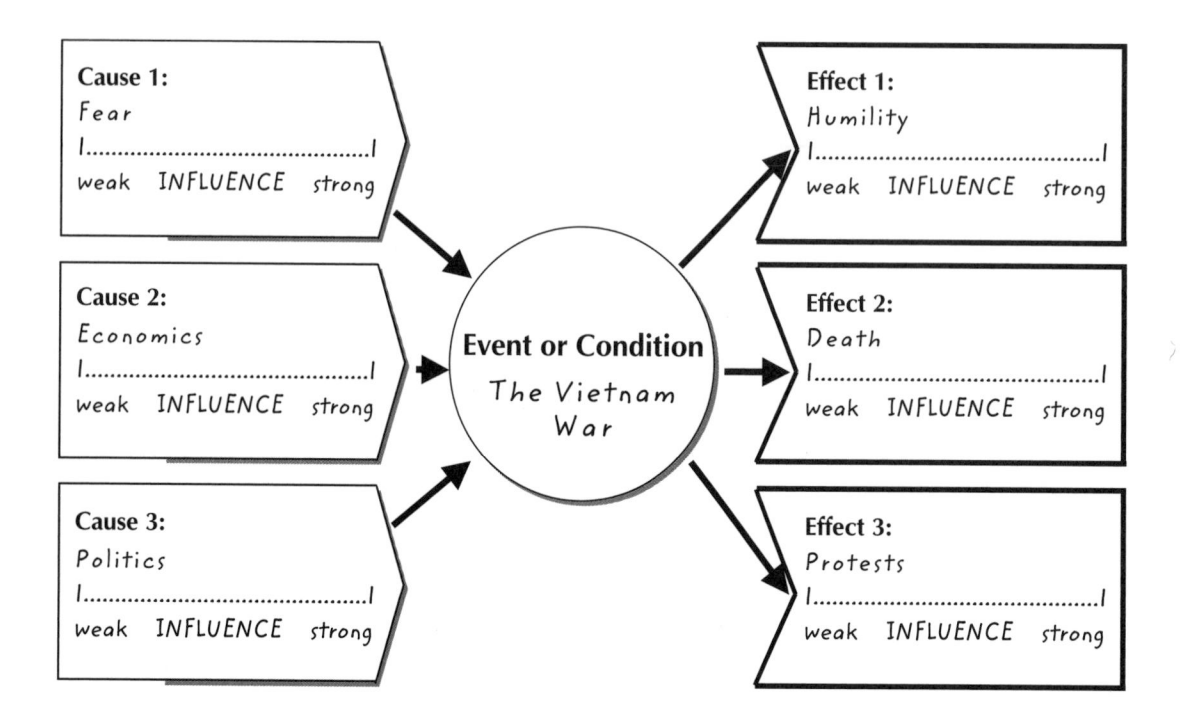

**4.** Model how to brainstorm possible causes for the event or condition (encourage guessing). Then choose three causes to write in the diagram, along the left side.

**5.** Consider *how much* you think the chosen causes influenced the event or condition and why. Write an X on the Influence scale to indicate either a strong or weak influence. Refer to the text to support your placement of the X. Students can help you decide on this and can bring up points for discussion.

**6.** Brainstorm various effects of the event or condition. These can be other events, effects on people involved, or effects related to the future. Try to come up with both positive and negative effects, even with an event that seems obviously positive (Emancipation of slaves) or negative (e.g., the Black Plague). Choose three to write in the Effects boxes.

**7.** Use an X to rate the influence that the event or condition had on that effect. Generate reasons and evidence for the rating.

**8.** Give students a new event or condition, or give them a list from which to choose, and have them go through the process on their own. Remind them that inference is important and that guessing is OK, as long as their guesses are logical.

**9.** Hold a discussion in which students can share their diagrams with the class.

**10.** Use the diagram as a scaffold for writing about cause and effect.

## Variation

Use another form of diagram with a tree, in which the roots are causes and the branches are effects. (A Cause and Effect Tree blackline master is provided in Part III, page 221.) Use this Cause and Effect Tree to show underlying and hidden root causes of complex systems and effects. For example, I have used the tree to describe culture in a social studies class: The roots were values and beliefs such as wealth, religion, education, and competition. The visible signs on the branches were sports, movies, advertising, consumer products, and music.

# CAUSE AND EFFECT VENN (Vi)

This is a visual organizer that shows what the brain is doing when it makes an inference about causes and effects. It looks at the text, thinks about how the text relates to an associated cause or effect scenario in the reader's background, and then makes an assumption or guess about possible causes or effects connected to the text information.

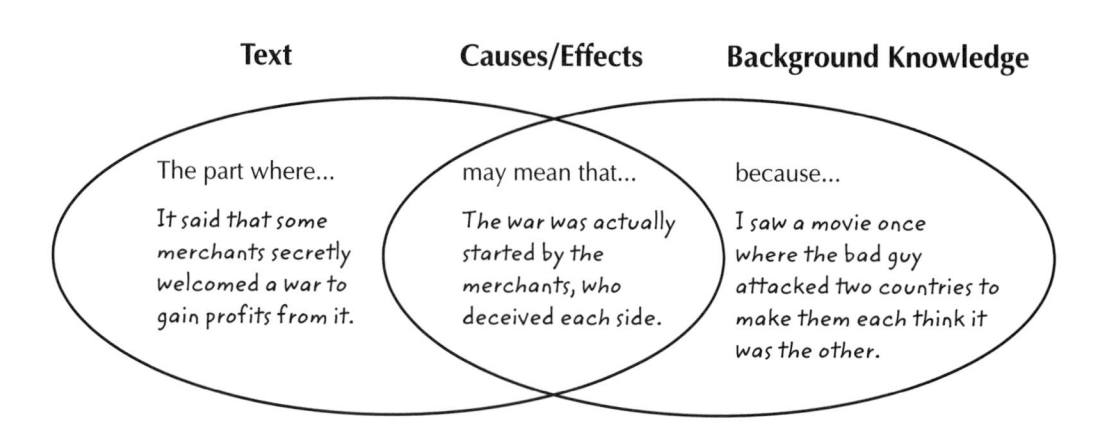

| Text | Causes/Effects | Background Knowledge |
|------|----------------|----------------------|

The part where...

It said that some merchants secretly welcomed a war to gain profits from it.

may mean that...

The war was actually started by the merchants, who deceived each side.

because...

I saw a movie once where the bad guy attacked two countries to make them each think it was the other.

## Procedure

**1.** Draw a Venn diagram like the sample shown above (Vi). Choose an important event in the text and note it in the Text side. You can also help students choose important parts from the text, if needed.

**2.** Although it may seem logical to fill in the Background Knowledge section next, you tend to generate the middle inference next. To create this inference, ask students to make a connection, conclusion, or educated guess about a cause or effect by thinking about the text. Consider the author's purpose, clues provided by the author, and vocabulary with new or multiple meanings.

**3.** Have students think about the background knowledge that they used to generate the inferred cause or effect. Write the reason for their inference based on background knowledge, another part of the same text, something they have done or seen, or past or present issues in the world.

**4.** Have students fill in the diagram on their own as they read, watch, or listen.

# HYPOTHESIZED CAUSES AND EFFECTS CHART (Vi)

This activity is helpful for training students to use good evidence for hypothesizing (or guessing, inferring, or predicting) the causes and effects of an event. This can help in problem solving as well. The chart below breaks down the process and shows how guesses should naturally happen in the brain while processing information. This chart is helpful for working with concepts in English, science, and social studies.

| Hypothesized Causes/Effects | Why? | True or Not? |
|-----------------------------|------|--------------|
| The boy will save him. | He is a good kid. | Yes |
| The boy's father taught him to be kind. | Kind actions resulted from his religion. | Don't know |

## Procedure

**1.** Discuss with students why it is important to hypothesize causes and effects. Create a list of ideas on the board. Point out to students that they already do this anyway when they make guesses about causes and effects in television shows, movies, and other stories. Tell students that they are to be somewhat like detectives, looking for clues and putting them together to give shape to their case. On an overhead projector, create a chart (Vi) with three columns similar to the one in the sample above. Students can draw a copy of it in their notebooks as well.

**2.** Read aloud or show a video. As you proceed, stop and have students write down the causes and effects that they hypothesize in the left column of the chart. Write some in your overhead sample as well.

**3.** Ask students to think about why they generated each of their causes and effects. Have them write their answers in the second column. Ask for solid reasons, and question ones that are weak.

**4.** Continue to read aloud the first few pages of the book (or show the first part of the video). Stop and check to see if any of the hypotheses have come true. Note this information in the third column of the chart.

**5.** Help students to continue making new guesses for causes and effects and providing evidence in the second column. Have them use language such as *cause*, *effect*, *resulted from*, *produced*, etc.

# CAUSE AND EFFECT TIMELINE (Ma, Vi, Mo)

The Cause and Effect Timeline helps students not only to determine sequences of events in a story or historical account but also to establish or infer the cause of those events. It helps students to see the ways in which events are connected. Students can, if desired, draw a line to connect each event from the upper part to its cause in the lower part. You can use this activity for stories, novels, history texts, biography, science observations, and more.

## Procedure

**1.** Make a copy of the Cause and Effect Timeline blackline master in Part III of this book (page 222). Cut out the two halves and fasten them together to make one long timeline (Vi) as shown:

**2.** Above the thick line, write events with or without time markers (e.g., years). Each event should go above one of the lower arrows.

**3.** Put the causes (if any) of the events below the line in the arrows. Make sure you can support each cause with evidence or solid reasoning.

**4.** Draw additional lines, if applicable, to connect upper events to causes below. Some causes will contribute to other events in addition to the ones written directly above them, or some events will, in turn, cause new events. Therefore, some of the connector lines you draw will be diagonal.

**5.** Connect more timeline halves, if necessary.

**6.** Optional: You can add a movement (Mo) component to this activity in the following ways:

- Have students pair up, and then give each pair a different event that they must research briefly (say for five minutes). They must find the possible causes of the event and the later effects it had on the future. They can hypothesize but they must be prepared to back up their ideas.

- Have each pair create a large card with their assigned event on the front and possible causes on the back.

- Have the pairs move around and arrange themselves in the order of the events as they happened. You will end up with a long line of students. Have one student in each pair describe the event, and have his or her partner present the event's possible causes and later ramifications.

- The next pair in line, if their event is connected to the previous event in any way, can agree or disagree with the first pair's ramifications when their turn comes.

**7.** Another option is using the timeline as a scaffold for writing a summary of the text that the timeline describes:

- Use an empty timeline, and show students how to create a logical story or account using the timeline's event and cause categories. Explain how different events will usually be covered in different paragraphs in the written text.

- Have students take notes on the sequence of events in a video or a science experiment, and then write a report on the experience.

## CAUSE CHANTS (Mu)

This is a chant frame that students fill in and then sing or chant to remember the material. It helps students to keep looking back and thinking about the causes of causes. The frame is meant to start you off, but you and your students will ideally modify it or create a completely different chant about the topic of study. Refer to chapter 2 for more specifics on how to create effective chants and how to get students to create them as well.

## Procedure

**1.** Analyze the topic and pull out key cause and effect elements. These will help you start off the chant.

**2.** Compose the chant on the overhead projector and have students copy it down on their own paper as you go along.

**3.** Fill in a cause and then ask students why it happened. Reflect on and discuss the question.

**4.** Have students go backward and continue to think about the cause of the causes.

**5.** Have students notice the different types of academic language used in the verses. Feel free to change it if you want.

| **Cause Chant for** _____ |
| --- |
| Let's think for a moment 'bout _____ |
| I often tend to wonder 'bout its cause |
| Some say it is because _____ |
| But I wonder what the cause of this was |
| |
| I think it was because _____ |
| But then I wonder what its cause was |
| Perhaps it was due to _____ |
| But then I ask what this came from |
| |
| I think it resulted from _____ |
| But why would this happen? |
| Perhaps it is a product of _____ |
| This leads me to ask why again |

**6.** If you like, have students finish the chant in groups or pairs, and have each group share their chant with the class. Have instruments or downloaded mp3 drumbeats to help with the beat.

**7.** You might want to have a "concert" in which you have a spotlight and let groups or individuals share their chants. Include in the concert a time for students to share a little about their songs or chants and why they chose or liked certain parts, in the way that pop singers often share this information about their songs in real concerts.

Following are sample cause chants on the topics of electricity and the Civil War.

### Electricity

Let's think for a moment 'bout ___electricity___
I often tend to wonder 'bout its cause
Some say it is because ___of hydroelectric power___
But I wonder what the cause of this was

I think it was because ___rain built up___
But then I wonder what its cause was
Perhaps it was due to ___evaporation of the sea___
But then I ask what this came from

I think it resulted from ___the sun's energy___
But why would this happen?
Perhaps it is a product of ___nuclear fusion reactions___
This leads me to ask why again

### The Civil War

Let's think for a moment 'bout ___the Civil War___
I often tend to wonder 'bout its cause
Some say it is because ___the South wanted to be separate___
But I wonder what the cause of this was

I think it was because ___of economic policies___
But then I wonder what their cause was
Perhaps it was due to ___Southern labor needs___
But then I ask what this came from

I think it resulted from ___wanting many crops___
But why would this happen?
Perhaps it is a product of ___selfishness and greed___
This is where this song must end.

## Variation

Students can write chants and songs without frames or scaffolds. The following sample cause and effect song gives students practice at saying difficult proper names. If desired, you can have students circle the causes and underline the effects in the song.

### A Very Brief History of Mexico

In the year 300 give or take a day, down in the Yucatan
Some Mayan students invented the zero to get a better grade in math
They studied the stars and played a high-stakes game a lot like basketball
They discovered chocolate (yay) and built great cities like Chichén Itzá and Uxmal
Then some mystery workers build the huge pyramids of the moon and sun
Further north around 600 in a place called Teotihuacan

But after 300 years those people disappeared, no one knows just why
Some say sickness or war or maybe they went to the beach and retired
Then the Toltecs built Tula in 1100, but their two gods had a big fight
Tezcatlipoca defeated Quetzalcóatl, who had to leave to save his life
Quetzalcóatl left to the east, and as he sailed away he said,
"Behave yourselves or when I return, you'll all have major problems!"

In 1300 the Aztecs passed Tula and heard about ole Quetzal's demise
They kept on moving 'cuz their god Huitzilopochtli said to look for a sign:
Where there's an eagle on a cactus with a snake, the journey for you is done,
There you'll build a great big city and call it Tenochtitlán.
The Aztecs built an empire by 1519 when the Spanish arrived
Cortes trekked up to Tenochtitlán with gold and treasure on his mind

And Montezuma, the Aztec king, thought the Toltec legend was true
That Cortés was really Quetzalcóatl who had returned to punish and rule
They finally realized that he just wanted gold and Cuahutémoc kicked him out
But in 1521 Spain finally won and said, "Now everything is ours"
Until 1810 when Hidalgo gave a shout to start the independence war
Ten years later, Spain was beaten and Mexico was born.

# Problem Solving

For most people—and almost all teachers—each day is full of problems to solve, challenges to overcome, and tough decisions to make. People solve problems in order to survive and to thrive. From the prehistoric problem of killing a mammoth to the modern problems of classroom behavior management, we all spend a large portion of our time and brain power on problem solving. The school experience, facilitated by teachers, offers students a variety of ways to practice solving problems, which prepares them for the many social and intellectual challenges just outside the school doors. For the purposes of this chapter, the skill of problem solving also includes making decisions, overcoming challenges, resolving issues, answering tough questions, or managing any other circumstance in which a solution or idea is needed.

According to noted researcher Robert Sternberg (1997), problems come in three types: analytical, creative, and practical. Analytical problem solving, just as one might guess, involves a hefty amount of analysis to find the solution. It is the most common type of problem encountered in many school settings, particularly in the United States where analysis is so popular. Analytical problem solving usually requires other thinking skills. For example, a teacher may give students the task of finding the cause of the Spanish-American War or of examining the environmental impact of a proposed dam. In these tasks, students will also likely use skills of synthesizing, identifying cause and effect, and evaluating as they go through the steps of problem solving.

Creative problem solving is more open-ended. It involves thinking processes such as imagining, inventing, designing, and hypothesizing. Creative problem solving is a vital skill that should play a greater role in our schools, as many of today's problems can only be solved by solutions that do not currently exist (or are not being implemented). Some basic examples of creative problem solving that some teachers have used are designing a book cover for a novel, inventing a solution for local air pollution, creating a sculpture that captures and expresses a moment in history, and writing a sequel to a popular movie.

Practical problem solving requires students to apply solutions to real-life issues. Students need to connect the problem to their lives or to the world around them. You may ask them to apply historical principles to present-day situations, or to apply algebra to real data from local businesses. By practicing problem solving in practical ways, students not only become more motivated to solve problems, they also acquire the skills necessary for automatic problem solving when they find themselves in the real world (e.g., in their future careers).

# Steps for Problem Solving

The steps for solving problems can apply to all three types of problems listed previously. It is important to train students to consider these steps whenever they come up against a problem, obstacle, hurdle, or puzzling situation. Numbered below are common problem-solving steps. However, real problem solving is seldom so linear; rather, it tends to be cyclical. For example, a possible solution in step 4 may lead a person back to step 2 and a best solution in step 5 may lead to the definition of a new problem, and so on.

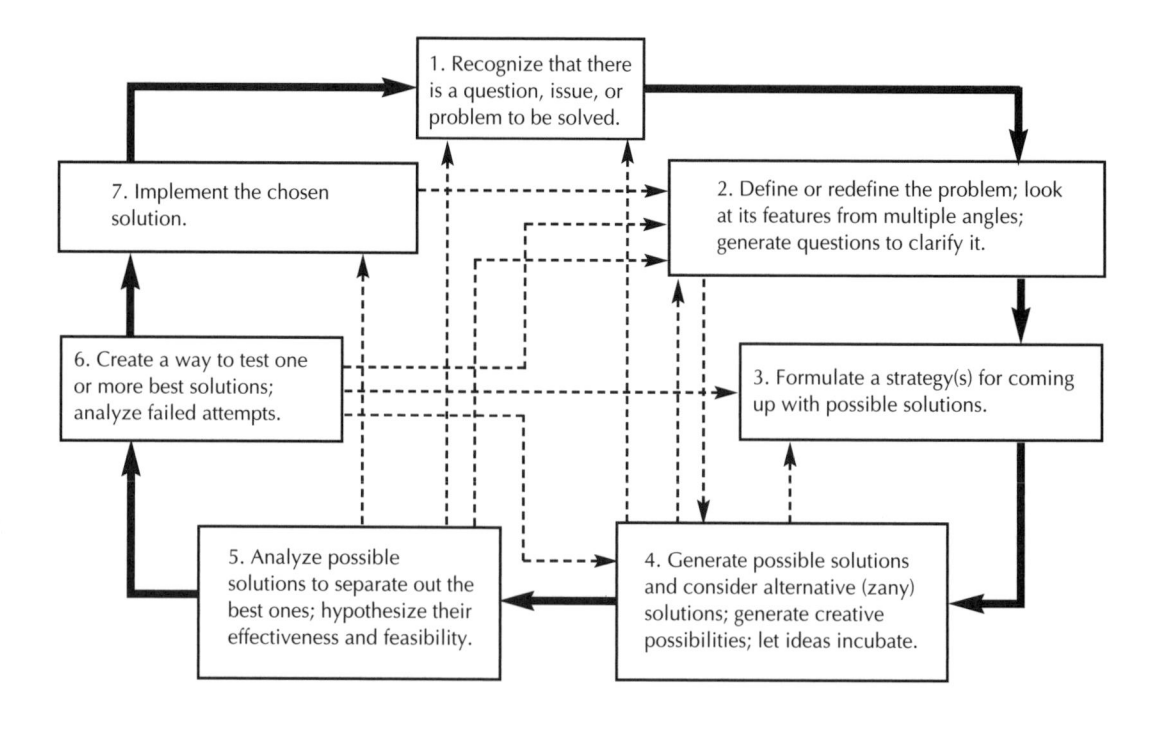

We must teach students these various steps and call attention to them when working through problems. (See Table 3 for questions to ask during each step.)

# Training Students in Problem Solving

Following are some suggestions for building the thinking skill of problem solving and its subskills. You can use these suggestions with the activities that appear in the latter portion of this chapter.

- Immerse students in problems. Students need to be exposed to a variety of problems. The most interesting problems, of course, are those that relate to their lives or the local community. Each day, you might designate two problems, questions, or issues for students to address. Students can try to solve both, or you can model solving one and then let students solve the other.

| Table 3. Questions to Ask During Problem Solving | |
|---|---|
| **Step** | **Questions to Ask Oneself in This Step** |
| 1. Recognize that there is a question, issue, or problem to be solved. | Is the problem even remotely solvable? Is it worth my time? |
| 2. Define or redefine the problem; look at its features from multiple angles; generate questions to clarify it. | What is causing this problem? Why is it a problem? If I were in others' shoes, would it be a problem? |
| 3. Formulate a strategy(s) for coming up with possible solutions. | How can I best use my time to generate solutions and analyze them? Are there charts, graphs, tables, visuals, computer programs, websites, books, people, etc., that I can use? What are the criteria that the solution needs to meet? |
| 4. Generate possible solutions and consider alternative (zany) solutions; generate creative possibilities; let ideas incubate. | What would be some outrageous answers? What has already been tried? Why didn't it work? |
| 5. Analyze possible solutions to separate out the best ones; hypothesize their effectiveness and feasibility. | What is good about this solution? What is bad? What are its long-term effects? Short-term effects? Is it viable/feasible, given the criteria above? |
| 6. Create a way to test one or more best solutions; analyze failed attempts. | How can I not waste too much time or money testing this? |
| 7. Implement the chosen solution. | How can I implement this solution in the most efficient way? |

- Model problem solving for students. As previously discussed, students need to see the invisible processes of expert thinking in action. This is because many of the struggling students have not "picked it up" during the years when other students were inductively learning it. We cannot assume that more of the same approach (inductive learning) will help. Instead, we need to slow down and go through the various steps with students clearly and methodically while modeling our thinking aloud.

- Explicitly teach the cyclical nature of problem solving. Create multiple and multimodal ways to show and tell students where they need to improve in solving problems. Write the steps on a big poster with corresponding symbols that you and the students create. Create hand motions for the steps also. Remember that some students may need extra work on defining the problem, whereas others may need to improve their brainstorming of solutions. Still others may have trouble discerning the feasibility of chosen solutions. Point to the written steps on the poster as you solve problems.

- Have students apply the steps to new problems and challenges. Give students related but different problems to which they can apply their problem-solving skills. Give them a chart like the one shown previously, in which they can fill in the cells for each step. Ask students to come up with their own problems that relate to the subject at hand and share them with the class.

Arthur Costa (2001) has generated the following helpful list of problem-solving traits (i.e., subskills). In addition to fostering these skills in students, we teachers can also benefit from developing these subskills in our own lives. In the list are several of the academic thinking skills from this book. Take a moment to think about why the following subskills might be important for being a good problem solver.

- Persisting
- Managing impulsivity
- Listening to others with understanding and empathy
- Thinking flexibly
- Metacognition
- Striving for accuracy and precision
- Asking good questions
- Applying past knowledge to new situations

- Communicating with clarity and precision
- Gathering data through all senses
- Creating, imagining, and innovating
- Responding with wonderment and awe
- Taking responsible risks
- Finding humor
- Thinking interdependently
- Learning continuously

Of course, to be good at solving problems, students must be given a wide range of problems to practice on, with well-modeled and well-scaffolded solutions. Table 4 offers a sampling of the types of academic problems, issues, challenges, and questions that are frequently found in different content areas.

| Table 4. Types of Academic Problems by Content Area | |
|---|---|
| **Content Area** | **Academic Problems** |
| Social Studies | Alternative scenarios: How would history have changed if ____ had happened differently? Would we be here? What caused that? What could have prevented this event? Will something like this repeat itself again? How might we prevent it in the future? Economic fiascos Historical mysteries and cover-ups Not-so-heroic heroes of the past Issues related to credibility of historical sources; conflicting sources Controversies (e.g., Vietnam, Iraq, etc.) |

(continued)

| Content Area | Academic Problems |
|---|---|
| Science | Environmental issues<br>Current physical limitations<br>Renewable energy<br>Word problems<br>Validity and reliability of a theory<br>Health and hunger problems<br>Issues related to space and deep ocean travel<br>Ethical controversies (e.g., stem cell research, abortion, assisted suicide, etc.) |
| Language Arts | Internal and external conflicts in a novel<br>Evaluate the importance of the characters<br>Figure out the author's purpose<br>Write a sequel to a story that resolves hanging issues<br>Write a prequel that explains characters before the story |
| Math | Designing a physical structure and figuring out costs to build it<br>Word problems<br>Making a scale model<br>Designing a musical instrument<br>Making graphs of observations<br>Creating a poster that explains a complicated math concept to others<br>Simulating a business<br>Challenges that engineers and architects face |

**Table 4.** Types of Academic Problems by Content Area (continued)

# Academic Language, Prompts, and Frames

The following expressions, prompts, and frame are for use with the skill of problem solving. Get to know these terms, and point them out when you and your students use them in discussions or written tasks. Refer to chapter 1 for ideas on how to use academic language expressions, oral or writing prompts, and paragraph frames to develop academic thinking skills and academic language.

Some common expressions used when problem solving include the following:

- We need to define the problem.

- The main problem is...

- The conflict is mainly between...

- This is a major problem for several reasons.

- There are different ways to solve it.

- The best solution is...because...

- I think that the answer is...because...

- I predict that...

- I'll bet that...because...

- Let's look at the roots of the problem.

- I hypothesize that...

- The negatives of such a solution are...

- When we break the problem down into...

- The main cause of this problem seems to be...

- This solution has been tried before.

- We need to identify the...

- There is a pattern that emerges when we look at...

Following are some prompts that encourage students to solve problems when speaking or writing:

- Debate the following problem.

- If you had the problem of...what would you do?

- Choose one side of an issue or problem; now argue for the opposite side.

- You have 30 minutes to solve this serious world problem. Put your heads together to solve it.

- We need to think outside the box to generate possible answers.

- Investigate the events surrounding...

- Write a letter to...to explain how to approach the current problem and solve it.

- Write a dialog for two persons with opposing solutions to a problem; describe how they solve it.

Frames like the one below help students to gradually pick up academic language and eventually use it to compose their own high-quality written products without help. One frame is given here to get you started on your own subject- and student-specific frames. This one is very generic, to allow you to fine-tune it or even to start from scratch. When creating your own frames, be sure to refer to the lists of expressions and prompts given above.

### Paragraph Frame for Scaffolding Problem Solving

The problem of _____ really boils down to the issue of
_____. In the past, the common solution was to
_____. However, this is only effective in terms of
_____. I propose several other options that might work. First,
they could _____. This would _____
_____. Second, they could _____
_____. Finally, even though it is costly,
they could _____.
This solution is ideal because it _____. These possible solutions
are worth considering and testing if we are to solve this issue in the near future.

Remember to start with student background knowledge when introducing activities that build this skill. You can create a starter board of background knowledge topics such as friendship, family, school, music, advertising, culture, sports, television shows, movies, famous people, wars, or recent units you have studied in class. Following is a short list of common problems to solve. (See Appendix B also.)

- Gang violence
- Gun control
- Drug addiction
- Drunk driving
- Health insurance coverage
- Truancy

- Large class sizes
- Cheating in schools
- Punishment for bad behavior in school
- Junk food's bad effects on health
- Curfews
- Television violence

# Activities for Developing the Skill of Problem Solving

## RIGHT AND LEFT BRAIN PROBLEM PAIRS (Gru, Vi)

This activity emphasizes the creativity and discernment needed for problem solving. It is also a fun way to discuss the theory behind right brain and left brain differences and to use them to carry out problem solving. This activity also is a way to practice certain dialog structures in cooperative situations.

### Procedure

1. Give students a brief talk on right and left brain differences in order to make the activity more interesting. To make things simpler, tell students that the right brain tends to be more artistic and spatial, whereas the left brain tends to be more logical and practical.

2. Give students a problem or set of problems to consider. Consider some of the issues found in Appendix B.

3. Model for students how you struggle to clarify and understand a problem before tackling it. Students should be able to define the problem to one another in their own words.

4. Photocopy the Right and Left Brain Problem Pairs blackline master from Part III (page 223) of this book, and give a copy to each pair of students. Let students come up with all the possible solutions they can generate, and have them write them all under the Right Brain column (Vi). Do not censor or criticize their answers or ideas. You simply want a large set of possible solutions.

5. Have students go through the list and move the most promising ideas to the Left Brain for further scrutiny and consideration. Students then will discuss the strengths and weaknesses in a more logical, left-brain manner.

6. Have students analyze the possible solutions and write their strengths and weaknesses in the appropriate sections of the boxes. Strengths might include low cost, time efficiency, or wide research base; weaknesses might be a lack of feasibility or inordinate expense. Think aloud to model for students what happens in your brain as you look at and consider solutions.

7. Have students choose the best solution and explain why they chose it. They usually will choose the one with the most favorable strengths-to-weaknesses ratio.

8. Give students a new problem or issue (or reassign different issues to different groups) and repeat the activity.

9. Students can share their results with one or two other pairs, then with the whole class.

# DESIGN A VIDEO GAME (Vi, Gru)

This engaging activity helps students to learn content standards and problem solving at the same time. The activity takes advantage of students' interest in video games and allows them to be creative in designing their own game (they can even send the game to an educational software company in proposal form). Most video games are motivating because of their problem-solving qualities, along with their increasing levels of difficulty and challenge (Gee, 2003). These qualities can be missing in many school activities, such as when we ask students to memorize information and then "regurgitate" it on a test. The Design a Video Game activity is mostly done on paper, but you can also have students create the game on a computer if you have appropriate software. An added bonus is that students learn to come up with multiple answers, some of which are decoys. Note that this activity is an idea starter that you will need to adapt to fit your context.

## *Procedure*

**1.** Choose a topic of study in the current unit to use for the game's theme. You can also give students choices of themes within the topic. For social studies, you might choose topics such as life in the U.S. colonies, the rise of the Aztecs, or the Cultural Revolution. For science and math, you might choose nuclear power, light refraction, nutrition, animal adaptations, or balancing equations. For English, you might choose the plot of a current novel; symbols and metaphors; or themes such as heroism, courage, faith, or love.

**2.** Talk about video games with the class. Find out which video games are their favorites and why. Have them discuss and make a chart of the good and bad characteristics of video games. You can use Think-Pair-Shares (see chapter 13) in this step.

**3.** Discuss the type of video game the students will be designing. Highlight the good characteristics on the chart made in step 2. Encourage students to be creative, but tell them that killing and violence (although contained in most of the best-selling video games) are not allowed in this game. Give students a list of requirements based on the content to be learned for the class and the problem-solving abilities to be cultivated. Remind them that this can be fun, but that they need to learn during the process.

**4.** Model for students how to develop a story line for the game. There should be characters, a main problem, and events that happen as the main character(s) try to solve the problem. You can use the story line in a movie as an example.

**5.** Use blank 8.5" × 11" paper for the screens. Assist students in designing their game:

   a. The first screen should give the background and main problem of the game—a problem is often a quest of some sort. For example, a game about the Cold War could have a main character who is trying to prevent nuclear war after hearing a conversation between two officials. If they like, students can give the player a choice of characters in the very first screen.

b. Screen 2 should contain the first scene of the actual game. It should contain some type of choice or challenge that the player must overcome in order to proceed to screen 3. The question or challenge can be written on the front of the page, and you should put the drawing of the scene on the back if there is not enough room on the front. Any questions used should be open-ended questions that force players to think. For example, "What could happen to the world if 20 nuclear missiles exploded?" One answer choice could lead a player to screen 3a, and the other answer could lead to screen 3b. If desired, you can use larger sheets of paper to fit more questions and drawings on one side of the page.

**(Screen 3a)**
The atmosphere probably wouldn't absorb enough radiation for us to survive. Please return to previous spot.

**(Screen 3b)**
Bay of Pigs
Probably, the radiation would kill most air-breathing organisms in the Northern Hemisphere.

Challenge: Why was the Bay of Pigs incident important?
a. It threatened to escalate.
b. We needed oil at that time.

c. Screens 4, 5, and so on should also have challenges or problems to answer. There can be more than two possible answer screens for each one.

d. Have students create an ending screen that shows a winner and how he or she solved the problem.

**6.** Have students revise the designs in pairs after they have a rough draft of their games (Gru). This will result in several different versions of the game.

**7.** Have students help one another play their games. If playing on paper, one player can simply hand the appropriate screens to another player while playing. If desired, students can set aside the "wrong answer" screens a player chooses, save them, and use them to subtract points from a player's score. When a player plays again, he or she can try to reduce these negative points to zero.

**8.** Play several students' games in front of the class, and discuss questions that arise and are especially relevant to the content you are studying.

# SOLUTION RANKING BOARD
## (Ma, Vi, Mo)

This is a kinesthetic and tactile way to rank possible solutions to problems. It allows the student to see and touch the process of evaluating the positive aspects of a solution versus the negative ones. You will need to model and scaffold this process very well, but it is worth it.

## *Procedure*

**1.** In pairs, have students cut out a main frame for the activity (Vi), as shown below. Then have students fold an 8.5" × 11" sheet of paper the long way once, then once again, to create four long strips that are each 2 inches wide. Have students cut the strips apart, then draw a line at 5.5 inches on each strip to split the positive side from the negative side. (Only three strips will fit into the frame at one time, but it helps to have an extra strip.)

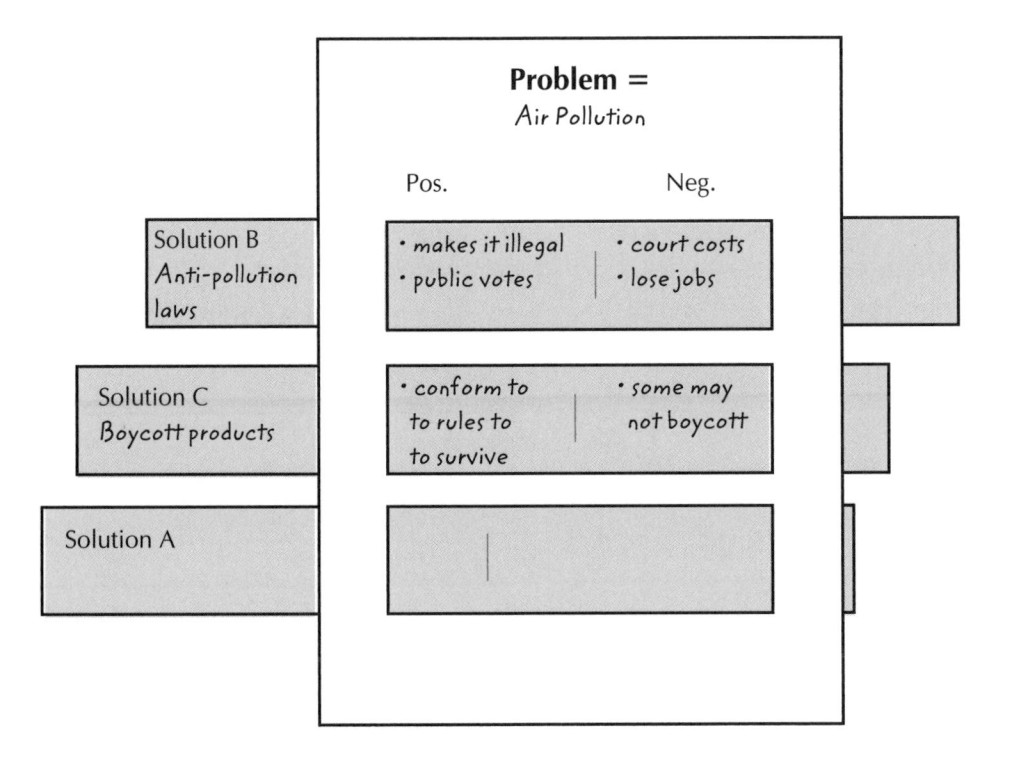

**2.** Present a problem or controversial issue to students and have them write it on the top of the frame. Choose a problem with three or more possible solutions.

**3.** Have the pairs of students brainstorm possible solutions, which they then write on the left side of the solution strips.

**4.** Have students come up with the positive and negative aspects of each solution. Ask them to write the positive aspects to the left of the center line on each strip, and the negative aspects to the right of the line.

**5.** Students should then evaluate which strip has the highest difference between its positive and negative aspects. They must be able to argue their choices with logical speculation and evidence. For example, students should say things like, "This solution's cost in dollars is worth it when we look at how many lives are saved"; "The chances of saving him are too slim to risk the lives of four others"; or "Doing the right thing outweighs the cost, doesn't it?"

**6.** After students fill in the strips, have each pair put three strips in their frame (Ma). They can then discuss which solution has the most positive and least negative outcomes. They can move the strips around in the frame to show the process of evaluating and choosing the best one (Mo). This is very subjective and should inspire lively conversations. The strips with more positive aspects can be pushed over to the right to emphasize positive aspects and make the prioritizing more visual for students.

**7.** Have each pair of students join another pair to form groups of four. Have each pair discuss their final solution(s) and reasons. The groups of four should try to come to a consensus.

**8.** Have the groups share their results with the whole class. If desired, you can make a chart on the board or overhead projector to show their solutions.

# PROBLEM CHANT PAIRS (Mu)

This is a chant frame that students fill in and then sing or chant in dialog response form. It helps students to think about how to solve problems in an engaging way. The frame is meant to start you off, but you and your students will ideally modify it or create a completely different chant about the topic of study. Refer to chapter 2 for more specifics on how to create effective chants and how to get students to create them as well.

## Procedure

**1.** Think about the topic you are studying and the possible problems or issues that can help drive the unit. Students can help in this process as well.

**2.** Compose the chant on the overhead projector and have students copy it down on their own paper as you go along. Do a sample problem from a past unit or from real life.

---

**Problem Response Chant Frame**

I have a major problem, it's a very big deal
I need to solve it right away,

If you tell me what it is, then maybe we can solve it,
Make your description crystal clear, OK?

The main issue is _____
And _____ you see

OK, let's generate possible solutions
Even if they're wild and crazy

I suppose we could _____
Or even _____, who knows?
Maybe we could _____
Or _____

Now we need to analyze each idea
And see what each one is worth
The idea of _____ costs too much
And the one about _____ will never work

But I think the idea of _____
Is better than the rest
Because it _____
Now let's take it to the test!

---

**3.** Fill in the first line with the problem and think aloud about it, going through the steps of problem solving.

**4.** Finish the rest of the chant on the overhead as a class.

**5.** Have students, working in pairs, take the problem and create a chant of their own. They can change it to fit more verses, if they want.

**6.** Have students notice the different types of academic language in the verses. Feel free to change the frame to add the language that you want.

**7.** Once the chant is finished, have the groups or pairs share their versions with the class.

**8.** Have instruments or downloaded mp3 drumbeats available to help with the beat.

Following are some additional chant frames to use with your students:

---

### History Mystery Chant Frame

Hello, you've reached the home of Sherlock Holmes
Leave a message; maybe I'll call
I went back in time to _____
There's a mystery I need to solve.

The place is _____
What happened? No one really knows
All we know is that _____
I need to figure it out, pronto.

First, I hypothesize the problem's cause
A _____, I think
Maybe it was _____
I need clues to help prove these things.

The fact that _____
Is the first important clue I can use
It suggests that _____
But could simply _____, too.

The fact that _____
Is another important clue
It supports the theory that _____
And _____, too.

The fact that _____
Is more of a lie than truth
It was fabricated by _____
To make us think how they wanted us to.

---

They wanted us to think _____
Because they _____, you see
But I'm Sherlock Holmes; I search for truth
I'm not easy to deceive

Now I've gathered all my clues up in my head
And to me, the answer is clear
That _____
It's elementary, my dear!

---

### The Scientific Method Chant Frame

_____
_____
That's our hypothesis

Because _____
And we're going to prove it.

First, we pick the thing we're gonna measure
The _____ in our case

Then we pick the variable we're going to vary
The _____ in our case

Then we make sure we have a control group
_____ in our case

Then we make sure that all the other factors
Remain constant and don't slip

Then we vary the _____ and measure the _____
And look for a relationship.

---

## Variation

**The Problem Office Chant:** In this variation for using music, students pair up and choose people with controversies, problems, or challenges to overcome. They adapt the chant's underlined parts to fit the subject's context. They can adapt it in other ways as well, such as elaborating on the problem and the solution. This activity, because of its question-and-answer format, is intended to put students in mind of a complaint department.

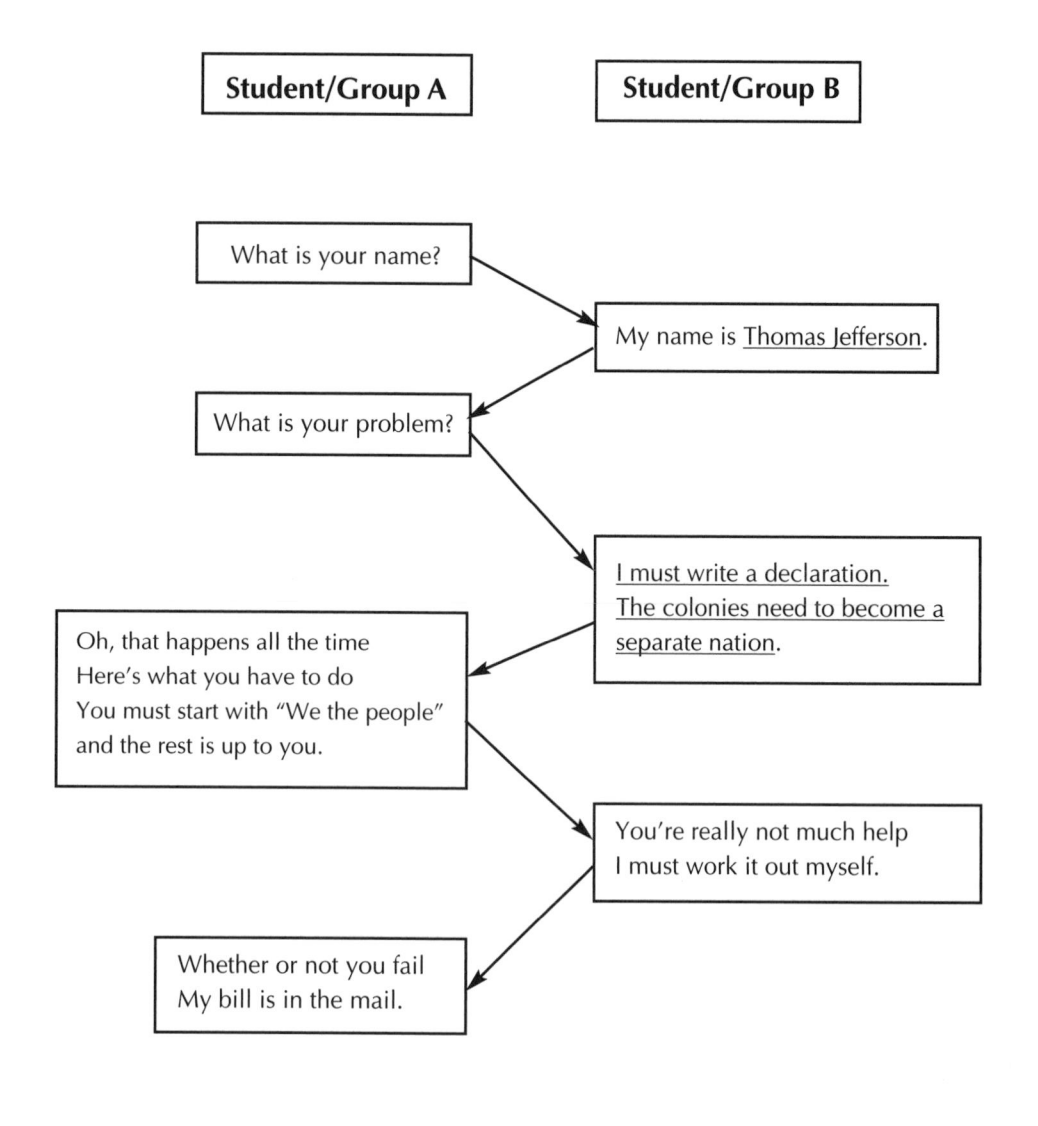

**Student/Group A**

**Student/Group B**

What is your name?

My name is <u>Thomas Jefferson</u>.

What is your problem?

<u>I must write a declaration.</u>
<u>The colonies need to become a</u>
<u>separate nation.</u>

Oh, that happens all the time
Here's what you have to do
You must start with "We the people"
and the rest is up to you.

You're really not much help
I must work it out myself.

Whether or not you fail
My bill is in the mail.

# CHAPTER 8

# Persuading

Life is full of persuasion. If you are not the one doing the persuading, someone is usually trying to persuade you. For instance, right now I am trying to persuade you that persuasive thinking is important. Students try to persuade us to give them less work, parents try to persuade them to study more, principals try to persuade us to work harder, spouses try to persuade us to work less (or more), and so on. Persuasion is also vital in many jobs. Think about how much persuasive thinking is needed by lawyers, social workers, doctors, politicians, and businesspeople. If we cannot persuade people to consider our ideas, we cannot contribute to problem solving, and, despite our intelligence or creativity, our ideas do not get a chance to shine. We all know students who have powerful ideas—they must learn how to promote them.

Chamot and O'Malley include persuasion as one of their 11 principal language functions in their popular *CALLA Handbook* (1993). Most state standards and assessments begin to require the skill of persuading in the middle school years. For example, in grade 7 of the California language arts standards, for listening and speaking we find "1.3. Responds to persuasive messages with questions, challenges, or affirmations." For writing in grade 8, we find "2.4. Writes persuasive compositions: include a well defined thesis...." In going through the English language development and English language arts standards for K–12, the terms *persuasive* or *persuade* appear 36 times (Carr, 2001).

Persuasion is what I call a "high-yield" thinking skill because as it develops, the other key thinking skills that support it also develop. These supporting skills include analyzing, comparing, evaluating, synthesizing, problem solving, and communicating. Persuasive thinking, more so than most other skills, has a knack for engaging students in a topic. Students like to learn how to get others to be on their side of an issue, and they like learning how to avoid being persuaded by adults and advertisers. There is more drama, more tension, and more energy in a persuasive situation. For teachers, persuasive thinking is useful in a wide variety of classes and contexts. When students are forced to argue their side and back it up with evidence, they show deeper learning of the concepts and better retention of them than when they are asked to perform the standard "right-back-at-you" assessments found in essays and answering test questions.

Another advantage of persuasion is that it lends itself well to group, oral, and written products. With group projects, speeches, and written pieces, you are better able to see how students are thinking than you might be with other, less visible skills. And, students might write more if they get a little emotion mixed in with the topic.

Persuasion, figuratively speaking, is tipping another person's scale to your side. It is showing the other that the reasons for your side outweigh the reasons for the opposite side. You must give evidence in support of your position to give it weight. Many issues, of course, require very subjective weighing and evaluating (see chapter 12) of the reasons and criteria involved. For instance, when considering the environmental impact of logging in a certain area, the jobs and livelihood of a group of people might be weighed against the severe depletion of an endangered species. Such weighing and comparing make persuasion an exciting way to teach a variety of content area concepts.

It is helpful to go over with students the common persuasive tactics that advertisers and politicians use to persuade people, such as the use of statistics, appeals to authority (e.g., "Doctors recommend..."), appeals to the bandwagon mentality (e.g., everyone believes this, and so should you), clever slogans, emotional language, exaggerated metaphors and analogies, hyperbole, promotions of a product or idea by famous people, the "common person" appeal, and the attribution of a cause to a factor that is merely correlational. For example, an author might find that more lunch consumed by students correlates to higher reading comprehension scores in an elementary school. Does that mean that eating more improves reading skills? Students should be trained to detect this type of faulty logic.

Learning the skill of persuasion helps students to recognize when, why, and how they are persuaded. Middle school through high school is an important time to develop this skill because it is when many real-life controversial issues start to surface. It is at this time of life that students start to formulate their opinions about the world and start deciding who they are, what they stand for, and what they will fight for (mostly figuratively, but sometimes even literally). They begin to realize that others want to persuade them to behave in certain ways and do certain things.

Finally, students need to learn when to be convinced by positive and helpful persuasion. They must start thinking about the future and about how some decisions they make now can help or hinder who they want to be; these decisions may even affect them forever. For example, I would guess that most students who were persuaded by counselors and parents to go to college have not regretted the decision.

# Academic Language, Prompts, and Frames

The following expressions, prompts, and frames are for use with the skill of persuading. Get to know these terms, and point them out when you and your students use them in discussions or written tasks. Refer to chapter 1 for ideas on how to use academic language expressions, oral and writing prompts, and paragraph frames to develop academic thinking skills and academic language.

Some common expressions used when persuading include the following:

- Although not everybody would agree, my position is...
- I have several reasons for arguing this point of view.
- My first reason is.... Another reason is...
- Therefore, although some people maintain that...
- There is a lot of discussion about whether...
- Even though the issue has two sides, I think I have shown that...

- These (facts, reasons, data) strongly suggest that...
- There are several points I want to make to support my point of view.
- Some argue that...
- They say (claim, maintain, hold) that...
- On the other hand, there are many who disagree with the idea that...
- They also argue that...
- A further point they make is...
- However, there are several reasons to oppose this point of view.
- Yet some argue vehemently that...
- After looking closely at both sides of the issue and the evidence, I believe it is best to...because...
- Granted, I admit that...
- Despite the fact that...
- Then again...
- It is also vital to consider...
- The statistics are misleading, however, because they do not show...
- Even though it seems that there is sufficient reason to do this, we must remember...
- Well, that is only partly the case. The other side of the story is...
- The advantages of...outweigh the disadvantages of...
- The issue is not so much a question of...but a question of...
- I completely understand what you are saying, but I would like to emphasize...
- That is a good point, but I think the evidence shows that...
- What it seems to come down to is...versus...
- Even though both sides have merits, the greater good will come from...
- We don't feel that the short run gains outweigh the long run losses.
- It is similar to...
- It is a difficult issue, but I feel that the (positives) of...outweigh the (negatives) of...
- If we look closely at..., we will see that it is better to...
- Based on the evidence so far, we should...because...
- We need to identify the key elements of this issue.
- We have a moral and ethical duty to...
- This finding is inconsistent with that one because...
- There is a pattern that emerges when we look at...
- When you take a close look at this part, you see that...

Following are some prompts that encourage students to use persuasion when speaking or writing:

- Debate the following issue/statement.
- Compare the two characters.
- Make a detailed description of…
- Evaluate the contributions of…to…
- Write a dialog for two persons with opposing points of view.
- Persuade a local government to…
- Convince a teacher to…

Frames like those below help students to gradually pick up academic language and eventually use it to compose their own high-quality written products without help. Two frames are given here to get you started on your own subject- and student-specific frames. These two are very generic, to allow you to fine-tune them or even to start from scratch. When creating your own frames, be sure to refer to the lists of expressions and prompts given above.

## Paragraph Frames for Scaffolding Persuading

1. Do you want a world with _____? This is what will happen if _____. For years, _____ _____. Unfortunately, they/we have failed to realize that _____. Therefore, I propose that _____ _____. This will _____ _____. Furthermore, it will _____. Opponents, of course, argue that this solution _____. These limitations are real, but greatly exaggerated because _____. Some also propose to _____. Yet this is not desirable because _____. Ultimately we must decide what we value. I, and many others, believe that we should place a higher value on _____ than _____. For this reason, we should _____.

2. The time has arrived for us to _____. Why? Because _____. Some say that _____. They are motivated by _____ _____. They also argue that _____ _____. On the contrary, such solutions only serve to _____. In the long term, our solution will be more effective because _____.

Remember to start with student background knowledge when introducing activities that build this skill. You can create a starter board of background knowledge topics such as friendship, family, school, music, advertising, culture, sports, television shows, movies, famous people, wars, or recent units you have studied in class.

# Activities for Developing the Skill of Persuading

## HOT AIR BALLOON (Gru, Vi)

In this activity, the class imagines that two or more people (story characters or historical figures) are in a hot air balloon that is too heavy. One person needs to jump out, and each balloon occupant must argue that he or she is more worthy of staying than the others. The actors in this activity need to summarize who they are and communicate their value and contributions. The audience then decides who jumps, based on the actors' speeches. This activity requires a high amount of synthesis and persuasion on the part of the actors and a high amount of evaluation on the part of the audience.

### Procedure

1. Put students into groups who will each study one person. For example, if you have three people to study, put students into three groups (or into six groups, with two groups each studying the same person).

2. Tell students that they need to build an argument that their good person is a really good person (i.e., better than other good people). Or, they must come up with arguments that their bad person is not as bad as other bad people.

3. Let the groups know who their study person's competitors are so they can think about how to weigh his or her own qualities against those of the other people in the balloon.

4. Have students practice their arguments within their expert groups, with other group members taking the roles of competitor persons to provide practice.

5. Tell the groups to choose a student to play the role of the person they were studying and to argue for that person's life in front of the whole class. Tell these chosen actors that they are in a hot air balloon that is going to crash if one or two people do not jump. Let the actors take turns pointing out their characters' good traits and deeds, or pointing out that their traits and deeds are not as heinous as those of their basket-mates.

6. As the balloonists plead and persuade, have the rest of the class take notes about who they think should stay and who should jump. Give students copies of the Hot Air Balloon blackline master from Part III of this book (page 224) and let them use the form for their note-taking. They can write on sticky notes the names of the people being discussed, and place these notes above the sandbags. They can write the arguments in the sandbags.

7. Give the class some time (around four minutes) to discuss their decision and then have them give their verdict, using solid reasons.

# BACK IT UP (Vi)

This activity (adapted from Dequine, 2003) gives much-needed explicit instruction and practice in supporting one's reasons with solid evidence. It shows students the different types of evidence that exist and lets them evaluate the relative strength of each.

## Procedure

**1.** Put samples of persuasive pieces on the overhead projector or in the hands of students, and model how to find the following types of support for backing up reasons. You can underline or highlight the examples of the various types, or create a chart like the one below, on which students can fill in appropriate examples from the persuasive text of each type of support.

| | |
|---|---|
| Fact/statistic | The World Health Organization (WHO) announced a 17% increase in death by malaria last year. |
| Quote from expert | Ultimately, we must address the issue presented by Marianne Stevens, chief spokesperson for the WHO: "It is getting increasingly difficult to reduce mosquito populations without using more toxic prophylactic substances." |
| Quote from person involved | A traveler to Nepal said, "We don't want to get malaria, but we keep getting crazy nightmares and other weird side effects." |
| Citation from credible source | In a recent WHO report, researchers estimated that certain strains of malaria will become totally resistant to current preventative medicines within the next five years. |
| Example | Last November, a high number of travelers with strange symptoms were brought to local health clinics. All had been using Larium. |
| Anecdote | On a recent trip to Nepal, I contracted malaria even though I was using the latest prophylactic medicine. |
| Hypothetical situation | Imagine a world with just mosquitoes flying around. |
| Rhetorical question | Will the mosquitoes win? Are we smart enough to defeat them? |
| Analogy | Can mosquitoes be spies? It seems like every attack strategy we have, they have prepared for and quickly adapt. |
| Comparison | This is similar to using certain types of radiation to cure cancer. The radiation often does unforeseeable harm to certain parts of the body. |

**2.** After students are familiar with different types of support and with the exercise of finding them in texts, they are ready to create their own reasons and support for their position. Model how to choose a position on a controversial topic, and let students watch and participate as you fill in a chart like the one below (Vi).

| My Position/Side | | | | | |
|---|---|---|---|---|---|
| Reason 1 | | Reason 2 | | Reason 3 | |
| | | | | | |
| Support Statement | Type | Support Statement | Type | Support Statement | Type |
| | | | | | |

**3.** Next, work on the counterarguments, also called concessions, counterreasons, or opposing viewpoints. Have students think about what the opponents of your side would argue, and put these counterarguments in a chart like the one below. Then, work with the students to come up with support for the arguments, and write those down along with the type of support each one represents. (Knowing the type of support is helpful because if the counterarguments only use one or two types, this can be a weakness you and the students can mention when refuting counterarguments.)

| Counterargument 1 | | Counterargument 2 | | Counterargument 3 | |
|---|---|---|---|---|---|
| | | | | | |
| Support Statement | Type | Support Statement | Type | Support Statement | Type |
| | | | | | |
| My response to this | | My response to this | | My response to this | |
| | | | | | |

**4.** Have students think about the counterarguments and prepare logical responses that acknowledge and respect the counterarguments, but then go on to explain that the counterarguments are not as strong as those that support your position. Explain to students that typical ways to respond to counterarguments include comparing statistics, questioning the validity and date of opponents' statistics, questioning the cause/effect explanations given by the counterarguments, questioning the credibility of the people or the value of the sources of information, challenging an analogy or comparison, or even exploiting an analogy to favor one's own side. Write down the responses the students come up with for each counterargument and include these on the chart.

5. Have students create conclusions that synthesize the points made and that leave the reader with the main argument presented in the thesis, without blatantly repeating the thesis. Ask students to work on creating clever and powerful closing statements that will make the reader think about the issue. (Students can write the closing statements on their own paper, or you can write them on an overhead transparency.)

# RATE THE REASONS (Vi)

This is an evaluation-based strategy that you can use to analyze persuasive texts that tend to contain varying levels of bias, opinion, and faulty reasons. This activity helps students through several steps that are vital to the academic thinking needed for persuading, evaluating evidence, reading critically, and supporting arguments.

## *Procedure*

1. Teach students to notice these various types of faulty reasoning that authors often use to support their opinions:

   - **False analogies**—Using a common illustration that seems similar, but does not match up with the argument in important areas
   - **False causality**—Attributing an effect to a cause without evidence
   - **False logic**—Arguing that a point is true because its opposite cannot be proved
   - **Weak generalization**—Using too few examples to make a claim or draw a conclusion
   - **Appeal to emotion**—Using emotional language and feelings as justifiable proof of a claim
   - **Fluff**—Using large amounts of text to give the appearance of large quantities of evidence, even though the text does not prove the point being made

2. Find a few editorials and put them up on the overhead projector to analyze for some of the reasoning fallacies listed previously.

3. Model the process of dissecting an essay and rating the reasons and evidence given. Use the Rate the Reasons blackline master in Part III (page 225); a sample is shown filled in here. Think aloud during this process, especially when you come to criticisms of evidence or when you think the author has a credible piece of proof.

4. In the top box, write the opinion statement that the essay is arguing for. Write the reasons that support the opinion in the Reason sections on the left side.

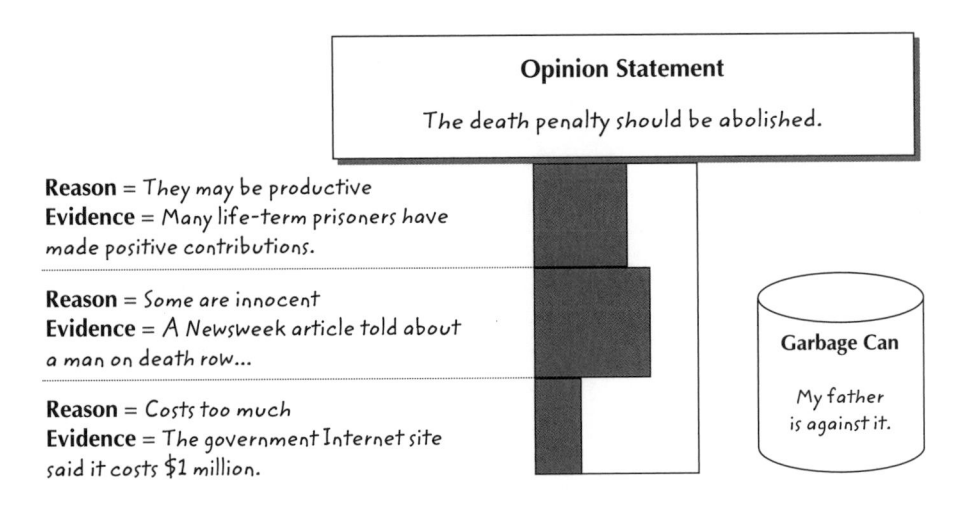

**Opinion Statement**

The death penalty should be abolished.

**Reason** = They may be productive
**Evidence** = Many life-term prisoners have made positive contributions.

**Reason** = Some are innocent
**Evidence** = A Newsweek article told about a man on death row...

**Reason** = Costs too much
**Evidence** = The government Internet site said it costs $1 million.

**Garbage Can**

My father is against it.

**5.** Write a short note about the evidence used to support each reason, such as statistics or the reasoning fallacies from step 1.

**6.** Decide how much weight each piece of evidence and each reason should have, and create a "brick" for the column holding up the opinion statement (Vi). The weaker or more faulty the proof or reasoning, the smaller the brick should be. Have students help you decide on the sizes of the bricks.

**7.** If a piece of text does not support the opinion or position, write it inside the garbage can on the right.

**8.** Create bricks for the reasons and evidence given (resembling a horizontal bar graph).

**9.** When finished, have students form pairs or groups to discuss the results and why they decided on the sizes of the various bricks. This discussion can be very lively; try to model some persuasive academic language for students during this process.

**10.** Have students create their own editorials or essays and rate their own writing using this procedure.

**11.** Optional: Use a rubric like the one below to rate the opinions, editorials, and persuasive arguments.

## Persuasive Evaluation Rubric

| Element | Rating | Comments |
|---|---|---|
| 1. Clarity of argument | 1 2 3 4 | |
| 2. Strength of reasons and claims | 1 2 3 4 | |
| 3. Effectiveness of evidence | 1 2 3 4 | |
| 4. Inclusion of key counterarguments | 1 2 3 4 | |
| 5. Response to counterarguments | 1 2 3 4 | |
| 6. Overall organization | 1 2 3 4 | |
| 7. Appropriate academic language | 1 2 3 4 | |

# PERSUADE PROCESS CHART (Mo, Vi)

The process charts used with this activity make effective posters or graphic organizers for discussions and persuasive essays. The Persuade Process Chart is a scaffold that students can remember when they are writing letters and taking written tests. Even more effective is using this chart in combination with the PERSUADE Acronym Chant-Rap and the Purse of Persuasion activity, both found in this chapter.

## *Procedure*

**1.** Photocopy the Persuade Process Chart 1 blackline master found in Part III of this book (page 226). Hand out a copy to each student.

**2.** Using the Persuade Process Chart 2 blackline master (page 227), create a poster that you can refer to while you analyze an essay on the overhead projector (Vi). To save time, use a poster-making machine at your school or local copy center.

**3.** Put a short essay sample that has all the elements from the chart, such as the following, on the overhead:

> "My back is killing me!" my friend told me the other day. He is only 12 years old. His back pain started when locker privileges were taken away from all students last year. Now he must carry his enormous textbooks all day long. The administration should allow us to use the lockers at our school to avoid problems such as these.
>
> Lockers allow us to store our books until we need them. My friend must carry a huge math book all day long until he needs it during seventh period. Carrying our books around creates extra stress and physical strain. In fact, in schools where lockers have been removed, the incidence of back and neck problems has increased 27%. Lockers also keep our valuables safe, as many students have lost money and other personal items through classroom theft. Furthermore, lockers provide some personal space, and even indicate respect and trust that we students can use them responsibly.
>
> Granted, we do realize that lockers can be used to store weapons and drugs. However, as they are school property, lockers can be opened for searching at any time without a warrant. Purchasing a home and classroom copy of each textbook is another option in some schools, but this is very costly and not what most taxpayers want.
>
> The potential health problems of not having lockers are more serious than the threats that lockers pose regarding weapons and drugs. So give us a chance to show that we can be responsible, and help us prevent long-lasting back problems at the same time.

**4.** Go over the chart with students as you analyze the sample essay or letter.

**5.** Optional: Do the hand motions for each persuasive element (see page 227) and explain why the hand motions will help students remember the elements (Mo). Even if the students do not want to do the motions, your doing the motions will help students remember the parts.

**6.** Explain the visuals in the right column of your poster and have students take notes on their charts using the sample essay.

7. Highlight the parts of the sample essay and label them directly on the overhead copy of the essay. You can also hand out a copy of the essay to students and they can highlight, circle, and label the parts of the essay as you go over them.

8. After you model the process, hand out a different essay, letter, or article and have students, in pairs, analyze and highlight the essays with the parts from the chart.

9. Have the pairs form groups of four and discuss and compare their findings.

10. Share everyone's findings in a whole-class format and discuss the purpose of the activity. Ask, "Why did we do this?" "How is persuasion useful?"

11. Have students organize their own persuasive essays by using the Persuade Process Chart.

# PRO/CON IMPROV (Mo, Gru)

This activity (adapted from Dennis, Griffin, & Wills, 1981) is a highly communicative thinking and language-building experience. It helps to build improvisation skills, sharpens student thinking about the pros and cons of a topic, and helps train students to use appropriate transitions and movements to communicate. It is fun and can be done easily in pairs. It provides a good foundation for many variations that you can use throughout the year as the complexity of subject matter increases.

## Procedure

1. Model the process by having a student (the director) pick a topic to be argued and then say "Pro!" while clapping once. You (the speaker) make up pro reasons for the topic for 30 seconds or so, being very convincing. Then the director says, "Con!" and you immediately switch to the negatives of the topic, often adding a transition such as *but, however, on the other hand, yet,* etc. Then go through the "Pro!" and "Con!" sequence once or twice more.

2. Give students a list of possible topics that lend themselves well to this activity. Students can also choose on their own, but a few to get you started are camping, rain, shopping, movies, the beach, watching television, dogs, parents, traveling, exercise, driving, computers, cars, and fast food.

3. Put students in pairs (Gru). Have each pair decide who will go first and then have the partners alternate between the roles of director and speaker. Encourage the speakers to show the pro and con sides not only in their voices but also in body language and movement. The director then begins by saying a topic of his or her choice. The speaker, if uncomfortable with the topic, can tell the director to choose another topic, but only once. The director claps and says, "Pro!" and the speaker begins (Mo). The director can respond with head nodding, showing engagement in the monologue.

4. After students have done the activity on their own, ask for some volunteers to do the activity again in front of the class. (It need not be the same as when they did the activity in pairs.) It is a good idea for the director (after asking the speaker to perform up front) to

say, "My speaker did an amazing job! We would like to go!" This validates the speaker's performance.

5. Have the volunteers perform in front of the class, and then let the students discuss what they liked about the performances on a verbal and a nonverbal level. What did they like about the speaker's communication? Did he or she smoothly transition from pro to con and back? You can also comment on good use of academic language and transitions.

6. Eventually, you can give students more substantive topics that pertain to your class or subject, such as these:

- the Vietnam War
- Albert Einstein
- Thomas Jefferson
- violence
- laws
- technology

- democracy
- nuclear power
- Napoleon
- radiation
- anger
- education

# PURSE OF PERSUASION (Ma, Vi)

The Purse is a catchy way for students to organize the vital elements of a persuasive argument. I have found that intermediate-level English-language learners, thanks to the Purse, have written better persuasive essays than many native speakers of English who have not used it.

## *Procedure*

1. Cut out the hook, pencils, and purse from a copy of the Purse of Persuasion blackline master in Part III (page 228), and fold the purse in half to make an actual functioning purse (Ma). Fasten the two halves of the purse together and staple along the seams between the pockets. Hand out photocopies of the master to the students and have them follow along with you, making their own purses as well.

2. Model the process of analyzing a sample persuasive essay or letter and filling in the parts of the purse as you look at the essay or paragraph. Take the hook from the essay and write it on the hook of the purse. Then proceed to the background information and persuasive points, which go on the pencils. Put the pencils in the appropriate pockets of the purse (Ma). (You can also create a larger visual that doesn't fold.)

3. After thus explaining and analyzing the points of persuasion in another writer's essay, have students use the purse to write their own. First, they must decide on a topic. You may already have one in mind, or you can give students a choice. Some teachers choose to put students in pairs and assign the partners opposing points of view on the same issue.

4. Model on the overhead how to construct a persuasive essay. Use colored pens to write the text for the hook (yellow), background (blue), thesis (red), topic sentences (orange), evidence (green), and conclusion (purple).

5. Have students cut out the purse, hook, and pencils and proceed to fill them in (Ma). They may need to do extra research to support their points with solid evidence and quotations. If they use a quotation, remind them to include an analysis or reason for using it.

6. Have students then use the filled-in purse graphic to create a draft of a written persuasive letter or essay. You should have a list of helpful academic language transitions on the board, such as *granted*, *therefore*, *on the other hand*, and *furthermore*.

7. Use the steps of the writing process, especially peer revision, to work toward publishable final products. Have students share their final products with the class or publish them in a class or school paper, if appropriate.

# PERSUASIVE 3-D BALANCE SCALE (Ma, Gru, Vi)

You can find a full description of the 3-D Balance Scale activity in chapter 12. The blackline master is in Part III of this book, on page 236. The activity described here is a persuasive variation of the scale in which students engage in a two-sided controversial or persuasive discussion with another person or pair. Students need to negotiate criteria as they work together to craft a well-constructed persuasive argument. This is a way to understand how to think about and "weigh" very subjective ideas. The goal is for students, all using the same criterion, to work together to agree, more or less, on which reason (and evidence) is better.

## Procedure

1. Refer to chapter 12 for how to set up the scale (Vi).

2. Choose a topic to argue or discuss. Put students in pairs or in groups of four (Gru). Have each person or pair take a side of the issue for the time being.

3. Have students work for a while on their arguments using their own paper. They should generate the criteria on which to judge, the reasons, and the evidence (including quotations and statistics) for their reasons. As a group, they should choose three criteria.

4. Have students summarize the information on the criterion cards. Have them use the MVP criterion card for the strongest point in the argument.

5. Emphasize that this is not a game and that the purpose is not to compete to see which end of the scale weighs more. As a group, they are to discuss and create the most insightful way to look at the issue possible.

**6.** Have one member of each pair (or one side of each group) read one of the smaller cards aloud and give it to his or her partner (Ma). Ask the listeners to think about the point on the card and to respond in writing on the back.

**7.** The group or pair must then come to some agreement as to how much weight the listener's response took away from the card's point. If only a little, have them snip a corner off the card. If the reason was significantly weakened, then have them cut off a quarter of the card, one third of the card, etc. If the response proved the point to be totally false, then have them rip the card in half and place it under the fulcrum. You can intervene when there are major differences of opinion. Remind students that the goal is not competition, but clarity.

**8.** When all the smaller cards are done, have students proceed to the MVP criterion and do the same.

**9.** Now, have students put the criterion cards on the scale and see which side weighs more. They should discuss whether their result makes sense. Remind students that they are trying to get a deep understanding of the issues.

**10.** Have the pairs or groups write a persuasive letter or essay using the notes and discussions from the activity to persuade readers to lean toward what they found to be the heavier side.

# PERSUADE ACRONYM CHANT-RAP
## (Mu, Vi, Mo)

This activity is meant to prepare students to write persuasive essays or letters. It is especially effective in concert with the visual Purse of Persuasion activity, also in this chapter. This is a powerful way to remember the many elements of persuasive writing in a musical way.

## Procedure

**1.** Have students look at examples of persuasive letters or essays, and describe to them what these letters and essays do. (You should have samples of persuasive essays in your district resources. If not, find them on the Internet in opinion-editorial articles from news websites or by doing a search for sample essays, benchmark essays, etc.) Tell students that they get to learn a song that hasn't quite made it to the Grammy Awards, but may in the future. Tell them the song happens to be a great way to learn how to write good persuasive pieces.

**2.** Get a percussion instrument or download an mp3 drumbeat to play on your computer. You can also have students snap their fingers or slap their laps to create a rhythm for the chant. Clapping and desk pounding, however, are not recommended because these methods can get too loud.

**3.** Write the following acronym chant (modify the verses if you want) on a large piece of butcher paper (Vi). You can even color code the lines of the chant to go with certain parts of a persuasive essay: for example, yellow for the hook, blue for the background, red for the thesis, orange for topic sentences, green for evidence, and purple for the summary. See Color-Coded Writing in chapter 13 for other color-coding ideas.

**P** Pick a side and prepare each part

**E** Excite the reader with a hook at the start

**R** Reduce it all into a thesis statement

**S** Stack up my side with evidence

**U** Understand opposing arguments

**A** Address opposing points and show their dents

**D** Describe how my side outweighs the other side

**E** End with a conclusion that pulls it all in tight

**4.** Optional: Do hand motions with the chant (refer to the Persuade Process Chart 2 on page 227). Teach students the hand motions as you go through each line (Mo).

**5.** Go through each line with the students while looking at a sample of a persuasive essay or letter.

**6.** Practice the chant with the students several times, and have pairs or groups of students come up and lead the class (Mu).

**7.** You can use the chant to create a persuasive writing rubric as a whole class. This helps students to gain a better understanding of the assessment process, increase buy-in, and helps them self-assess to create better products of learning.

## PERSUADE CHANTS (Mu)

This is a response chant that helps students to remember the elements and language of persuasion. The following frame is meant to start you off, but you and your students should feel free to modify it or create a completely different chant about the topic of study. Refer to chapter 2 for more specifics on how to create effective chants and how to get students to create their own.

## Procedure

1. Consider the target concepts and pull out key ideas that you want to use in persuasion. These will help you start off the chant. Students can help in this process as well.

2. Compose the chant on the overhead projector and have students copy it on their own paper as you go along.

3. Have students share ideas for lines as you continue to fill in the song. Remind them that they can modify the existing words or delete them to fit their needs.

4. When you think the students can do some on their own, let them try to finish the song in groups or pairs.

5. Call attention to the different types of academic language in the verses. Feel free to change the language if you want.

6. Once the groups or pairs finish their chants, have them share their chants with the class. Let them rehearse in advance, if needed. Have instruments or downloaded mp3 drumbeats available to help with the beat.

---

### Persuade Chant Frame

Do you want a _____?
Well that's what will happen
If we let _____
You'll see I'm right in the end.

Why? Well, first _____ no lie.
For example, _____
_____. That's why.

Furthermore, _____
_____ you see
Because _____
That's solid evidence, most would agree.

Granted, it's true that _____
And this could help out in the short run
But this doesn't outweigh the _____
_____ in the long run.

I also concede that _____
This is partly true, I must agree,
Nevertheless, we must remember _____
_____ I believe.

Therefore, before _____
Think about these words of mine
And choose to _____
In the long run it's what is right.

---

The following page features a sample persuade chant frame on the greenhouse effect.

## The Greenhouse Effect

Do you want a _____world covered with water_____?
Well that's what will happen
If we let _____the world keep getting warmer_____
You'll see I'm right in the end.

Why? Well, first _____it's the glaciers_____
_____they are melting fast_____ no lie,
For example, _____the ones in Alaska have dwindled_____
_____it's the Greenhouse Effect_____. That's why.

Furthermore, _____the oceans are already raised_____
_____several centimeters_____ you see
Because _____U.S. Oceanography did a study_____
That's solid evidence, most would agree.

Granted, it's true that _____they say there are cycles of warmth_____
And this could help out in the short run
But this doesn't outweigh the _____excessive flooding_____
_____and the loss of land_____ in the long run.

I also concede that _____we are starting to act_____
This partly is true, I must agree,
Nevertheless, we must remember _____all the heat_____
_____each day adds up_____ I believe.

Therefore, before _____you start your car_____
Think about these words of mine
And choose to _____walk or ride a bike_____
In the long run it's what is right

# Empathizing

Not only does empathy improve a person's social skills, it influences one's overall ability to think and succeed in school. In fact, noted researchers on curriculum argue that empathy is one of the top six facets of understanding that teachers must help students to develop in order for them to understand concepts at deep and enduring levels (Wiggins & McTighe, 2000).

A student's ability to empathize facilitates deep learning because in order to be able to think "in the shoes" of another person, one must learn a lot about that person and about the circumstances that surround him or her. Empathizing is particularly useful in social studies and language arts. However, there are some exciting empathy-based activities in science as well, such as having students write and even act from the viewpoints of different types of glaciers. Such activities allow students some freedom to be creative while at the same time digging into the content. You will find activities in this chapter that can be used in most classes, with a touch of creative adaptation.

Empathy is stepping into another person's (or animal's or thing's) shoes to think and feel as he, she, or it does. It provides a student with a way to participate in the lives of others, and by doing so, to better understand and remember the others' experiences and thoughts. But there is a catch: We humans must battle our deep-rooted narcissistic tendencies to perceive life as being the way we ourselves have experienced it. Sam Wineburg says, "Paradoxically, what allows us to come to know others is our distrust in our capacity to know them, a skepticism about the extraordinary sense-making abilities that allow us to construct the world around us" (2001, p. 24). We must be humble and open-minded when we set out to walk in another person's shoes, whether he or she lived 3,000 years ago or currently lives down the street. We must remember the countless influences that have bombarded us since we were born—such as television, school, movies, music, trips, family, and friends—things that all work in concert to shape how we might think when we step into another's shoes.

We need to learn as much as we can about the person (or group, animal, or object) with whom we are trying to empathize. What were the details of the person's childhood, relationships, goals, actions, words, failures, and successes? How did these life factors affect this person's personality and actions? Once we gain this knowledge, we can close our eyes and begin to visualize what the person might have seen or still sees. We must strive to filter out the many thoughts and feelings from our own experiences that bias our perceptions of the other person. Then we can generate a possible and evolvable set of thoughts and feelings. In a sense, we are trying to put together a puzzle that will never be complete.

During the entire process, it is vital to ask lots of questions, such as, "If she knew that... then why would she...?" or "What did those words mean in that time and place?" or "What did *freedom* mean in that context?" Such questions help us consider the validity of our assumptions and inferences, strengthening them or pruning them away as we gain new knowledge.

Empathy also involves broadening, or diversifying, our perspectives and viewpoints. Wiggins and McTighe say, "Empathy is a form of insight because it involves the ability to get beyond odd, alien, seemingly weird opinions or people to find what is meaningful in them" (2000, p. 56). This is difficult because we must leave who we are behind. We must think outside the box created by our limited cultural and temporal influences. Many students have had little practice thinking outside their particular paradigms. In fact, the Bradley Commission on the Teaching of History states that the primary purpose of teaching history is to help students break free from their ethnocentric and present-centered views (Gagnon, 1989).

Empathy is useful for many academic purposes. First and foremost, empathy improves our ability to communicate with others. One of the keys to communication is knowing how others will perceive our message. This helps us tailor our message to maximize its clarity. A related purpose is being able to perceive what others are thinking as they communicate to us, even though their words may not be crystal clear. Second, empathy can teach us about how past humans thought and felt. Third, empathy helps us explore the vast diversity among humans today: how we currently think, feel, live, and grow. Fourth, empathy engages us in a story as we walk in the shoes of characters and think about what we would do in similar situations. This helps us understand ourselves better as a result. Finally, empathy opens our minds to new ways of solving social and political problems and new avenues for understanding other people's opinions and arguments.

# Academic Language, Prompts, and Frames

The following expressions, prompts, and frames are for use with the skill of empathizing. Get to know these terms, and point them out when you and your students use them in discussions or written tasks. Refer to chapter 1 for ideas on how to use academic language expressions, oral and writing prompts, and paragraph frames to develop academic thinking skills and academic language.

Some common expressions used when empathizing include the following:

- To echo what they were saying, we think that...
- I feel the same way, with a slight difference...

- If I were in (person)'s shoes, I would...
- I think (person) felt...because...
- Let's remember the time in which (person) lived and what (he/she) went through.
- First...I'll bet (person) was thinking...
- How would you feel if you were (him/her)? I would...
- Do you have any idea how she might have felt?
- By his reaction to the situation, I think he was probably feeling...
- Each experience played a key role in the formation of his personality. First...
- If we lived back then, how might we have...
- In her eyes, she sees it to be...
- From their perspective, they think of it as...
- The person probably considers it to be...
- But in his mind, he believes that...
- We can only speculate about what they were thinking when they...
- Yet from her point of view, she thinks that...
- I was thinking along those same lines...

Following are some prompts that encourage students to empathize when speaking or writing:

- Debate the following issue/statement.
- Compare the thoughts and feelings of two characters.
- Write an "autobiography" of (person).
- Analyze the contributions of... to...
- Investigate the events surrounding...
- Create a personality profile of...
- Write a dialog for two persons with opposing points of view.
- Write a journal entry from the perspective of...

Frames like the ones shown on the next page help students to gradually pick up academic language and eventually use it to compose their own high-quality written products without help. Three frames are given here to get you started on your own subject- and student-specific frames. These are very generic, to allow you to fine-tune them or even to start from scratch. When creating your own frames, be sure to refer to the lists of expressions and prompts given above.

# Paragraph Frames for Scaffolding Empathizing

1. _____ (person) responded to the _____
   by _____. If I were _____
   (person), I would have reacted to the situation differently. I would have _____
   _____ because _____. In addition, I would
   have _____.

2. I am a/an _____ (object/animal). I enjoy _____
   _____. I like to spend time with _____.
   Sometimes I get in trouble when I _____. I never _____
   _____ because _____.
   Other _____ (objects/animals) envy me because
   they _____.

3. If we consider the time and events through which _____ lived, we can
   better understand him/her. I argue that he/she wasn't as _____ as
   many people think. Rather, because of _____, he/she
   became more _____. This is evidenced in the part of the
   book when he/she says, "_____."

Remember to start with student background knowledge when introducing activities that build this skill. You can create a starter board of background knowledge topics such as friendship, family, school, music, advertising, culture, sports, television shows, movies, famous people, wars, or recent units you have studied in class.

# Activities for Developing the Skill of Empathizing

## EMPATHY ROLE-PLAY MINGLER (Gru, Mo)

This activity builds on the ideas of the Hot Seat and is similar to what many teachers call a Tea Party activity. It emulates a workshop mingler in which participants take on the persona of a character or historical figure as they converse with others. Students share their feelings and thoughts as if they were the person, based on the text and on class discussions.

## Procedure

1. Choose the people from the text or unit that you want the students to play in the mingler. Assign each student a role to learn about and portray. (More than one student can play the same role if needed; for example, in a class of 30 that is studying 3 people, 10 students will play each role.) Have students research their person's motivations, feelings, and any other important information pertaining to their role and take notes about the character on a colored sheet or card. Tell them to focus not only on important outer achievements and events but also inner motivations, thoughts, and feelings, which may not be explicit in the text. They may have to infer some of these.

2. Optional: Select important quotations, facts, and concept summaries from the text that pertain to the characters or historical figures. Write the information pieces on half-sheets of paper, a different color for each character, historical figure, author, or famous person. Give these half-sheets to the students whose roles correspond to the characters. This step helps to provide information that students might not otherwise find or deem important.

3. Have students compare and add the information from your teacher notes to their own notes. They are now "experts" on their characters and will share their information with other students through role-playing.

4. Tell students to mingle with other people and get to know them better, especially how they thought, felt, and were motivated to do and say what they did in the text. Choose a student and model with him or her how it is done. You can give the student a couple of sample questions to ask you in order to get the interaction going. For example, for the role of Napoleon, the student might ask, "What did you do?" and "Why did you want to conquer Europe?" You might respond, "It's complicated. I thought that Europe needed a strong leader, to be united under one ruler." The student could then ask, "How did you feel when you were defeated?" You could respond, "Distraught, angry, confused. I couldn't believe the people would do this to me. Then I vowed to rise again because I knew I was destined to rule! The world needed me! It still does!"

5. Give students a grid sheet like the following to fill in as they mingle. They should also carry with them the colored notecards they made in step 1 above. Tell the students to look for

others whose cards are different colors from theirs (i.e., who are playing a different character than they are) and to converse with everyone as if they were actually the character or historical figure. They should use *I* and *you* and act out the character's passions and emotions when speaking. Circulate and help them act their parts.

| Person (Animal/Thing) | Motivations What motivated you to...? Why did you...? | Feelings How did you feel when...? | Important Details What did you do? |
|---|---|---|---|
| 1. | | | |
| | | | |
| 2. | | | |
| | | | |

**6.** When the mingler is finished, ask the class if any students were particularly convincing. Ask those chosen students to do a role-play in front of the class. Have the other students share what they liked about the acting after the role-play is finished.

**7.** Have a brief class discussion about what the students learned through this activity. Ask students to talk about what they learned about other characters as well as their own.

# HOT SEAT (Gru)

The Hot Seat provides motivation to thoroughly understand a text by empathizing with a person or object. Students need to understand varying viewpoints and act them out. For example, if a student assumes the role of a historical figure or a character in a narrative, he or she will have to infer reasons for actions by referring to evidence from the text or other sources. The student must empathize to understand the person or object he or she is portraying.

## *Procedure*

**1.** First, model the process by assuming the role of an author, historical figure, story character, expert on a topic, or scientific subject (e.g., raindrop, moon, molecule, octopus, tectonic plate, etc.).

**2.** Give students sample questions or question starters on 3" × 5" cards and have them ask you the questions as you sit in a seat at the front of the room (the hot seat). For example, you might say, "I am Huck Finn. What would you like to know?" or "I am General Lee. Shoot your questions at me," or "I am a carbon molecule. Fire away," or "I am Steven Hawking. Any questions?" Answer the questions as the chosen person would answer them.

**3.** Have students practice this process in pairs or groups of four to six. One student in each group should assume a role and take the questions.

**4.** The other students in the group should ask questions about purpose, motivations, feelings, actions, or other content. They can use questions such as these:

- Why did you do this?
- How did you feel about the other characters?
- How did you change? Why?
- What will you do now?

- How did your invention change the world?
- If you had...how would the event/ story have changed?
- Why are you relevant to my life?

**5.** Optional: Play a whole-class version of Hot Seat. Groups can nominate a student who did well in the small groups to go to the front of the class and take questions. Give students some time to prepare good questions. You may want to chart questions into three levels (explicit, implicit, and life applications) and evaluate them in terms of their helpfulness in understanding the text.

# SCIENTIFIC PERSPECTIVE WRITING (Gru)

Similar to the Historical Narrative Perspective Writing activity in this chapter, students take on a different perspective in this activity. However, in this one, you will ask them to walk in the shoes of a scientist, animal, organism, mineral, or vegetable. Before you start, look at the standards and concepts to be learned, and generate a possible set of subjects that students can use. Shown here are some past examples from classes I have taught and observed:

**A Water Molecule**
I am $H_2O$, a water molecule. I am not very complex, but I am very important. The bonds between my oxygen atom and the hydrogen atoms are interesting. They...

**The Sun or Moon**
No doubt you've seen me up in the sky at night. But I am more than a romantic ball of rock. Without me, life would be very different down there on Earth. I am vital...

**A Glacier**
About 60,000 years ago I was born, very slowly. Snow started to fall and build up over many years. It turned to ice. Once I reached about 80 feet tall, I started to move. I guess I was like a teenager ready to move on.

**A Blood Cell**
I am a white blood cell. I like to travel and take care of problems, such as bacteria that invade the body. They usually get in through cuts or food. When I find these evil little organisms, I surround them and...

**A Tectonic Plate**

**An Astronaut**

**An Electron**

**A Galaxy**

**A Whale**

**A Volcano**

**An Amoeba**

**A Guitar**

## Procedure

1. Use ideas from the previous samples or generate your own from content standards and vocabulary.

2. Have each student choose a person, object, or process to write about in the first person point of view. Students must remember to try to teach as much content as possible through their stories, as if writing for younger students.

3. Remind students to include various functions and parts of the subject, as well as its purposes, problems, effects, desires, and any humor that may make the story more entertaining to read.

4. Have students find or draw pictures to include with the text. They can create a small book if there is time.

5. Students should share their stories in small groups for suggestions and comments (Gru). They can then share them with students in younger grades as well.

## Variation

Have students write a scientific perspective chant, song, or poem in narrative form, such as the following:

**Riding the Water Cycle**
Ouch! I hit the mountain with my raindrop friends
We join together and make a stream again
More friends join in and we become a raging river
And the waterfalls get bigger and bigger

At last we flow into the open sea
Then the sun comes out and evaporates me!
I become a vapor and I'm hard to see
If you've seen a teapot, well I'm like the steam

I'm riding the water cycle
I'm a raindrop or a cloud or sometimes snow (when I'm cold)
I'm riding the water cycle
Round and round and round I go

I wave goodbye to my watery friends
And float back up to be a cloud again
Then the wind nudges me toward dry land
I get colder as we reach mountains

So I huddle together with my vapor friends
And suddenly we begin to condense!
I become a raindrop once again
And I start falling down next to my friends
Hey, I'm gonna hit another mountain
And the water cycle commences again!

# EXPERT POINT OF VIEW ARTICLE (Vi)

This tool helps students to understand an issue by becoming an expert in the field. Students write an article or report about a topic as they take on the role of the expert. Pace, Pugh, and Smith (1997) suggest three points of view to help students think like historians: They become detectives, judges, and lawyers as they write. For science, students can take on the points of view of scientists, environmental engineers, or politicians as they uncover the important elements of a topic to write about it. Writing from these different viewpoints gives students a taste of real-world work and thinking.

## *Procedure*

**1.** You must first teach students how to think like the experts they will emulate. This may take a while, but it will be worth it in the long run because many other thinking skills are cultivated in the process. Make a poster (Vi) from the Expert Point of View blackline master in Part III (page 229) of this book.

**2.** Choose five main thoughts that you think the chosen expert may think. Some general ways of thinking are given here, but you may want to get more specific when you use this activity.

- A detective might think about defining the problem, finding clues, figuring out causes and motives, resolving conflicting evidence, and inferring bias in witness responses.

- Judges and lawyers might think about the credibility of evidence, previous similar cases, motive and intent, appropriate punishment, the importance of the act, evaluation of claim and responsibility, future ramifications of any decision made, and character references.

- A scientist might think about the scientific method (observation, hypothesis, experimentation, conclusions), validity of experimentation, the overall value of the topic or theory, extraneous variables in the experiment, and ramifications of success and failure.

- A politician might think about maintaining popularity among voters; making government spending efficient; evaluating the worth of a new bill in terms of dollar cost and ultimate benefits to people; radically changing a large part of the health, education, or social services program; and saying the right thing at the right time to the right people.

**3.** Have each student take on an issue from the perspective of the expert he or she decides to emulate. The activity is especially interesting when two students pair up and take on the same issue from different expert points of view. For example, one partner can be a scientist and the other a politician; they can describe opposing points of view on stem cell research. The scientist can point out facts and research, and the politician can refer to public opinion and moral considerations.

**4.** Have students organize facts and statements in an outline or web and then begin their articles. Remind them that they are writing to persuade the general public unless you just want to have them inform.

**5.** Publish the finished pieces and use some as examples for pointing out empathy and persuasive language, if appropriate.

# HISTORICAL NARRATIVE PERSPECTIVE WRITING (Vi, Ma)

Many English teachers already use a variation of this activity to teach students to write from the viewpoint of characters in literature. Perspective writing means having students empathize with other people, animals, or things in social studies, science, and literature-based classes and then write from that perspective. Historical narrative is a creative way for students to see life through the eyes of another and to learn more about him, her, or it. The student becomes a historical figure, famous or not, and describes life from that person's perspective. This can be in the form of a journal or a story.

## *Procedure*

**1.** Show students several good writing examples of the perspective(s) you would like them to take and of possible subjects. You can even create a list of standards (written in student-friendly language) that students can aim for in this activity. Help students understand the topic by breaking it down into the three concepts: historical, perspective, and narrative. Review what these mean and how yo u and the students will synthesize them to create the desired product.

**2.** Have students take notes on sticky notes (Ma) from their reading. Place the sticky notes on three different-colored sheets of paper, taped together and labeled like the sample shown below (Vi). You do not need to use the categories shown here; these are just ideas to get you started.

| Daily Life | Conflict/Event | Changes |
|---|---|---|
| Me: | Causes: | Me: |
| Family: | | |
| | Events: | Family: |
| Education: | | |
| | | Education: |
| Politics: | Effects: | |
| | | Politics: |
| Work: | | |
| | | Work: |
| Culture: | My role: | Culture: |

**3.** For the daily life page, students should record details and important ideas from their readings that fit into whatever categories you use. The middle section is for use when the student learns about a major event that touched the character, such as a war or political situation, that brought about change in his or her life. Finally, the student should describe and infer (with good evidence) the changes that occurred in various categories of the person's life.

**4.** When their notes are finished, model for the students how to consider audience and purpose when writing a story. The audience for this activity will include other students and you. Point out that, although one's audience may be generally acquainted with the parts of history one is studying, readers are probably not experts on the topic. Most likely, they will only know major facts and dates and will not necessarily know other colorful details about that time period—for example, the clothes people wore, the kinds of food people ate, what household items were common (toasters? butter churns?), or the details of major conflicts. The student's purpose is to tell a realistic story with a beginning, middle, and end that includes historically accurate information.

**5.** Have each student write his or her story, using the ideas from the notes. Students should remember to use a first person narrative format to teach readers as much as possible about the important events, ways of thinking, and culture in the chosen time period. This means they will be writing sentences using *I*. For example, "I awoke to sounds of horses galloping past." Students can take on the role of a real or an imagined character of a specific time period and place. See the sample shown here.

### The Strangers at Plymouth

Mother lit the fire to cook the fish I had caught that day. She thanked the guardian spirit of the fish for their sacrifice. Then she carefully placed the vegetables in the coals so that they would all be ready at the same time. The aromas all mixed together in my nose, and I sat down, eager to begin the meal.

My mother smiled at me because she knew how much I liked to fish, even though it wasn't a Wampanoag custom to let girls fish or hunt. When I finished with chores, I often sneaked away to fish or hunt. My parents knew this, as did many others, but they didn't care. I provided food, didn't I? I didn't tell them my secret that one day I wanted to be the sachem, or leader, of our people. I didn't think the boys around me were any wiser than the girls my age.

A short while later, we ate dinner. It was perfect. My father told stories of our Wampanoag ancestors and the strange creatures that roamed the Earth and sea. We lived on the edge of the world, on the east coast of what is now called North America. Wampanoag meant "people of the dawn."

I had a weird dream that night in which there were hundreds of giant brown and white beasts floating into our harbor. When I woke up, it was almost light. I stared at our simple home. The posts were made of tree trunks, and they stayed here all year. We covered them with grass mats when we came here each spring. We lived in this house until we returned to the forest in the fall to hunt and stay protected by the trees in winter. In the forest we hunted deer, bear, moose, turkey, and other animals. We cut holes in the ice on lakes to catch fish. One time I fell through the ice, and my father had to save me.

I got up early and put on my leather clothes and shoes to go to the field where we had planted corn, beans, and squash. Corn was precious. It was a gift from our god Kiehtan, and every time we ate it, we give special thanks. We planted on a different piece of land each year. The sachem, or leader, decided on the location each year. We got a good section this year that was close to the beach. I picked some beans and a couple of squash and put them in a basket. I walked to the beach where my little sister, Shayla, was gathering shellfish and firewood.

"The tide is low, and it's a beautiful day. How are the crops?" Shayla asked me.

"Growing well. We should have enough for a good winter," I said.

Then she stood up and pointed out to a brown and white ship floating on the horizon. It reminded me of my dream. I had seen ships before, just like this one, but somehow it felt different.

**6.** You may need to give a minilesson with examples of how to expand a fact or event into a fictional account, trying to make it as believable as possible. See the examples that follow.

### Fact: During the American Civil War, sometimes brothers fought against brothers.

As I finished lacing my boots and putting on my gray uniform, I felt a surge of excitement to join the rest of the Confederate soldiers in the fields of battle. As I hurried to my brother's room to have him share in my excitement, my jaw dropped as I noticed that he was putting on a blue uniform. The blue uniform meant he was fighting for the North.

I suddenly realized that I was entering a war in which I would not only be fighting my fellow Americans, but my own brother. I felt confused and upset at the same time. I began to question what went so wrong in this country that a brother was forced to fight his own brother.

Perhaps I should reevaluate my reasons for fighting this war and think about which side is the right side. Is there a right side? My confusion continued as I closed my brother's door and left our house for Fredericksburg.

### Event: The passing of the Indian Removal Act

I was playing in the fields with my friends when we received the news. My uncle had returned from a trip, and all the men in our tribe hurried to him when they saw him coming. Their faces looked very stern and serious; the news didn't look good.

I ran to my father and asked him why he looked so sad. He was in shock. He could barely speak. After several minutes, he finally told me that we were being forced off our land.

I was confused. My family had lived here for many generations, and suddenly we were being forced off our land. I didn't understand why someone would want to take our land after so many years.

**7.** Give students a checklist of requirements for a historical fiction narrative. For example, tell them that they must do the following when writing their stories:

- Tell the story from the first person point of view.

- Write a clear beginning, middle, and end.

- Include a conflict (i.e., a problem) and a resolution (i.e., a description of how the problem is solved).

- Include details about the setting (time and place), the major character(s) (what he or she says, does, looks like, thinks, and what others say about him or her), and so on.

- Reveal the following about the major character: gender, age, ethnicity, family life, and background up to the point story begins.

- Give details about the historical context (situation), such as time period, government, socioeconomic situation, major current events, and societal expectations of major and minor characters.

- Include some pictures with their story.

- Do a Story Map Tableau (chapter 3) activity during prewriting.
- Write a first draft and get a peer response to it.
- Write a second draft and receive help when editing it.

# EMPATHY RESPONSE CHANTS (Mu)

This is a response chant that gets students to empathize with people or things. The frames will help start you off, but you and your students should modify them or even create a completely different chant about the topic of study. Refer to chapter 2 for more specifics on how to create effective chants and how to get students to create them as well.

## Procedure

1. Consider the topic of study and pull out key target learning concepts that you want to highlight through the skill of empathy. These will help you start off the chant. Students can help in this process as well.

2. Compose the chant on the overhead projector and have students copy it on their own paper as you go along.

3. Fill in the first line with an appropriate entry in order to model how to begin.

4. Have students share possible lines as you continue to fill in the chant. When you think students can do some on their own, let them try to finish the chant in pairs or groups.

5. Call attention to the different types of academic language in the verses. Feel free to change the wording if you want.

6. Once the chant is finished within different groups or pairs, have students share their chants with the class. Let them rehearse, if needed. Have instruments or downloaded mp3 drumbeats available to help with the beat.

### Empathy Response Chant Frame

If you were _____, what would you do?
I'd _____, how 'bout you?
I might do that too (That's not what I would do)

If you were _____, what else would you do?
I'd also _____, how 'bout you?
I might do that too (That's not what I would do)

If you were/had _____, how would you feel?
I'd feel _____, if this were real
But it's not, so no big deal.

Tell me, _____ (person/object), why would you feel that way?
Because _____, that's all I'll say,
Will one more question be OK?

If you were _____ what's your one big wish?
I want _____; it's number one on my list.
Because I _____. That's it.

### Object Chant

I am a _____ and I am proud
Because _____, right now.
The benefits are _____
And I get to _____.

Yet it is not always fun and games
There are some drawbacks, they are quite lame
For instance, _____
And I have trouble _____.

# Synthesizing

Synthesizing, in a nutshell, means taking information from different places and combining it all with our existing background knowledge. We then see patterns emerge and formulate novel concepts about the information. Further research or reading leads us to new perspectives and insights that can only be formed from the unique combination of information we take into our brains, our unique backgrounds, and our thinking processes. Synthesis is one of the most creative skills of thinking—and, therefore, one of the most challenging ones to teach.

Synthesizing is like making a quilt out of a variety of cloth pieces gathered from different places. You make patterns with the cloth pieces as you combine them into one big whole that you call a quilt. The pieces, now in the form of a quilt, have a new purpose that they could not have achieved individually. Synthesizing is similar in that the ideas and the pieces of information are sewn together by the student in his or her brain to achieve novel purposes, to spark insights, and to create content knowledge connections.

I like to separate synthesis into three facets. The first facet can be remembered by using its word parts: *syn-* to synchronize, or bring together, and *thesis* to make a main point. Therefore, this first facet means bringing together the main points of two or more concepts, ideas, or messages. This aligns well with Marzano's (2000) description of synthesis as the process of identifying the basic structure of knowledge, the sequences and relationships among the parts, and critical versus uncritical information.

The second facet of synthesis is the ability to make connections and take increasingly larger perspectives (Berman, 2001). It is the skill of thinking in a broader way, zooming out, so to speak, in order to elucidate the importance of interrelationships. Good synthesizers, as Berman says, "are open to new information, new points of view, and new experiences in order to enlarge their perspectives.... The lens through which synthesis thinkers view the world is a wide-angled lens" (2001, p. 16). This means that to build the skill of synthesis in our students, we must teach (i.e., model, scaffold, practice, assess) students to be intuitive, global, and creative.

The third facet of synthesis is combining elements into a pattern not clearly evident before thinking about it, or doing something new and different with the information. Synthesizing differs from summarizing in that when you summarize, you focus in on one concept or text and reduce it to its main points. There is often agreement between individuals on what this summary needs to contain. Synthesis, on the other hand, means that you create a new way of seeing and using the knowledge. Agreement on the perfect synthesis can vary widely, especially when evaluating essays and tests that ask students to synthesize.

Consider a science class, for instance. If I read conflicting articles about the changes in the ozone layer and want to write a report, I first come up with the key points and compare them. Then I make connections to other sources and to my own background knowledge. I pull it all together to see how to recommend changes in the current laws. I then formulate a conclusion of the issue and a statement of any next steps involved. In a social studies class, I may need to synthesize the information gathered from primary sources and information from a textbook. I may then be assigned to write a mock letter to a publisher with recommendations about changes that need to be made in the science textbook.

# Academic Language, Prompts, and Frames

The following expressions, prompts, and frame are for use with the skill of synthesizing. Get to know these terms, and point them out when you and your students use them in discussions or written tasks. Refer to chapter 1 for ideas on how to use academic language expressions, oral and writing prompts, and paragraph frames to develop academic thinking skills and academic language.

Some common expressions used when synthesizing include the following:

- In a nutshell, it means that...

- Other sources also argue that...

- It all boils down to...

- Even though it seems that the text is about...I think that...

- The author is essentially saying...

- If we think about all the issues, we come up with...

- One source is not enough to make such a decision.

- Upon gathering all these facts, we can conclude that...

- The elements (parts) are related in the following ways.

- When we put the pieces together, we see that...

- Its most important traits are...

- If history is any indication, then...

- Which research supported that?

- There is more than one way to approach this issue.

- That evidence is hardly applicable to the issue because...

- This is related to (extraneous to, not applicable to)...because...

- That finding is inconsistent with this one because...

- There is a pattern that emerges when we look at...

- When you take a close look at this part, you see that it...

Following are some prompts that encourage students to synthesize when speaking or writing:

- Write a journal entry from the perspective of...
- Create a sculpture that relates to...
- Design a greeting card for...to send...
- Write a letter of appreciation to a historical figure.
- Compose a modern folk tale about...
- Write a science fiction story about...(with a certain character in it).
- Create a song or poem expressing your feelings about...
- Write a fairy tale titled *The Wise Woman Who...*
- Compose a short story from the point of view of a...
- Create a proposal with different alternatives for making a major change in your community.

Frames like the one below help students to gradually pick up academic language and eventually use it to compose their own high-quality written products without help. One frame is given here to get you started on your own subject- and student-specific frames. This one is very generic, to allow you to fine-tune it or even to start from scratch. When creating your own frames, be sure to refer to the lists of expressions and prompts given above.

### Paragraph Frame for Scaffolding Synthesizing

In order to gain a proper perspective on the issue of _____, we must synthesize information from the following sources: _____, _____, and _____. The first source claims that _____ and uses _____ as its evidence. This is valid but may not be strong enough to _____. The second source, _____, reports that _____. This implies that _____. Finally, the third source offers the most compelling argument, which is _____. The evidence is _____ _____. Therefore, even though many conflicting views on this issue exist, a synthesis of these three sources strongly suggests that _____. Further research down the road, of course, may change all this.

Remember to start with student background knowledge when introducing activities that build this skill. You can create a starter board of background knowledge topics such as friendship, family, school, music, advertising, culture, sports, television shows, movies, famous people, wars, or recent units you have studied in class.

# Activities for Developing the Skill of Synthesizing

## CREATE A BOARD GAME
### (Gru, Vi, Ma)

This activity, similar to the card game activity in this chapter, requires students to gather the most important details and concepts from various places and synthesize them into an educational board game. The board game, when it is finished, need not be particularly exciting to play or even particularly educational. The point is that the process of creating the game gets students to think and speak academically. Also important are the skills that are developed by coming up with a clear set of written directions for the game. The choices in design, the manipulation of objects, the creation of the visuals, and the chance of sending the idea to a game company all tend to increase students' interest and motivation.

Below is a very simple procedure for creating a game; you might, however, want to purchase a book on game design if you like the idea and want to do the activity in more depth. Feel free to add other helpful and fun elements of popular games. The game that students design can be for future students of the class, current students, or younger students.

## *Procedure*

1. Ask students which they would choose between writing a 40-page paper and designing a board game. (This gets you some buy-in.) Ask if they would be interested in submitting a proposal for the game with a chance for some money and a contract. Most students will likely be interested, as it often means a brief break from essays and tests and a time to be creative. Explain that some of the work will need to be done at home.

2. Bring in some sample board games and explain why you like them or not, and have students offer their opinions as well. Generate a list of characteristics that a board game should have. You will need to add the educational part to it and explain what types of knowledge and skills will be required to play the game. You can also explain the skills required to design the game (synthesis, analysis, application, communication, categorizing, evaluating, comparing, and so on).

3. Put students into groups or pairs to work on the game (Gru). Give them a choice of board and playing formats or let them create their own (Vi). Here are a few possibilities; students can also come up with another design or pattern that the players can proceed along during the game.

   - **The mountain**—a cardboard piece folded once and standing like a mountain between or in front of both players. A path zigzags its way up the mountain. The questions or tasks get harder as you near the top, with reaching the top being the goal of the game.

- **The spiral**—sequence of spaces that denote tasks or questions form a path that spirals into the middle of a flat piece of cardboard. The first player to reach the middle wins.
- **3-D shape**—some sort of 3-D shape (e.g., a large cube, cylinder, pyramid, prism) made out of cardboard that allows players to manipulate it or travel around it as the game progresses. It can have windows in it that allow players to see answers inside the shape.

**4.** The students may be tempted to have spaces or cards that have low-level questions, such as "What does DNA stand for?" or "Who was the fourth U.S. president?" A few of these are acceptable, but challenge students to create a game in which players must think harder about what they have learned in class. Refer to the core knowledge and skills of the lesson. Also refer to syntheses that students have already done in other projects and activities.

**5.** Have students create the cards and game spaces (Ma). This is the most challenging and time-consuming step. Try having them create three different-colored spaces on the game board or object. Each space can correspond to a deck of cards in the same color. Each card can have one question, which is worth 1, 2, or 3 points depending on its difficulty level. You can throw in a few really challenging 5-point questions, too. One deck can be the verbal deck, another the drama deck, and another the drawing deck (these will give the game Mo and Vi elements). Here are some examples of the type of questions students should come up with:

- **Verbal**—Why did Montezuma think Cortés was a god? How has the floating property of ice helped animals and humans survive? How did Johnny die?
- **Drama**—Act out the arrival of the adults on the island. Act out the water cycle. Act out the last scene of *Romeo and Juliet*.
- **Drawing**—Draw the water cycle. Draw the city of Tenochtitlán. Draw the last scene of *Romeo and Juliet*.

**6.** Have students decide on the type of movement device: dice, spinner, etc. They can make these out of cardboard or other materials.

**7.** To play the game, use the following rules: The game is played with teams of two or more. A team member draws a card and asks the specified question (or draws or acts out the specified concept) for his or her teammates. If the teammates get the correct answer, the team moves their game piece a number of spaces equal to the number of points on the card. If that team does not get the correct answer, the opposing team can try to answer and can claim the points and move their game piece if they are correct. The first team to reach the finish line wins the game.

# LATEST CARD GAME CRAZE
## (Gru, Vi, Ma)

This activity capitalizes on the game-playing interests of many middle school and high school students. Latest Card Game Craze is simpler than, but similar to, these card games that have become so popular with students. It also provides an extra motivation because it is a project that may be of practical use to other students besides your class. The process of making the game builds more content knowledge and thinking skills than actually playing it. To create it, students must synthesize, evaluate, communicate, and negotiate about the importance of various events and people.

## Procedure

1. Near the end of a unit, quarter, or semester, let students know that one of their final assessments will be to make an engaging card game (Ma) that teaches younger (or future) students what your class has just learned. Give them two colors of card stock paper from which to make two different types of cards. One color is for the context deck, and the other color is for the detail deck. The size of each card should be 2" × 3".

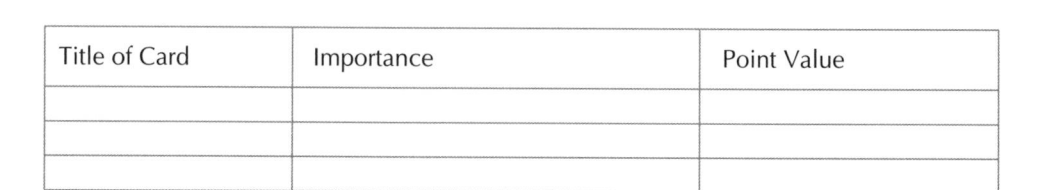

2. Set up the context deck. These are the simple cards that will guide what players will lay down from their hands (see the example). The context deck should contain cards labeled with main events, situations, concepts, and general categories that you want students to synthesize from the unit of study the class has just completed. You will doubtless have some already in mind, but you can work with students to add more. Four or five contexts are sufficient, but you may add more if you like. The context deck should have around 20 cards, so duplicate cards will probably be necessary (i.e., if you only have 5 different contexts, there will be 4 identical cards for each context).

3. Next, work with students to plan the detail deck. These cards should show specific actions, events, and objects that pertain to the more general contexts in step 2. This deck should consist of families of cards that connect to each other in some way. Each card family should contain one or more persons. For example, a family may consist of Hernan Cortés, searching for gold, burning his ships, horses, and cannons; or Montezuma, thinking the Spaniards were gods, temples, and idols. Create a few sample cards for students to get them going on theirs. Have students fill in a chart like the one below or a rough draft sheet before marking up the final card sheets; this way, students can edit, revise, and delete cards before they make the final versions.

| Title of Card | Importance | Point Value |
|---|---|---|
|  |  |  |
|  |  |  |
|  |  |  |

**4.** Have students work with partners to discuss and agree on the number of importance points given to each card. Important people, their actions, and key objects get 4 points; less important ones get 3 and 2 points. Cards that are interesting, but not as important to the subject being studied, get 1 point. This step is good for developing the skills of evaluating and using criteria to figure out importance. (Remember, creating the game generates more learning than playing it.)

**5.** Let students make the actual detail cards. Each card should have a title and a family symbol on the top; a point value for the card's importance, denoted by one to four small symbols; a drawing of the card's subject; and an explanation of its importance (Vi). See the sample shown here. If desired, you can use the Latest Card Game Craze template in Part III on page 230; this template is designed like some of the cards that are currently popular with students. You can also let the class create their own design, of course. Each family of cards should have around four to eight members, but this can vary. The detail deck should contain around 40–50 cards or so, but it can have more, if needed.

**6.** Have students create a full written description of the relationships among the cards and why the cards have their given point values. Students can even write a proposal letter to send to game companies.

**7.** Have students design the box cover and create an advertisement for the game. Designing the box cover can develop interpretation skills, and designing the advertisement can develop persuasive thinking skills.

**8.** Let students create their own variations on the rules below. Writing the rules is a good way for students to build skills of clear, practical communication. Your students can let other students play or test the game; they can then revise their rules for clarification, making changes based on anything these testers do not understand.

**9.** Use the following as a preliminary set of rules: Shuffle the details deck and give half of it to each of the two players (Gru). Have players then take five cards each from their own detail stacks. Turn over the top card of the context deck and read it. Each player chooses two cards from his or her hand that best fit the context and will score the most points. If both are in the same family, the player receives an extra 2 points. The player who puts down the most points wins the other player's cards, but the winner must explain how the cards related to the context and to one another before taking the loser's cards. If he or she is unable to do so, each player takes his or her cards back. If the round is a draw with regard to points, then both players put down a third card. When both players have gone through their stacks of detail cards, the winner of the game is the player who has collected the most cards.

# SYNTHESIS NOTES (Vi, Ma)

This activity helps students take a meta-look at the levels of thinking needed when reading a complex text. We seldom think about a text's thinking demands, use of language, structures, or devices. This activity is a way to scaffold these metacognitive skills of synthesizing so that they become automatic over time. It is also visual and tactile: Students take notes on colored strips of paper (Vi) and then turn them into shapes that fit inside one another.

## *Procedure*

**1.** Fold three different colors of 8.5" × 11" paper the long way into thirds, and cut it into strips. Distribute the paper to students so that each student has three strips in different colors. Then have students cut two of their strips down to 10" and 9" long, leaving one strip 11" long. Have students label the strips with the labels shown here.

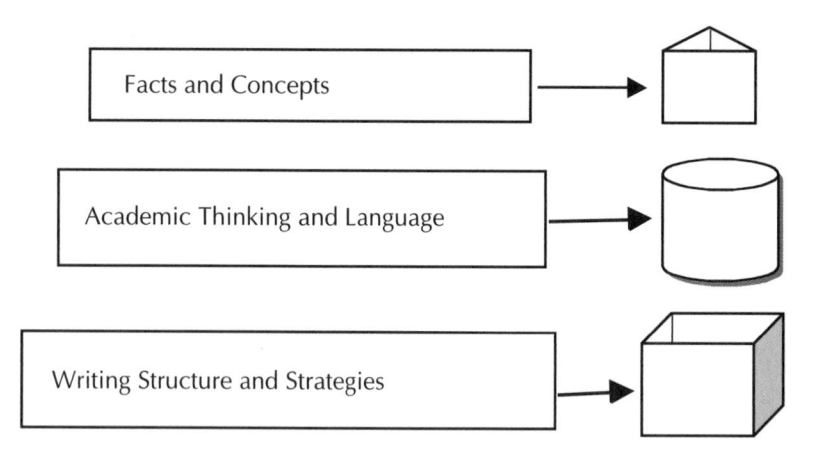

Think aloud as you go through a text, and take notes on strips of your own while looking at the text. Describe how you decide which are the most important facts and concepts to put down, how you think about the author's purpose, and how the text fits into the current content learning objectives of the class.

**2.** Describe how you identify the academic thinking and academic language in the text: for example, "Here, it says *whereas*, which means that an opposing point is going to come up in the sentence," or "The author expects me to analyze these two events and compare them, and then I think I need to evaluate which is more influential." You can bring up many of the thinking skills presented in this book.

**3.** Describe the author's strategies for maximizing communication of the concepts. Perhaps there are rhetorical questions, anecdotes, metaphors, subheadings, effective visuals, bolded words, flashbacks, or poor transitions. Mention how you might put the information into a semantic organizer such as a web, T-chart, table, Venn diagram, cause and effect diagram, or sequence diagram.

**4.** When you have finished writing your notes on the strips, show students how to fold or form them into the shapes shown above (Ma). The Writing Structure and Strategies strip becomes the shape of a square that holds everything else inside. The Academic Thinking and Language strip becomes a tube that fits inside the square. Finally, the Facts and Concepts strip becomes a triangle that fits inside the tube. This is a three-dimensional way to show, more or less, the ways in which many texts communicate their messages.

**5.** Have students take notes on their own strips, and then have them work in pairs to test each other on the text. With the shapes between them, one partner lifts up one of the shapes and reads the side silently. He or she then asks a question relating to the notes. These can be fact and concept questions for the triangle; questions such as "What type of thinking did we use when...?" and "What were some academic language terms we learned?" for the tube; and questions such as "What strategies did the author use?" for the square.

**6.** In a whole-class setting, have students share especially good questions and answers asked during the pair work.

**7.** Optional: You can do this activity on a piece of paper, calling it Flat and Sticky Synthesis Notes. Have students take notes as above, but have them write their notes on sticky notes and then organize them in rows or columns on a sheet of paper. The rows or columns are labeled the same as the strips.

# TRANSMEDIATION TEXT TRANSFORMATION (Vi, Mu)

Transmediation is a combination of *translate* and *media*. In this activity, students transform one text into a different type of text or genre. The new form should retain, augment, and clarify the important ideas that the student synthesizes. This activity requires a large amount of inference, synthesis, and comprehension of the important parts of the text. Students might do the following transmediations:

- Turn a textbook chapter into a newspaper article, poster (Vi), biography, interview, letter, narrative, poem, or news program with video.
- Turn a narrative into a poem, letter, commercial, diary, play, song (Mu), comic book, or book jacket.
- Turn a biography into a letter, interview, poem, short story, comic strip, or poster.

## *Procedure*

**1.** Model how to transform a variety of texts. In the beginning of the year, you will probably concentrate on only a few types of transformations.

**2.** Model the types of thinking skills that you want students to practice, such as cause and effect, fact or opinion, sequence, and persuasion. Tell students that you want to see evidence of this thinking in their text transformations.

**3.** Emphasize that students must concentrate on the most important information in the text in order to carry it over to a different text. Tell them to think about what the author of the original text would want them to not leave out when creating a new version of his or her text. Also, have students refer to the standards for the current unit to get ideas for what must be left in and what can be taken out.

**4.** If needed, you can use an intermediary scaffold, such as a graphic organizer (e.g., semantic map) for main idea, to capture the elements needed for the new version of the text. See examples below of some transformed texts.

---

**Balloon Rocket Haiku**

(A haiku that describes the balloon rocket experiment in a physics class)

First fill it with air
As much air as possible
To traverse the room

The hooks and the sticks
Must be balanced exactly
To avoid crashing

The force of the air
Through the balloon's opening
Propels it through space

It would never stop
If it didn't have friction
Or gravity, too

---

**Black Hole Chant**

My name is Joe,
I live in a black hole
The neighbors complain,
but I call it home

We can't see straight,
we can't decorate
Because gravity's so strong,
not even light escapes

It's hard to see past
the event horizon
And the sun got sucked in
so it won't be risin'.

---

**Dear King George,**

We are sick and tired of all your laws and rules. We do not have representation in your government and therefore we should not be taxed.

Some of the colonists have talked about revolution, but we simply want what is fair. Consider our request to have representatives with voting rights to hear our needs. If not, we don't know what will happen, but it might not be pretty.

Sincerely,
The colonists

---

**Glacier Play Script**

Glacier:    Excuse me, but since I am now 90 meters high, I must start moving downward.

Mountain: OK, what choice do I have? But do you have to make the valley U-shaped? And do you have to pick up so many rocks?

Glacier:    Yes, I can't help it. It's called plucking and ...

---

# ADMIT AND EXIT TICKETS (Ma, Vi)

This activity can be very effective at helping students synthesize what they have learned. Admit tickets generally function as passes to get in the door at the beginning of class or to participate in a classroom event or activity. Exit tickets allow students to leave the room, say, for lunch.

## *Procedure*

**1.** Several options exist for creating tickets. Students can design them, and the class can vote on the best ones. Or, you can give students colored sheets of paper, which they can cut in four to nine pieces that become simple blank tickets. You also can design a more elaborate ticket like the ones shown here (an Admit and Exit Tickets blackline master is provided in Part III, page 231) that contains the elements you want students to synthesize (Vi).

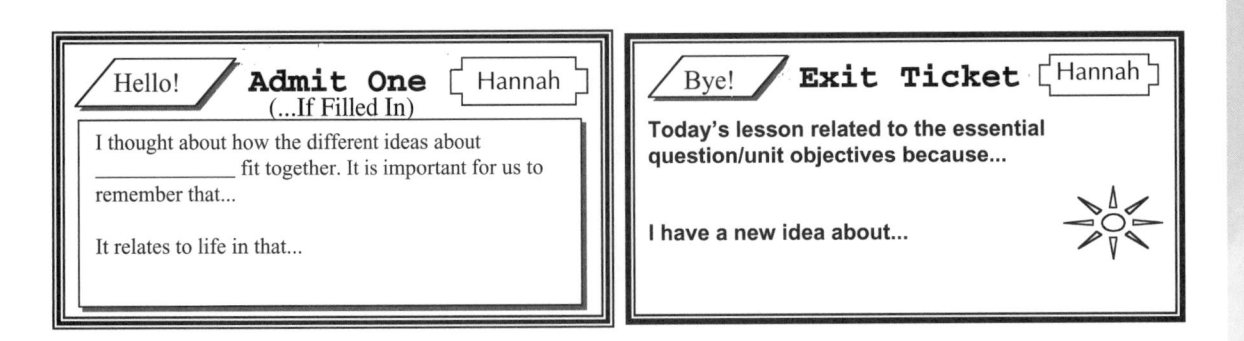

**2.** Choose the best times and ways to give out and explain the tickets (Ma). For example, you can give out Exit Tickets at the beginning of the class period and tell students what they will need to focus on during the period in order to clearly and succinctly fill out the Exit Ticket before they leave. Give them time to fill in the Exit Ticket, and save a little time to have them share their completed tickets with the class and turn them in while you check them. If you catch a blank one or a bad one, have the student stay and get it right, either with or without help from another student. Emphasize the self-monitoring nature of this activity: Students need to own their learning and thinking so that they can develop habits of lifelong learning.

**3.** At another point in the class, or preferably on a different day (different days make the tickets less confusing), explain the Admit Ticket. This can be a chance for students to reflect on and synthesize learning when they are between classes and at home. It can also be used as a warm-up question for the next day's lesson (i.e., you can give the students time to think outside of class in order to maximize class time). Put any prompts that you wish to use on the ticket or on the overhead or chalkboard.

**4.** Optional: As students enter the classroom and turn in their Admit Tickets, stop a couple of students as they enter and have them verbally explain to you what they wrote.

**5.** If you have a minute or two, it is effective to read a few of the tickets (after asking those students' permission) at the beginning of class. This validates the responses and can be a great warm-up for the lesson to come. You can even ask students how they think the ticket relates to the lesson learned yesterday or to today's lesson.

**6.** Have students store their tickets in a special spot in their binders or portfolios.

# SYNTHESIZE CHANTS (Mu)

This is a response chant that gets students to consider different sources of information, bring them together, and draw original conclusions about them. The frame will start you off, but you and your students should modify it or create a completely different chant about the topic of study. Refer to chapter 2 for more specifics on how to create effective chants and how to get students to create them as well.

> **Synthesize Chant Frame**
>
> It's taken me a while to compile
> All the info for this song
> I'll give you the scoop about _____
> And tell you what's really going on.
>
> First the _____
> Even though you might hear otherwise
> Evidence comes from _____
> Which shows that _____, no lie.
>
> Furthermore, the _____
> I believe it to be key
> Evidence comes from _____
> Which shows that _____, you see?
>
> Yet the _____ and the _____
> were conflicting facts in my eyes.
> So I concluded that _____
> This is how we synthesize.

## Procedure

**1.** Consider the topic of study and pull out key target learning concepts that you want to synthesize. These will help you start off the chant. Students can help in this process as well.

**2.** Compose the chant on the overhead projector and have students copy it on their own paper as you go along.

**3.** Fill in the first line with an appropriate entry in order to model how to begin.

**4.** Have students share possible lines as you continue to fill in the song. When you think students can do some on their own, let them try to finish the song.

**5.** Call attention to the different types of academic language in the verses. Feel free to change them if you want.

**6.** Once the chant is finished within different groups or pairs, have students share their versions with the class. Let them rehearse, if needed. Have instruments or downloaded mp3 drumbeats to help with the beat.

**7.** Optional: Have students write their own chants (without using a frame) that synthesize the content learned in the unit.

Following is an example chant about a cultural anthropologist. This can be sung to the tune of "We Will Rock You" by Queen; students slap their laps twice and snap their fingers once for the beat.

I went to see the cultural anthropologist
To ask her exactly what culture is
She said, "It's what is shared by most in a group,
The way people think; what they make and do."

She said we should start with seven elements
These reflect what goes on in people's heads
If you look closely, you can see their values
And how to see the world from their points of view

    These are elements of culture—just a few
    They can symbolize values—of a group

The first is how a group spends its leisure time
Like playing games or sports or chatting online

The second is the power of music to the ear
The lyrics can tell you what people truly feel

Religion is a way to see into people's heads...
And their beliefs about purpose, life, and death

We should analyze holidays and ceremonies
Like weddings, independence days, and Sweet Sixteen

    These are...

Art can show with colors, shapes, and themes
What people love and admire and fear and dream

Movies and TV reflect how watchers want to be:
Heroic, wealthy, cool, and pretty

A group's literature uses stories and poems
To teach and touch them deep in each soul

There's much more to culture, this is just a start,
You'll soon discover that each culture is a masterpiece of art!

# CHAPTER 11

# Interpreting

Interpreting allows people to figure out many of life's messages that are not directly stated. We spend a lot of time making sense of the many small and large signals that fill our days. Our students, of course, are immersed in their own worlds of interpreting, too. We can build on this to academicize their skills at interpreting. In addition to being a key facet of the work of Wiggins and McTighe (2000), the skill of interpreting is also mentioned in the California English Language Arts and English Language Development standards 35 times (Carr, 2001).

As this chapter primarily focuses on academic interpretation, it highlights the interpretation of information sources most commonly found in school. These texts have been created to communicate meaning, most often in the form of music, spoken words, visuals (images, paintings, graphs, diagrams), actions (theater), written words, or combinations of these. The meanings of these texts that surface in class are often the ones intended by the author or actor, but not always; poetry and other literature cultivate interpretations beyond the scope of the author's intentions. For example, Langston Hughes (1994) intended (most likely) to teach about perseverance with his poem *Mother to Son*, yet a student may read it and, after connecting it to his or her own background, may interpret the poem to be about a mother's love. In contrast, most authors of expository material (such as social studies and science) prefer that their readers not have divergent interpretations. They want the material to be communicated as efficiently and effectively as possible.

When interpreting, we take in observable clues and use our background knowledge to create a meaning that we think is intended, but that is not explicitly given. Successful interpretation depends on several key abilities: relating to background knowledge, seeing cause and effect patterns, inferring, and comparing results and contexts.

Interpretation ranges from figuring out the "big picture" of a text to deciphering the meaning of an individual word. We teachers need to train students to interpret the big, the small, and everything in between. At the "macro" end of this hypothetical spectrum of interpretation is the ability to see the implied overall meaning of a text. This means the ability to figure out the life-enriching insights that the author intended for the message's users (readers, viewers, listeners) to put together. Authors know that often the deepest truths in life are solidified when readers construct them on their own. This is why most authors of narratives write: to create a story that sticks in our minds because we have taken the time and energy to process it, feel it, and connect it to our own lives. They want us to interpret meaning that can only come through story or poetry. For me, a powerful story or poem can even become a foundation upon which I construct key thoughts and feelings about life that I could not conceptualize without it. For example, when the topic of memories comes up in conversations, I think about the role of memories in society in the young adult novel *The Giver*, by Lois Lowry (1993). When I contemplate friendship, I sometimes think about events and dialog in *Holes*, by Louis Sachar (1998).

At the more "micro" end of the spectrum of interpreting is being able to decipher and use figurative language such as analogies, metaphors, similes, symbols, and multiple-meaning words. I call this metaphorical thinking. When we think metaphorically, we typically use concrete ideas to describe abstract ideas. We also discern abstract concepts from concrete concepts and then recognize connections between the two. The use of metaphor can open entire worlds of thought to students. They can not only better understand poetry and literature but also content area concepts as well. Many of the most complex concepts in science and social studies can be better comprehended and remembered through metaphor.

Of course, it also helps to be able to recognize when and where analogies break down, given that metaphors and analogies are often used to fortify persuasive arguments. Many authors and speakers use metaphors and other figurative expressions to their advantage when they are making arguments. The metaphors are meant to clarify a person's message, but they almost always reflect the person's viewpoint and bias toward the issue as well. If used frequently enough, many metaphors become accepted as truth, despite obvious flaws and limitations. Metaphors then become the persuasive instruments of advertisers, propagandists, and politicians, many of whom are trying to influence the thoughts and buying patterns of our students. Fortunately, in this case, students are very motivated to learn how not to be manipulated by adults. They also tend to be interested in analyzing metaphors' strengths and weaknesses.

Interpreting figurative language is a gatekeeper thinking skill. This means that students must develop this skill in order to succeed in high school and beyond, both in academic settings and in many real-world settings. Because we live in a world that values information and ideas, our students must be prepared to understand increasingly complex messages, images, and language. We cannot invent a new word for every new idea or concept, so we combine the ones we have and assign them abstract meanings. Many of the academic language terms in these chapters are examples of this phenomenon: *boils down to, sidestep the issue, read between the lines, outweigh,* and so on. Likewise, technical jargon is often borrowed: *mouse, boot up, overhaul, frozen, link, surf,* etc. This necessitates a certain mental flexibility and an openness to seeing expressions, connecting to background knowledge, understanding the context, and making the leap of interpretation.

The study of literature demands high amounts of interpretation. Contrary to what many students think, literature is one of the exciting keys for understanding what it means to be human. "The teaching of literature inevitably involves the conscious or unconscious reinforcement of ethical attitudes," writes Louise Rosenblatt in *Literature as Exploration* (1996, p. 16). When we read narratives and poetry, we are given brief windows into the lives of others, through which we can reflect on the right or wrong nature of events and actions in the text. Through literature, we can better understand our own thoughts and feelings through characters and metaphoric language (Pugh, Hicks, & Davis, 1997). We can see into the thoughts of countless other people, present and past, to learn how they lived and thought about life.

# Academic Language, Prompts, and Frames

The following expressions, prompts, and frames are for use with the skill of interpreting. Get to know these terms, and point them out when you and your students use them in discussions or written tasks. Refer to chapter 1 for ideas on how to use academic language expressions, oral and writing prompts, and paragraph frames to develop academic thinking skills and academic language.

Some common expressions used when interpreting include the following:

- It really means...because...
- This is analogous to...
- The analogy breaks down at this point...
- One way to interpret this is...
- The...is an important symbol for... because...
- This part meant that...
- For us in modern times, it could mean that...
- This...teaches us that...

- The...is a metaphor for...
- The...is like a...because...
- If we read between the lines, we see that...
- The author used that analogy because...
- In the same way that people..., the...
- This is a figurative way to describe how...
- This is not literal—that's the author's way to describe how...
- This is similar to my life in...
- From the part where...I infer that...
- In this context, the word means...

Following are some prompts that encourage students to interpret when speaking or writing:

- Explain how the concrete idea of...helps to describe the abstract concept of...
- Compare...with...
- Infer the meaning of this section of text.
- Create a metaphor for...
- What can this (event, etc.) teach us about how to act today?
- What did his/her/their actions mean?
- Change the ending of this story.
- What conclusions can you draw from this?
- What assumptions can we make about this?
- What did he really mean by...?
- Create a skit to dramatize the use of...
- Design a museum exhibit for...
- Write a memo to...during a crucial moment.
- Make sense of...

- Provide a helpful analogy for...
- Make a graph or chart to show...
- Imagine you are...and map out your strategy for...
- Write an entry from the diary of...
- Show the importance of...
- Explain how this story or event teaches us a lesson about life.
- You must introduce a person at a banquet. Describe the person and include an anecdote.
- Design a poster to advertise for...
- Create a symbol for...
- Come up with ways in which these two very different concepts are similar.

Frames like those below help students to gradually pick up academic language and eventually use it to compose their own high-quality written products without help. Three frames are given here to get you started on your own subject- and student-specific frames. These three are very generic, to allow you to fine-tune them or even to start from scratch. When creating your own frames, be sure to refer to the lists of expressions and prompts given above.

### Paragraph Frames for Scaffolding Interpreting

1. The author of this article was clearly biased in favor of _____.
He (she) tried to influence us to _____ by using persuasive techniques
such as _____. He (she) conveniently omitted important evidence
such as _____. And even his (her) language was used as a tool to
sway us. For example, he (she) uses the word _____ instead of _____.

2. On the surface, _____ was a _____ story about a _____.
Yet I believe the author used the story to teach readers a deeper lesson about _____
_____. For instance, when the main character, _____, proceeded to
_____ , this showed _____. Also, when
_____ said, "_____," this implied that _____.
Finally, _____.

3. People are basically _____. This aspect of human nature is reflected in the novel
_____, by _____, in which the protagonist _____.
At various points during the story, she (he) _____. For example, near the
beginning, she (he) _____. Later, she (he) says, "_____."
This shows that _____. Not only is this evident in the novel, but it is found in life
as well. For example, _____.

Remember to start with student background knowledge when introducing activities that build this skill. You can create a starter board of background knowledge topics such as friendship, family, school, music, advertising, culture, sports, television shows, movies, famous people, wars, or recent units you have studied in class.

# Activities for Developing the Skill of Interpreting

## ART INTERPRETATION TRIANGLE
### (Gru, Vi, Mo)

This is an enhanced version of the Transmediation Text Transformation activity found in chapter 10. It is similar to the classic telephone game in which a message is passed from student to student and becomes somewhat distorted along the way due to interpretation. Even though you can start at any point on the triangle, I have found it most effective to start at the Story stage and move to Tableau, then to Picture, and back to Story.

### Procedure

1. Find four short stories or historical events that relate to your content.

2. Divide the class into four groups and give each group a story (or divide the class into eight groups and let two groups work on each story) (Gru).

3. Story to Tableau—Have one group interpret their story and turn it into a tableau (a scene in which the students create a scene [Mo] in which they pose silently as if frozen in time) that highlights the most important scenes and characters. They then will present this tableau to another group (see below). You might want to have the tableau's participants speak for added effect and clarity, but they should not move (Mo). If desired, a narrator from the group can explain to the audience what is going on in the tableau. One tableau is often enough, but the group may decide to have two or three tableau scenes. Groups must keep the written story from getting into the hands of the next group.

4. To present the tableaux, stagger them in this way: Group A presents to group B while group C presents to group D; then group D presents to group A while group B presents to group C (Vi). In each case, the group watching the tableau should not have seen the original story.

5. Tableau to Picture—Next, each of the groups must interpret the tableau(x) they saw in order to create an image on a poster that they think approximates the original story. At the end of this step, you should have four posters. Group B makes a poster from group A's tableau; group C, a poster from group B's tableau; group D, a poster from group C's tableau; and group A a poster from group D's tableau.

6. Picture to Story—The next group, without seeing the original story or the tableau, should then interpret the poster in order to make up a short narrative about it. They should look at the poster's characters and invent possible events and dialog. Have them write down their story and give it to the group that had the original one. Group C should rewrite group A's story, group D rewrites group B's story, group A rewrites group C's story, and group B rewrites group D's story. Use a pocket chart to keep track of the sequence of the activity.

7. Comparison—Each original group now has two stories, the original they read and the one they received from another group. Have students go through the new story and compare it to their original, noting the similarities and differences on a chart, if desired. Have them make positive comments about the new story's accuracy and show the previous group the chart they made.

8. Wrap-Up—Do a final discussion on the findings, and examine what students learned about the content and about interpreting stories, tableaux, and pictures.

# ACADEMIC LANGUAGE INTERPRETATION CHART (Vi)

The Academic Language Interpretation Chart is a powerful way to help students develop the skill of thinking about multiple meanings, idioms, and other figurative language such as analogies, metaphors, and symbols (adapted from Bean, Singer, & Cowan, 1985). In addition to its usefulness in language arts classes, this activity is very effective in science and social studies classes: These classes have texts with words and terms that students may already know at a literal level, but for which they now need to learn new and abstract uses and meanings.

## Procedure

1. Make a transparency from the Academic Language Interpretation Chart blackline master in Part III (page 232) of this book. In the right-hand column, write an unknown word or expression from the text. This word may be figurative, such as an idiom, symbol, or metaphor, or it may be a new or additional meaning for a known word (e.g., *mouse* for a computer).

2. In the left column, write down what the word actually describes (Vi).

3. In the middle arrow, write an explanation. Write down how the two (the literal and the figurative) are similar, what the author was trying to emphasize, or why you think the author (or people in general) used this particular word. See the filled-in sample on the next page.

4. Have students notice whether any language used in the middle or left columns is figurative. If so, put those terms in the right column and keep filling in the columns. In the example, the word *precious*, used in the right column, is in turn examined in the middle column.

5. You may scaffold the activity by filling in certain boxes or columns beforehand (or on an overhead) and letting students fill in the rest on their own copies.

6. You may also introduce new vocabulary terms to help students be clear and explicit when they fill in the middle column.

7. Students can build up a large set of these analyses throughout the year. You can turn the box-and-arrow graphic into a simple grid with three columns that students can easily draw in their binders.

## Explanation

**What It Describes** (Literal)                            **Text** (Figurative)

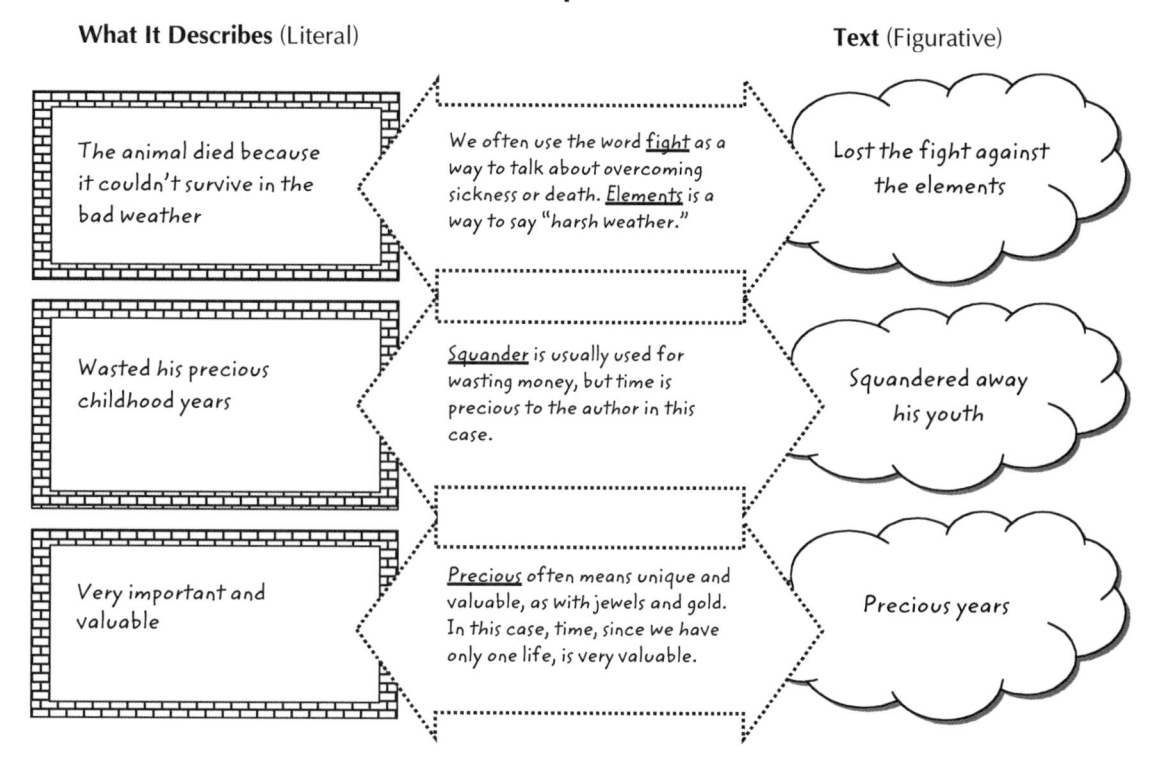

The animal died because it couldn't survive in the bad weather

We often use the word <u>fight</u> as a way to talk about overcoming sickness or death. <u>Elements</u> is a way to say "harsh weather."

Lost the fight against the elements

Wasted his precious childhood years

<u>Squander</u> is usually used for wasting money, but time is precious to the author in this case.

Squandered away his youth

Very important and valuable

<u>Precious</u> often means unique and valuable, as with jewels and gold. In this case, time, since we have only one life, is very valuable.

Precious years

**8.** Optional: You can use the following song, which has around 40 idioms, for this activity. Have students pick the idioms out of the song and use the graphic to examine and explore them.

### 'Til the Cows Come Home

Now I'm in the doghouse for putting my foot in my mouth
But I'll swallow my pride and beg your pardon somehow
I won't beat around the bush or mince any of my words
In plain English I'll tell you I won't let you slip through my fingers

I know it ain't no picnic, on our merry-go-round of love
Wiping the slate clean is easier said than done
But now I'm at the end of my rope, I've turned over a new leaf,
Give me a break, Rome wasn't built in a day
Be patient and bear with me. Because...

      I'm gonna love you 'til the cows come home
      And even if they don't come back,
      I'm gonna go out on a limb for you,
      I'm gonna give you my heart, no strings attached.

Last night I saw the light, like a bolt out of the blue,
That not even for the whole wide world, could I part with you.
I'll burn all of my bridges and make a beeline to your heart,
Inch by inch we'll iron out our problems from the start.

I'll go the extra mile and take the bull by the horns
I'll never throw in the towel, or run from the storms.
Love ain't no stroll down easy street, play it safe and you'll never win,
I may be out in left field but I'll stick by you through thick and thin.

I'm gonna love you 'til the cows come home...

No man is an island, and you're the only fish in my sea
I feel like I'm walkin' on air, falling head over heels,
And if any part of what I said ain't true I'll eat my hat,
So for Pete's sake, give me the scoop, will you take me back?

# METAPHOR WRITING (Vi)

This activity is mainly used in social studies and science classes as a way to help students think metaphorically, abstractly, and figuratively. Furthermore, it strengthens their understanding and recall of content vocabulary and concepts. An added bonus is the building of analyzing and comparing thinking skills.

## Procedure

**1.** Create some sample metaphors for understanding concepts in your class. Use concepts from previous units of study. For example, you could use canals of water to explain electrical currents, a village to describe the world's population, a seesaw to explain how to balance equations, a car engine to describe the human body, or a recipe to explain friendship.

**2.** Create a drawing, if possible, to show the metaphor (Vi). It can be symbolic and silly; in fact, a silly visual is almost always better than no visual at all. You might draw a seesaw with numbers on both sides, a bridge between two stick figures, a tree with names in the roots and other names in the leaves and fruit, or a train that gets shorter as it approaches the speed of light.

**3.** Scaffold the process of writing about the metaphor or analogy. Do this by coming up with phrases that describe how the abstract concept compares to the concrete analogy that describes it. You will want to emphasize the main concept to be learned from the metaphor. For example, to show how a governor and a legislator battled one another like a bullfighter and a bull, you can emphasize the tactics they used to strike and defend. Perhaps at one point, one of the two is down for a while, then gets up and comes back to win. Because some students may not know what a bullfight is, you may need to change the metaphor or explain what it is.

**4.** Write down how the metaphor or analogy breaks down. That is, explain the ways in which the concept and the metaphor are not similar. This can be just as important for describing the concept. For example, you might say, "Unlike real bullfights, however, the

155

legislator (bull) came back to win against the matador (governor) by his perseverance and patience."

**5.** Model how to put a paragraph together on the overhead, using these concepts. For example, you could write,

_____

When the governor and _____ went head to head on the issue of _____, it was similar to a matador taking on a raging bull in a bullfight. The governor is the matador and _____ is the bull. When the governor _____, it was like waving the bright red cape for _____ to charge.

_____

**6.** Have students create their own metaphors and analogies and do the activity on their own, with some help from you, if needed. You can create a list of possible metaphors for them to pick from: tree, house, car engine, human body, mountains, ocean, river, storm, clock, war, cave, fishing, sports, food, butterfly, snake, bullfight, traffic jam, etc.

## SHALLOW–DEEP NOTES (Vi)

This is a very simple tool for introducing students to the skill of thinking about deeper, hidden, and implicit meanings in texts. Remind students that there are few wrong answers here, especially in the deep part. This is where they will write their inferences, interpretations, and guesses about the text.

### Procedure

**1.** Have students draw a note-taking form like the one shown here (Vi).

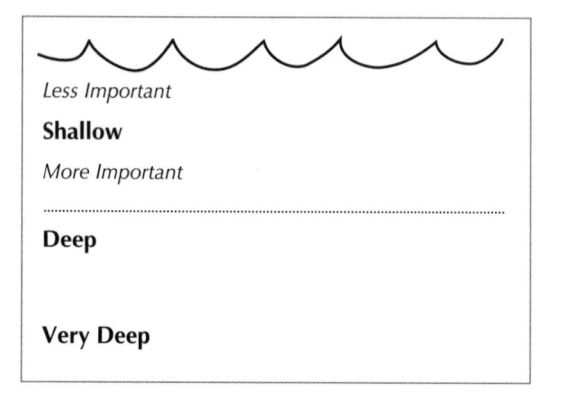

*Less Important*
**Shallow**
*More Important*

**Deep**

**Very Deep**

**2.** Discuss the differences in the notes that they will take as they go through a text. Tell them that the shallow notes will be explicit, "right-there" facts and observations that are stated clearly in the text. They are important to remember in order to maintain comprehension of the details, characters, events, and plot of a text.

3. Tell students that the real gold, however, is in the deep part. This is where students need to keep track of their thoughts related to the author's purpose. Remind students that most authors have a dual agenda: to tell a good story (concrete) and to teach an important life lesson (abstract). Students often get caught up in the story, the concrete, but they often do not use the skill of looking for the deeper meaning, the abstract moral or lesson the author intends. The very deep part is where students write about connections to their own lives and the world around them. They answer the question, How can what they have read apply to them?

4. Model for students how to take notes in all three sections of the graphic. The Deep section will have inferences and interpretations that relate to the book and its characters. The Very Deep section will have bigger life questions that do not have answers but can generate a lot of discussion.

5. Have students share their notes in pairs. Have them trade two or three good ideas with their partners.

6. Have students share ideas with the whole class.

# SYMBOL SEMANTIC WEBS (Vi)

This activity is more commonly used in literature and reading classes, but it can work for social studies as well. It involves the analysis of symbols and their purpose in the text. Symbols are typically metaphors that have evolved to the point of being commonly understood by many people. Some symbols common in Western culture include the dove for peace, the eagle for freedom, the heart for love, the owl for wisdom, and the cross for Christianity.

## *Procedure*

1. Briefly discuss the purpose of symbols in life and literature. Ask students why they think symbols are so commonly used. Tell students that they need to explain how symbols are used to develop themes in texts.

2. Work with the students to use pictures, images, and objects to generate a definition of *symbol*. Explain how symbols are different from metaphors.

3. Examine some symbols found in the media, popular songs, or previously read texts. Discuss whether these fit the definition you created in step 2.

4. Choose a text (story or poem), and model for the students how to look for symbols in the text.

5. Draw a semantic web like the one on the next page, and choose a symbol from the text to study. Write the symbol in the center oval (Vi). Find a quote or portion of the text that relates to the symbol, and write them in the upper right box.

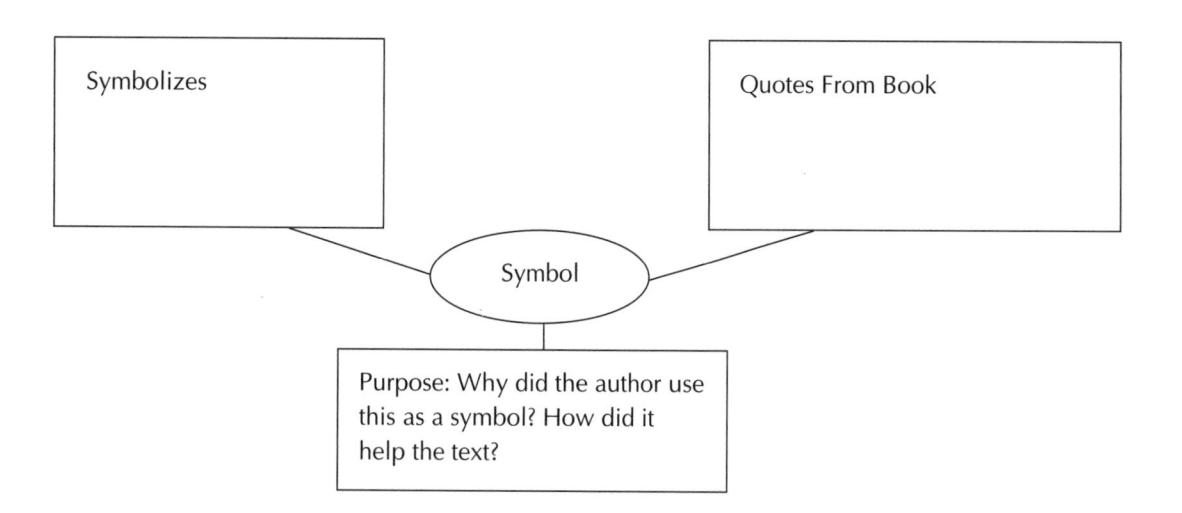

6. Think aloud as you consider what you will write in the Symbolizes box in the upper left of the web. You can put more than one concept in the box, if needed.

7. Now, discuss why the author used the symbol and why you and the students even interpret it as a symbol. (That is, the author may not have meant it to be a symbol.) Think about why the author used the symbol and how it added to the text; write your and the students' ideas in the bottom box. Allow this box to branch off and lead to more writing and open-ended thinking.

8. Have students do another web exercise in pairs. Have the pairs discuss their answers, and ask some pairs to share their ideas with the whole class.

9. Optional: Have students write a quick paragraph on their findings.

10. Optional: Use the same web with backward symbolizing: Tell students what it symbolizes first (the upper left box), and then have them find the symbol, a quote, and the symbol's purpose.

## PROP MAKING (Ma, Gru)

Props, in a sense, "prop up" and support the meaning of verbal concepts with solid, touchable, visible, manipulative objects. The more props we make, use, and have in any class, the better the learning, generally speaking. Props are obvious supports for narratives in literature classes, but they can also be helpful in supporting learning in social studies and science classes. In this activity, students interpret a text and figure out which props might best communicate the main points or concepts (note that this activity also builds the skill of communicating). A key aspect of this activity is the motivation it gives students to understand and re-refer to the text. They must also evaluate which aspects are important enough to warrant making props for them.

## Procedure

**1.** Before students make their own props, you will need to show them some possibilities. Most teachers tend to use one or more of the following:

- Flannel board figures
- Laminated pictures and cutout figures
- Props made out of construction paper
- Overhead transparencies and cutouts
- Costumes
- Puppets
- Salt and flour clay (the kind that is baked) (Ma)
- Real clay (the kind that dries without using an oven) (Ma)

**2.** Pick a challenging text that you need students to understand and that lends itself well to making 6–12 props to aid in its explanation or retelling. For example, you could pick a textbook explanation of plate tectonics, a chapter on the New Deal, or a short story about heroism.

**3.** Model for students how to go through a text and make a list of 10–20 possible items or props that might help another student understand it. I like to tell students to prepare a short presentation with props for teaching younger students. This places less pressure on them than presenting to peers, even though I can usually convince most of them to present to their own class also.

**4.** Think aloud the process of choosing from the 10–20 possible props to pare them down to 6–12. This helps students think about what is most important and feasible.

**5.** Have students, working in groups or pairs, read the text and consider which props might support it best (Gru). Have them then decide on 6–12 of their own most helpful and feasible props to make.

**6.** Give students the materials and time to make the props. Circulate through the classroom, and ask students for their reasons for choosing the props they did.

**7.** Have the groups or pairs write notes on what they will present, in what order, and how. They can add dialog and movement, such as mime and hand motions, if needed.

**8.** Have students volunteer to present to the class or to students in younger grades. They can also present to another group in the class.

# INTERPRETATION CHANTS (Mu)

This is a response chant that gets students to interpret concepts below the surface level. The frame is meant to start you off, but you and your students should modify it or create a completely different chant about the topic of study. Refer to chapter 2 for more specifics on how to create effective chants and how to get students to create them as well.

## Procedure

**1.** Consider the topic of study and pull out key target learning concepts that you want to interpret. These will help you start off the chant. Students can help in this process as well.

**2.** Compose the chant on the overhead and have students copy it on their own paper as you go along.

**3.** Fill in the first line with an appropriate entry in order to model how to begin.

**4.** Have students share possible lines as you continue to fill in the chant. When you think students can do some on their own, let them try to finish the chant in groups or pairs.

**5.** Call attention to the different types of academic language in the verses. Feel free to change them if you want.

---

### Interpretation Chant Frame

Let's look closely at _____
What does it really mean?
Maybe it means _____
I hope at some point we'll clearly see.

The author wrote _____
What was he/she trying to say?
I think it is a metaphor for _____
I'm not sure, but I see it that way.

The _____
Was a symbol used to emphasize
The _____
I'll remember this a long time

The text/movie tried to teach us _____
And/by _____, I say,
I can apply this to my life by _____
_____, starting today!

---

**6.** Once the chant is finished within different groups or pairs, have students share their versions with the class. Let them rehearse, if needed. Have instruments or downloaded mp3 drumbeats available to help with the beat.

**7.** Optional: Have students learn popular songs or ones that you have created. Most songs exist to be interpreted. One song I sometimes use to introduce the interpretation of metaphors is the one below titled "What Is Love?" The sample "Cultural Anthropologist Thinking Song" can be sung to the tune of "La Bamba."

### What Is Love?

I used to wonder 'bout a thing called love
So I asked everyone and all things what it was
The glue said love is sticking together
The clothespin said it's hanging out forever
The front door said love is always open
The marathon runner said it's persevering till the end

The nighttime whispered, it's the morning sun
The soaring eagle cried, "It's freedom!"
The sailor said it's the wind that fills the sail
The eraser said it wipes all wrongs away
The gourmet chef said it's the perfect spice
The baseball player said it's joyful sacrifice

### Cultural Anthropologist Thinking Song

That's an interesting product
or practice I see

Is it shared by others
Or is it unique?

Is it just practical
Or does it symbolize more

If so, then what
Beliefs and values does it show?

I'm a cultural anthropologist
That's what I do
I'm a cultural anthropologist
I'm studying you

# RESPONSE TO LITERATURE
## RAP-ACRONYM (Mu, Mo)

The use of music to promote learning rarely fails to engage students in some manner—even in high school. Music offers key ingredients to learning such as rhythm, repetition, concise language, and fun. The verses given below are full of academic language and many of the thinking skills that we want students to engage in as they respond to literature. It is not that easy (especially in a test setting) to respond to a piece of literature without some strategies already embedded in our brains, ready to work for us; this activity helps get a few such strategies engraved in the brain in a fun way. Of course, teaching effective use of the thinking skills embedded in the verses takes a bit longer. I use the following song as a rap with an mp3 drumbeat. You or your students might be able to sing it to current tunes.

"How's it going?" you ask, "What's going on?"
Well, I'm reading a book and I want to respond,
I want to share my feelings and my thoughts
Here's how I was taught to write a written response.

First, I reflect on the title, plot, and scene,
And what I learn about the characters, flat or deep,
I empathize with them, I "walk in their shoes"
I infer how they feel by what they say and do.

    This is the lit, (snap snap) this is the lit response
    This is the lit, (snap snap) this is the lit response

I look for the main challenge or problem to solve,
And watch how the characters change and evolve,
And all throughout the story I keep one eye
On the underlying purpose the author had in mind.

The author wrote the story to teach important things,
With clever lit devices to describe meanings
The plot on the surface is interesting
But gold nuggets of wisdom are found beneath.

    This is the lit...

I use the other eye to search for universal themes,
Like love, faith, commitment, culture, justice, hope, and greed,
And I relate them to my own experience in life,
I let it teach me how to think about what's wrong and right.

I reflect on how the book has touched my heart and head
And compare the piece to other works I've read
I look for key quotations and text for support
I interpret figurative language such as metaphors

    This is the lit...

I become a tough book critic for a moment
I evaluate the plot and character development
Finally, I organize it all so it flows like a stream
And becomes the best response to lit you've ever seen!

## *Procedure*

**1.** Explain to students that they will be learning a complicated rap about how to respond to literature and that those who learn it will be rewarded in some way, such as being smarter, enjoying books more, or getting higher grades. They will also have fun in the process.

**2.** Explain that the rap is so long that it will help to learn an acronym that gives clues to the verses, just in case the song fades from students' memory (Mu). The acronym is RESPONSE TO LIT; it is shown on the next page. Explain the lines of the acronym to students, and use examples from a sample text. If desired, make copies of the Response to Literature Rap Organizer blackline master, found in Part III of this book, page 233.

**3.** Along with each letter of the acronym, you can also use a hand motion to help students remember it (Mo). After teaching the acronym, cover any classroom or overhead copies you might have showing, and have students practice the acronym in pairs. Then see if anyone can perform it for the class.

**4.** Teach the rap shown on the next page. (Feel free to modify it, if you want; if you do, remember to modify the acronym if needed.) Use an mp3 drumbeat or an instrument to keep the beat.

**5.** Have students explain the verses in Think-Pair-Shares (see chapter 13) and use examples. For example, a student might say, "In the second verse, 'learn about the characters, flat or deep' means that we need to figure out which characters are important to the story and might change and which characters are flat, which means that some characters don't get described much and just serve certain purposes. They might not even show up at the end."

| Acronym Letter | Line From the Rap | Motion |
| --- | --- | --- |
| R | I **reflect** on... | Put index finger to forehead, thinking |
| E | I **empathize** with them, I "walk in their shoes" | Walk (with feet or fingers) |
| S | I infer how they feel by what they **say** and do | Make a talking motion with the hand |
| P | I look for the main challenge or **problem** to solve | Place hand over eyes, looking, then scale an imaginary mountain |
| O | I keep **one** eye on the underlying purpose | Point to one eye |
| N | But gold **nuggets** of wisdom are found beneath | Move the hand like a stream, down low |
| S | I use the other eye to **search** for universal themes | Place hand over eyes, looking out |
| E | And I relate them to my own **experience** in life | Hold up both hands, all fingers pointing to self |
| T | I reflect on how the book **touched** my heart and head | Point to heart, then head |
| O | And compare the piece to **other** works I've read | Pretend that each hand is one side of a scale |
| L | I **look** for key quotations and text for support | Check pockets for keys |
| I | I **interpret** figurative language such as metaphors | Make a digging motion |
| T | I become a **tough** book critic for a moment | Slap fist on palm of other hand |

# Evaluating

In Benjamin Bloom's original taxonomy (Bloom et al., 1956), evaluating was the highest level of thinking. Other researchers, such as Robert Marzano (1988) and Barry Beyer (2001c), also have included evaluation as an important information-processing skill that students need to develop for academic success.

Evaluation, as its name implies, means assigning value to something. We assign value when we judge a thing (object, idea, event, person, etc.) or its parts according to certain criteria. For example, when evaluating the ramifications of cutting down the rainforest, I use the criteria of short- and long-term financial gains, water runoff, loss of habitat, loss of potential medicines, and the ethics involved in each issue. Of course, in communications with others, we all must agree on the criteria used, and on how the information matches, or is described by, the criteria.

Sometimes the criteria are straightforward and even quantifiable. For example, we can say, "This will take more time than that," "This item costs more money than that item," or "Both appear to be of the same quality." Yet in school (and life), we must grapple with more "apple and orange"–type issues. We might, for instance, be asked to evaluate the contributions of a historical person, such as Christopher Columbus. What value did his actions have for the world? He started the colonization and trade between the Americas and Europe. Yet slavery was also a product of his "discovery." And millions of Native Americans died in the years following his meeting with them. Did he do more harm than good? Should we no longer celebrate Columbus Day? Answering these types of questions requires evaluation.

The core ability in evaluating is effectively using criteria. A criterion is a rational principle or category used for judging the value or logic of an idea (Marzano, 1988). Criteria are derived and defined from a variety of sources: teachers, classrooms, school systems, governmental agencies, parents, and a person's own background experience and culture. All of these, as you might guess, tend to vary from one person to the next. The set of criteria that one person uses to evaluate are the rational, "common denominator" categories that must be understood and agreed on by the others in a collaborative setting. Therefore, criteria need to be negotiated to a large extent by all parties involved. For example, student A may decide to evaluate the quality of a movie. If student B does not agree on the criteria used to determine quality, such as plot, character development, and special effects, then both may disagree about the movie and the process goes nowhere. (By contrast, in a dictatorial setting, the dictator or boss alone decides the criteria.)

Students need to understand the many ways in which evaluating takes place in the world. That is, they must be able to understand how various people in various settings use criteria to assess the worth of something. Being a good employee, for example, means more than satisfying the criterion of arriving on time and staying late. One must also be professional, dress a certain way, be productive, and so on. Likewise, people in any domain in which students may think or work (e.g., politics, medicine, history, law, education, technology) each have criteria for evaluating. Students need to learn how these others evaluate, in order to better understand those domains. At the same time, students must continue to develop their own way of evaluating life's wide array of "valuables."

I teach three basic steps for evaluation. I call them the ICH questions: What is the **i**ssue or idea being evaluated? What are the **c**riteria we will use to decide the value of the issue or idea and its aspects? and **H**ow do the facts and evidence meet or support the criteria? This last step is the most challenging. This is where the student must analyze the facts and decide how well they fit the criteria being used to measure the worth of the issue or idea's aspects or sides. This is often subjective and needs extensive clarification and negotiation (which can be good for language development). For example, to evaluate whether to fund a tutoring program, one might have to place a value on student and teacher comments and weigh them against the monetary figures. Both sides need to negotiate how much weight to give the comments.

Negotiation of criteria is common in courts of law. One side of a legal issue may emphasize one or two criteria, and the opposing side may emphasize different criteria to build a case. For example, many lawsuits end up arguing how reasonable or acceptable an action or inaction was. One person's idea of "reasonable" can drastically differ from the opposing side's definition. Ultimately, a jury must decide if the criteria on one side outweigh the different criteria on the other side. This can be some of the most challenging and abstract thinking done by humans. Teachers must therefore extensively model the use and discussion of criteria to evaluate (i.e., model how to weigh apples and oranges) in their classes.

Here is a simplified illustration that shows part of the ICH process used in a two-sided issue.

## Step 2. Establish the Criteria (for Both Sides)

| Criterion 1: | Criterion 2: | Criterion 3: | | Criterion 1: | Criterion 2: | Criterion 3: |

**Side A:** | **Side B:**

Step 3. How this side meets each criterion | Step 3. How this side meets each criterion

Step 1. The Issue

Because the formation and use of criteria are unfamiliar to many students, I give minilessons that introduce and model their use. I start with the question "What are criteria?" We then discuss how criteria are like requirements with different levels and degrees. Then I move on to the use of examples, which I put on a poster that evolves during the year. Common criteria include scientific advancement; morality and ethics; environmental impact; justice; human rights; and the loss or gain of human lives, time, money, and freedom. The more subjective and abstract the criteria are, the more modeling and practice the students will need in using them to evaluate.

Remind students that they are using criteria all the time, often without consciously naming them. A good way to get students to understand the concept of using criteria is to have them identify reasons for their opinions on a hot topic. You can then look at the given reasons and point out what criteria they fit under. "Because it's wrong" is not usually a good enough answer to this question; a student must have a clearer reason for wrongness according to logical and agreed-upon criteria. "Because all people have the legal right to be heard," on the other hand, might indicate that a student's criterion for objecting to an action is human rights. If a student objects to an action by saying, "But what about the negative impact it has on children?" this could fall under the criterion of societal growth or that of morality. Finally, you and the students might end up weighing the "apples" of the degree to which human rights should be allowed against the "oranges" of the degree to which morality is pursued. The result would be an engaging discussion in which students dig deeper into criteria and practice evaluation-rich thinking.

One of the most interesting criteria for evaluation is ethics. Ethical decisions and practices are those that we determine are right or wrong, depending on who is doing the determining. Because people often have differing senses of right and wrong, we tend to disagree on many issues. This ties up a lot of tax dollars in our courts, but it can make classroom discussions more interesting. Ethics tend to be influenced by religious and cultural norms. We teachers must respect religious and cultural differences and be open to discussing them in our classes. You might want to introduce the subject and hold a short discussion on ethics before diving into discussing ethics in relation to criteria. Mention that ethics is made up of our ideas about our rights to be free, respected, and heard; our human growth and potential; our survival needs; justice; equality and equity; interpretation of laws and rules; fair practices in games and business; hard work; and so on.

Another element of evaluation is the ability to discern fact from fiction and opinion. A practical use of this skill is the ability to judge the credibility of written information. This is important, especially in these days of Internet research. Anybody can put anything on the Internet to be found by students. Students should be trained to evaluate immediately the source and quality of the content of a website, article, or book. In history class, students should learn how to compare primary source documents with the textbook. You will need to model how to constantly question the texts that you read. The more critical questions you can model and encourage students to ask, the more they will evaluate. Questions might include these: "Was the author biased in any way?" "Is there language in here that shows the author's biases?" "Am I biased about these issues in any way?" "What do I believe?"

# Academic Language, Prompts, and Frames

The following expressions, prompts, and frames are for use with the skill of evaluating. Get to know these terms, and point them out when you and your students use them in discussions or written tasks. Refer to chapter 1 for ideas on how to use academic language expressions, oral and writing prompts, and paragraph frames to develop academic thinking skills and academic language.

Some common expressions used when evaluating include the following:

- Assess the importance of...by using the following criteria.
- Decide whether...has the moral right to...
- Critique the actions of...
- Evaluate the contributions of...
- Research shows that....
- We must not lose sight of the number one criterion for.... This is the...
- Was he thinking about this issue when he committed the act?
- The...meets the criteria of...in the following ways. First...
- The possible consequences of this option are dangerous because...
- They want to throw out the baby with the bathwater...
- Estimate the chances over the next 20 years of...
- My points are supported by research that shows...
- Granted, the opposing side does meet certain criteria, such as.... But...
- When we break it down into the components of..., we can see that...
- Considering..., decide whether or not...
- From a practical stance..., yet from an ethical point of view...
- On one hand we have...; on the other, we have...
- We must judge them according to...

Following are some prompts that encourage students to evaluate when speaking or writing:

- Debate the following issue/statement.
- Write a newspaper article supporting your opinion.
- Criticize the decision to...
- Defend the decision to...
- Write an essay supporting your opinions.
- What criteria would you use to decide whether a movie is good? Why?
- Write a classic comic strip or paper that argues your point of view.

- Generate and use criteria to decide which character is more...
- Write a letter, puppet show, or role-play supporting your opinion.
- Evaluate the importance of this historical event.
- Create a philosophical question and answer it (e.g., What is love?).
- Evaluate the impact that this novel had on...
- Write an argument between two persons with opposing points of view.
- Which is more valuable (moral, effective, logical, valid, appropriate, lasting): _____ or _____?
- What is the likelihood (probability, chance) that...

Frames like those below help students to gradually pick up academic language and eventually use it to compose their own high-quality written products without help. Two frames are given here to get you started on your own subject- and student-specific frames. These two are very generic, to allow you to fine-tune them or even to start from scratch. When creating your own frames, be sure to refer to the lists of expressions and prompts given above.

### Paragraph Frames for Scaffolding Evaluating

1. Before we blindly head down the road of _____, we must evaluate the decision to _____. First of all, it will mean that _____. Research shows that _____. Second, the decision meets the criterion of _____, but not that of _____. Finally, we must consider the ethics of the issue. Is it right to _____? Does the _____ outweigh the_____? Further research and dialog will perhaps get us closer to the answers.

2. Should we _____? I believe we should _____. A decision of this magnitude needs to meet several important criteria for. The first criterion is _____. What I propose meets this criterion because _____. Second, (my side) meets the criterion of _____ by _____. Finally, even though the opposing side does _____, my proposed solution has a greater chance of _____.

Remember to start with student background knowledge when introducing activities that build this skill. You can create a starter board of background knowledge topics such as friendship, family, school, music, advertising, culture, sports, television shows, movies, famous people, wars, or recent units you have studied in class.

# Activities for Developing the Skill of Evaluating

## CHARACTER TRAIT GRAPH (Gru, Vi)

The Character Trait Graph is, in a sense, a melding of language arts and math. Students who excel at math but dislike literature get more interested in this reading activity than they would in most. This activity produces a visual representation that shows how students evaluate certain traits of characters in a story.

### Procedure

**1.** Decide on possible personal traits and qualities that you want to evaluate: self-assured, mischievous, secretive, creative, persevering, patriotic, greedy, patient, naive, caring, heroic, compassionate, etc. Choose a story and a character to evaluate.

**2.** Draw a box on the chalkboard or overhead like the one shown below. Write one or two key story events along the bottom. This can be a helpful process in itself because it helps students recall the most important parts of the story in sequence.

**3.** Model how to look for concrete behaviors that show the trait you are measuring. Also show students how to look for dialog that helps you to infer. Tell students that they will have to be ready to defend their choices if asked how a quote relates to the trait.

**4.** Have students help you create a graph on the chalkboard or overhead (Vi). Decide on a scale for the left side. You can use ratings such as Not at All, Some, Average, A Lot, and In Excess, or you can use number ratings (e.g., 1 = not at all; 5 = in excess).

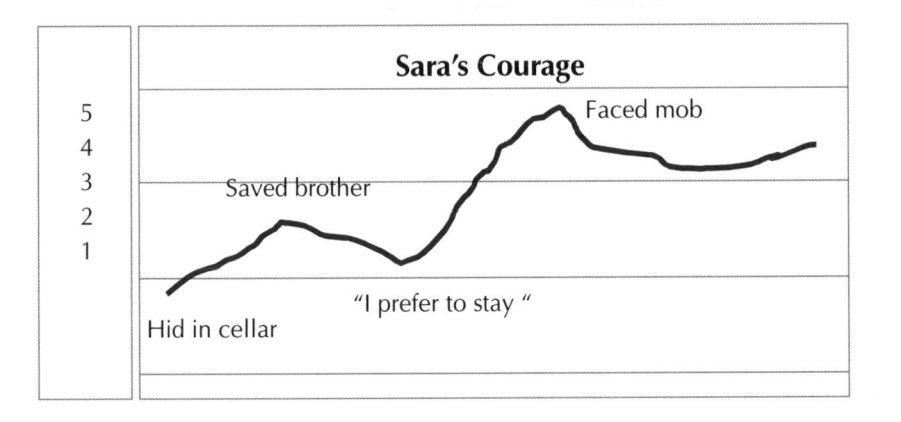

**5.** Discuss the placement of each chosen behavior on the graph (Gru). Discuss whether the act or quote was an exception to the character's normal behavior or whether it was a sign of the character's basic nature.

**6.** Have students do the activity on their own in pairs. Have pairs put their graphs on an overhead transparency and share the results with the class.

# EVALUATION SCORE CARDS (Gru, Vi)

This activity allows students to practice the challenging skill of assigning value to very subjective categories. For example, it encourages students to think about why their society values certain traits, products, and ideas more than others—and it gets them to ask whether their society has good values. This activity can be used with other comparisons of texts and of concepts such as heroes, novels, movies, choices in war, types of experimentation, aspects of culture, and laws. You will need to model the process on the overhead projector several times before asking students to do the activity on their own.

## Procedure

**1.** Choose two characters, concepts, sides of an issue, etc., that you want students to evaluate. Let students know that they will be evaluating two things that are not easy to compare. Tell them that this is much more difficult than comparing prices or comparing the quality of two tangible items.

**2.** Students must first come up with solid criteria for evaluating. Have them brainstorm, in pairs, about the qualities or traits they will consider (Gru).

**3.** Have students create a list of traits that you can turn into a scorecard, like the one shown here (Vi).

| Evaluation Scorecard | |
|---|---|
| **Person A** | **Person B** |
| Brave<br>1-----------------5<br>Because... | Brave<br>1-----------------5<br>Because... |
| Passionate<br>1-----------------5<br>Because... | Passionate<br>1-----------------5<br>Because... |
| Important<br>1-----------------5<br>Because... | Important<br>1-----------------5<br>Because... |

**4.** Have students evaluate the two characters or concepts using the scorecards. They can do this individually or in pairs.

**5.** Have students then share their evaluations with a partner (if students are working in pairs, have each pair share with another pair). They should refer to evidence or background experience and then evaluate how solid or credible this evidence is. Have the pairs or groups discuss any discrepancies and come to a final agreement.

6. Ask students to write a final summary paragraph that answers a final question you pose to them about the two items being compared. You might try some of the following for your final question:

- With whom would you prefer to have dinner, and why?
- Which is more applicable to your life?
- Which is more important to history?
- Which is more ethical?
- Which is worth more monetarily?
- Which would be missed more if it did not exist?
- Which will be best remembered in 100 years?

# CENTRAL QUESTION DIAGRAM (Vi)

The Central Question Diagram, adapted from Alvermann (1991), trains students to connect to evidence in their background knowledge in order to answer complex questions posed about a text. It teaches students to compare their opinions and reasons with those mentioned in the text. It also requires students to see both sides of an issue and to modify background knowledge when necessary. This also connects nicely to work by Wiggins and McTighe (2000) on asking essential questions that drive the curriculum.

## *Procedure*

1. Photocopy the Central Question Diagram blackline master found in Part III of this book (page 234), and give a copy to each student. Work with students to generate a central question for the text and have them write this question in the central box. Refer to the standards for the unit you are studying to find some ideas for a central question.

2. Have students individually generate their reasons in the YES and NO side boxes before reading (Vi).

3. Optional: Have students discuss their reasons with a partner before reading.

4. Have students write additional reasons on both sides of the diagram as they read. Optionally, students can take notes on sticky notes and later transfer them to the diagram.

5. Ask students to come to a conclusion in which they decide which answer is better, if any.

6. Conduct a discussion on the students' conclusions and come to a consensus as a class. Emphasize the evidence used to support both sides of the issue.

7. Optional: Have the students write essays about their opinions, using the filled-in graphic as a visual aid. Show students how to structure the essay and explain the common language that can be used to introduce opposing points.

8. Model how you use the central question to write your thesis and explain the importance of concession and of addressing a reader's potential concerns and counterarguments. Show students how to refer to the text and how to either refute it or use evidence from it.

# CRITERIA BAR GRAPH (Vi)

The ability to measure components against specified criteria is vital for evaluation, yet it is extremely challenging in most cases, given how subjective and abstract the measuring is. The Criteria Bar Graph is a very visual way to show how well a concept's components or outcomes meet the criteria and, more important, to explain the evidence or rationale for the degree to which it meets the criteria. Model the procedure several times before doing the steps with students.

## Procedure

1. Discuss with students the issues that you want to evaluate. These might be core content questions or simply likes and dislikes. For example, you might choose to evaluate a book, the contributions of a historical figure, the importance of an invention to human progress, the need for poetry, the beauty of a painting, the importance of trust in a friendship, or whether an act qualifies as a racially motivated crime. Ideally, you should generate two or three issues that are central to the current topic you are studying (Vi).

2. Photocopy the Criteria Bar Graph blackline master found in Part III of this book (page 235). Give one copy to each student or pair. Individually or in pairs, students can choose which issue they wish to evaluate. Have them write this issue in the top box.

3. Have students then generate three criteria that make up the core idea being evaluated. For example, the "goodness" of a book might have criteria such as plot twists, character development, and educational value.

4. Put students in pairs or groups with the same issue, and have them negotiate which criteria to use. Some students will have different criteria than others, which provides good fodder for discussion. When they agree, have them write the criteria in the tabs that hang from the issue box.

5. Have students individually think about the aspects of the idea that relate to each criterion. They can list these in the lower columns and even include quotations, if desired. They must write notes that are clear enough to give good reason for the bar graph they will fill in. They will need to explain their evidence to classmates and to you.

**6.** Let students decide how well the evidence in the lower columns meets the criteria described in the tabs on the top of the page, and then ask them to create a shaded or colored bar for each one up to the appropriate level (Not at All, Somewhat, Well, Very Well, or Completely).

**7.** Have each student meet with one or two others who evaluated the same issue and discuss their different levels. See if students can come to an agreement on the bar graph levels.

**8.** Have students share their results with the class. You can have a couple of overhead transparencies of the graphic to fill in as students describe and discuss their work. Have them use academic language such as "We found that _____ partially met the criterion of _____ because it _____," or "However, one person argued that criterion 3 carried the most weight in deciding...."

**9.** Optional: In a two-sided issue, put two Criteria Bar Graphs on opposite sides of a 30" strip of paper with a fulcrum underneath to make it look like a scale, as shown. Each side needs to have the same criteria. Then go through steps 1–8 and decide which side outweighs the other. This is similar to the 3-D Balance Scale activity in this chapter. This activity also works well for tasks of persuasion.

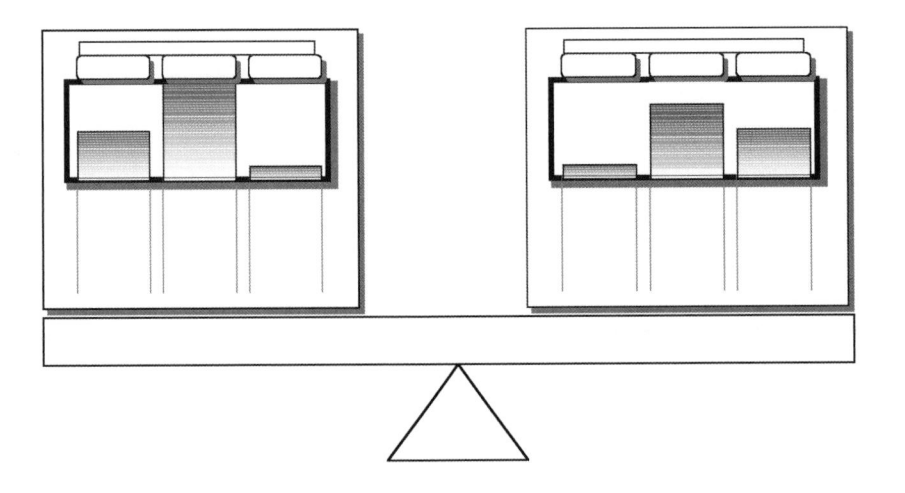

## DEEP QUESTIONS (Vi)

The thinking it takes to answer deep questions can generate and cultivate top-notch evaluation. Wiggins and McTighe (2000) use the term *essential questions* for questions about core issues and concepts that are central to what we teach. Such questions, like those listed on the next page, are mostly controversial and philosophical questions that challenge students to continually reconstruct and reevaluate their answers. These questions also force students to generate and use criteria as they think abstractly and subjectively about the topic. See if any of the questions here relate to your current topic of study. Most have direct connections to literature, science, and social studies. They can also be used with other activities in this and other chapters.

## *Procedure*

**1.** Model aloud the thoughts you generate when answering a tough question such as "Are humans basically good or evil?" "Should we drastically limit the emission of greenhouse gases?" or "Should we have waged the war in Iraq?" Describe how you look at all sides objectively and generate evidence for each. You can even stand in different sections of the room when discussing different sides. Bring up the limitations of each side, as well.

**2.** Give students a different question or set of questions to examine. Have them think about their ideas, then write them, then share with a partner, and then share with the class.

**3.** Discuss with students why this is an important question (or not) for them as students and for all of us as humans.

**4.** Design a graphic organizer that will effectively "hold" the discussion information, such as a T-chart, Venn diagram, or semantic web (Vi).

**5.** Encourage students to bring in deep questions that come up in other classes or when watching television, reading the paper, or in discussions with others. Following are some examples:

- What do you think the world will be like in 500 years? In 1,000 years? Why?
- What person from the past or present do you admire, and why?
- What animal(s) has characteristics that you think more humans should have?
- Are media messages about women harmful?
- If there were to be a nuclear war in two weeks, what would you do and why?
- Should parents be able to refuse medical treatment for their children because of religious reasons?
- Should tobacco advertising be banned?
- Is television viewing harmful?
- Is it ethical to clone animals? Humans?
- Do the mass media influence a society's values?
- Should drugs be legalized?
- Should Native Americans receive their original lands back?
- Is technology the answer for improving education?
- Is it right to use animals for research purposes?
- Did the early American colonists commit genocide?

# COURT CASE SIMULATION (Mo)

Some of the most intense evaluating goes on in courtrooms. Courts tend to decide society's challenging issues, the cases with difficult answers, unclear facts, and complicated laws. This activity is particularly effective for students who like to talk, act, and improvise and who are drawn to verbal and drama-type activities. However, even students who do not enjoy such pursuits might come out of their shells if given the right role. This activity takes several days or more, so you must choose a meaty and high-mileage topic to make it worthwhile. If you choose well, though, you can get exceptional levels of analyzing, comparing, evaluating, and persuading from your students.

## *Procedure*

**1.** Choose two similar issues that relate to what you are studying, and assign a group of students to each issue. Choose controversial and unclear issues that need to use criteria to stack the evidence on each side. For example, a case may be about whether a crime was political or not, whether a medical practice is ethical or not, or how evil a person is. Remember, just about anything can be turned into a court case.

**2.** Discuss what a court case is and how criteria are used to make the decisions. Remind students that they must present the evidence in their favor in the most persuasive and powerful way possible. Point out that they will need to practice their roles, but they will also need to be ready for unexpected situations.

**3.** Describe the order of a trial. Write the process on the chalkboard if needed:

   i. Opening Arguments

   ii. Questioning the witness(es) for the prosecution

   iii. Cross-examination of defense witness(es) by the defense

   iv. Questioning the witness(es) for the defense

   v. Cross-examination of prosecution witness(es) by the prosecution

   vi. Closing arguments

**4.** Have students read the background information needed to form their arguments, questions, and answers. Have them center their research and notes around the central issue and the criteria that form it. Remind students to think about the ICH (Issue/Criteria/How met) questions: For example, "Was it a political crime?" "What are the criteria for a political crime?" and "How did this specific action fit the criteria?"

**5.** Model for students how to build a case for one side of an argument. Point out that certain words and ideas will emphasize what they want to stick in the minds of the jury, and that they should think about the questions and comments that will do this. Have students put their notes and ideas in order from least to most powerful. Have them predict the questions that the other side will ask and the comments they will make, and prepare counterarguments and comments that address them.

6. Optional: Design a graphic organizer, such as a chart or web, that shows the strengths and weaknesses of the evidence. For example, a grid might have six criteria down the left side and the two sides across the top. Students could fill in how each side fits each criterion, if at all. See the example shown here.

| Criteria | For Amnesty | Against Amnesty |
|---|---|---|
| Criterion 1 | | |
| Criterion 2 | | |
| Criterion 3 | | |
| Criterion 4 | | |

7. Hold the court simulation in the classroom or, ideally, in a more "official"-looking room (Vi). (For example, I acted as a judge for high school students who rented space in the county courthouse and held the simulations in real courtrooms.)

8. The jury for case A should be the students who were working on case B, and vice versa. The judge (most likely you) should use and model typical courtroom lingo: "This hearing is now in session," "Defense, please call your first witness to the stand," and "In your closing argument, you mentioned that...." Scaffold the language and clarification of points along the way. Help both sides as equally as possible.

9. When the process from step 3 is finished, have the jury deliberate on the facts presented, with the help of the judge. Help them discuss the facts on both sides and do not let them think you favor either side.

10. Have the jury return to the room when they are finished with their discussion, and have one jury member deliver the verdict and explain the rationale for the jury's decision. You can clarify any points to bring final closure to the activity.

11. Repeat the process with Case B, whose jury will be the students who worked on case A.

12. It is very helpful to have students afterward reflect on the simulation and what they learned in the process. Even discussing their feelings of like and dislike, with reasons, are helpful. All students should understand both cases and the arguments for both.

13. Optional: Have students write a paragraph or two, or even a newspaper article, that describes the proceedings, the decision, and the reason for the decision.

# 3-D BALANCE SCALE (Ma, Vi)

This is a very manipulative-based (Ma) activity that allows students to grasp, literally, the process of weighing criteria on two sides of an issue. You can create the working scale with one piece of 8 1/2" × 11" paper, a pair of scissors, and some tape. Simply photocopy the 3-D Balance Scale blackline master from Part III of this book (page 236). You might want to model this activity with a large replica of the scale made out of construction paper.

## Procedure

1. Show students how to cut out the parts of the scale and put them together: You simply cut on the solid lines and fold on the dotted lines. Tape the triangular fulcrum together and then fold the crossbar into an upside-down V and place it on the fulcrum. Each side has one larger MVP (Most Valuable Persuasive) criterion card and two smaller criterion cards. You may not need to use all of these, or you may need more. Each student should cut out and assemble his or her own scale and work on both sides of the argument.

2. Model the activity as you help students go through the steps. First, clarify the issue and write it in the center box on the crossbar (Vi). Then, clarify each side of the issue to write in the side boxes.

3. Decide on criteria. Show students how to decide which elements of the issue will become the criteria by which they will evaluate each side. Write each criterion on one of the smaller cards. Use the larger cards for each side's MVP criterion, the most important or most valuable criterion for that side. This step prompts students to prioritize criteria, a key skill within this skill. Following are some criteria you may want to discuss with students:

   - **Money**—What will it cost? Is the measure of better health, for example, worth the money invested? How much environmental protection, beauty, freedom, etc., is worth how much in monetary terms?

   - **Time**—How much time will the solution take? How valuable is time?

   - **Long run versus short run**—Long-term gains must be considered and evaluated fairly against short-term (sometimes selfish and greedy) gains.

- **Future impact**—Students must use their skills of prediction and may refer to similar events in history that relate to the issue at hand. If a historical event cited is different from the current issue, students must be prepared to say why it is similar enough to make the prediction.
- **Health**—How will the issue affect both our mental and physical health?
- **Environment**—What is the issue's impact on our planet and its ecosystems?
- **Culture and religion**—Many attitudes and behaviors are shaped by culture and religion; does this make them right? Are some morally wrong behaviors perpetuated in the name of culture? If certain aspects of a culture were changed, what would happen?
- **Ethics, morals, and human rights**—Students must develop the ability to decide what is right and wrong by measuring it with one of the most subjective yardsticks of all: What is the better of the two options for the individuals involved and society as a whole?

4. Have students explain how each criterion can be used to make a reason that supports its side of the issue. For example, if the criterion is money, then the reason against a particular side might be that it will cost too much. Have students write their reasons on the cards for each criterion; they can use the back of the cards, if needed. They should also write down any evidence that they have found, including quotations and statistics, for each reason.

5. Have students put the "weights" on the scale: They should slide their cards into the slots, placing their most important (MVP) criterion cards in the outer slots.

6. Have students then compare the arguments to see which are more valuable, convincing, and have the strongest evidence. They should then tear pieces off cards whose evidence is less convincing. For example, a student may have one card that says, "High cost of incarceration" and another that says, "Rehabilitation programs are more effective." She may decide, after examining the evidence, that the cost of incarceration is too high and that the money could be used for other rehabilitation programs. She would then tear a corner off the "High cost" card so it weighs less when put back on the scale.

7. Have students write notes as they go about why they tore off each piece and why another card had a higher value.

8. When done, each student's scale will tip in the favor of one argument or the other. Have students then compose written products that demonstrate their evaluation of the concepts.

# EVALUATION CHANTS (Mu)

This is a chant that gets students to define the issue being evaluated and come up with appropriate criteria to decide on a conclusion. The frame will start you off, but you and your students should modify it or create a completely different chant about the topic of study. Refer to chapter 2 for more specifics on how to create effective chants and how to get students to create them.

## Procedure

**1.** Consider the topic of study and pull out key target learning concepts that you want students to evaluate. These will help you start off the chant. Students can help in this process.

**2.** Compose the chant on the overhead projector and have students copy it on their own paper as you go along.

**3.** Fill in the first line with an appropriate entry in order to model how to begin.

**4.** Have students share possible lines as you continue to fill in the chant. When you think students can do some on their own, let them try to finish the chant in groups or pairs.

**5.** Call attention to the different types of academic language in the verses. Feel free to move the words around or to delete and add words, if desired.

**6.** Once the chant is finished, have the groups or pairs share their versions with the class. Let them rehearse, if needed. Have instruments or downloaded mp3 drumbeats available to help with the beat.

---

### Evaluation Chant Frame

The issue of _____
Is important to evaluate.
On one side, _____
The other side _____, OK?

In order to judge _____
We need some good criteria
The first one is _____
Let's start with this one.

The option to _____
Meets this criterion
In the sense that it _____
Not crystal clear, but enough.

Yet the option to _____
Also meets criterion one
In the sense that it _____
Not fully, but enough.

Criterion two is _____
It is important to the issue because
It _____
Let's see how the sides measure up.

The option to _____
Meets the criterion well
Because it _____
As far as I can tell.

But the option to _____
Doesn't meet this requirement
Because it _____
That's fairly solid evidence.

So by adding it all up, it looks to me
That _____ is slightly ahead
Since it was better at meeting the criteria
That we agreed upon when this began.

CHAPTER

# Communicating

Communicating is not a skill you will typically find on most lists of thinking skills. I included it in this book because I have noticed the high amount of thinking and creativity required in order to communicate well through oral, written, and nonverbal means. During the course of a school day, we communicate countless thoughts, messages, emotions, and ideas to our students and other adults. Shouting louder than others doesn't always work; we must be creative in communicating and in modeling effective communication to our students. In turn, we often ask students (i.e., require them) to communicate what they have learned *after* they have learned. In addition, they must communicate *while* they learn and even *in order* to learn.

Communication directly intertwines with the development of academic language. I have seen many students fail to communicate their academic knowledge—even though they know it very well—to other students and to the teacher who is grading them. Students deserve extensive modeling and explicit instruction of a variety of communication methods so that they become equipped with the ability to demonstrate their thoughts. Many of the students who struggle the most in school have what is needed in their brains; they just have not developed a versatile set of strategies to make what is in their brains clear to others. Fortunately, there are ways to fortify the skill of communication within our students. This chapter presents some exciting communication activities I have seen and used in middle school and high school classrooms.

Good communication is also necessary for what many educators call socially constructed learning, or constructivism. Constructivism stems from much of the work of John Dewey (1938). This approach encourages social interaction and dialog during the learning process. Humans have a long history of communicating knowledge to one another. It is how we have survived and progressed as a species. Somewhere along the line, however, it was mistakenly theorized that humans were more like computers that perceive, then think, and then act in a linear fashion. Educational practices were thus stripped of the methods that encouraged interaction and dialogic communication of ideas. Many classrooms became like factories in which the students worked individually as the boss (i.e., the teacher) told them what they needed to do and know. Sadly, this factory model can still be seen in many classrooms. Educators such as John Dewey and Paolo Freire (Freire & Macedo, 1987) were pioneers who attempted to revive communication as a central component of students' development of concepts and language.

# What Is Academic Communication?

Classroom communication comes in two types. One is discussion communication, in which messages are exchanged during the *process* of learning. Discussion communication then leads to the other type, presentation communication, in which the messages are turned into a *product* of learning. Presentation communication is often in the form of summative assessments: essays, presentations, tests, posters, and so on. These tend to be the most visible (or audible) ways in which we teachers evaluate the learning of content and language standards.

Discussion communication is vital to develop in the classroom, but it is the harder of the two to teach because extensive social interaction is needed. Discussion communication, also known as discourse, is the exchange of messages in a face-to-face setting. A large part of academic discourse is the process of negotiating meaning, which means the continual adjustment of what and how one says something in order to be understood. It means bridging the gap of meaning so that both people involved in the conversation have a clear grasp of the message. One must be adept at asking questions, paraphrasing, using gestures, creating facial expressions, inferring misunderstandings, and empathizing. Modeling and scaffolding such discussions in the classroom are challenging. One way is to have a "fishbowl" session in which you and another person have a discussion about academic content while being observed. While in the fishbowl, you can call attention to transitions, turn-taking techniques, questions, and discussion continuers. Write these on the chalkboard for the students, if needed.

Presentation communication is communicating to more than one person in a mostly one-way direction. There is much less negotiation of meaning in presentation communication than in discussion communication. This second type of classroom communication includes oral, written, and visual means of communicating. Presentation communication involves finding the best way to reach the audience with your message. The trick is to know the possible ways to present to your audience and then pick the best one. Often, a combination of verbal and nonverbal methods is effective. Verbal presentation communication, even on its own, requires a wide range of skills in order to be effective. Many books and seminars in the "real world," for instance, are dedicated solely to the ins and outs of public speaking. Some of the top presentational speaking skills are gestures, facial expressions, voice projection, eye contact, rate of speech, word stress, and tone.

There are three basic steps to developing effective presentation communication. Step 1 is honing the message. Students often learn the content standards at a somewhat unrefined and surface level. Learning deepens when they are asked to communicate to others what they have learned. They must figure out how to best "cook and season" their "raw" thoughts in order to serve them to others, in a sense. They must be able to discern important information from unimportant information and then to organize the points into a coherent message. For example, they may use a semantic map or outline to understand the relationships and come up with appropriate examples and evidence.

Step 2 is the big "how." Students must decide on the medium of communication. This step is often decided by the teacher, or sometimes students choose from a list of methods. Students should be given choices, as this will train them to be more creative and versatile in their thinking about communication. To make good decisions, students must consider the following: audience age and size, attention span, interests, linguistic and cultural backgrounds, and background knowledge of the topic. Step 2 options might include posters, videos, essays, letters, speeches, photos, recipes, songs, poems, analogies, allegories, drama, gestures, acronyms, references to pop culture, webpages, or murals.

Once this medium is decided, students must proceed to step 3, the little "hows." They must figure out which words, details, academic language, visuals, and/or movements best communicate their message to the particular audience. Step 3 is challenging. It is when the other academic thinking skills and academic language play key roles. An important thinking skill that is useful here is empathy. Students must be able to step into the audience's shoes to guess how they will receive the message. Students might ask, "What do they already know? What would they like to know? What interests and learning styles could I utilize to prepare my thoughts?" Depending on the message, which may be anything from a comparison to a judgment to a persuasive argument, students must synthesize their thoughts well enough to organize them within sentences. These sentences must be clear and concise, and they must contain language that the audience can understand. If not, students may need to use different language and incorporate other visual aids.

# Academic Language, Prompts, and Frames

The following expressions, prompts, and frames are for use with the skill of communicating. Get to know these terms, and point them out when you and your students use them in discussions or written tasks. Refer to chapter 1 for ideas on how to use academic language expressions, oral and writing prompts, and paragraph frames to develop academic thinking skills and academic language.

Some common expressions used when communicating include the following:

- We ought to distinguish between...
- Let's consider not only...but also...
- I'd like to build on what you said about...
- It is not a case of...but rather...
- What struck me was...
- I would like to add that...
- We have all heard that..., but I propose a new way of looking at...
- We should make a distinction between...
- This isn't all that relevant because...
- Let's see how the pieces fit together to make...
- So what you are saying is...
- One aspect of this that is particularly important is...because...

- It is analogous to...
- I have two points that relate to what you said. First...
- This leads us to ask the question...
- Can you clarify your last point?
- We must dig deeper into the idea of...
- The issue is essentially...
- This doesn't seem to be as important as...
- The most essential statements are...
- I think it is more helpful to look at...
- They seem to conflict because...
- There is a pattern that emerges when we look at...

Following are some prompts that encourage students to utilize their communication skills when speaking or writing:

- Convince us to...
- Compare the two characters.
- Make a detailed description of...
- Analyze the contributions of...to...

- Investigate the events surrounding...
- Create a personality profile of...
- Write a dialog for two persons with opposing points of view.

Frames like those below help students to gradually pick up academic language and eventually use it to compose their own high-quality written products without help. Two frames are given here to get you started on your own subject- and student-specific frames. These two are very generic, to allow you to fine-tune them or even to start from scratch. When creating your own frames, be sure to refer to the lists of expressions and prompts given above.

### Paragraph Frames for Scaffolding Communicating

1. For connecting literature to life: "_____," says _____.
This quotation on page _____ captures the essence of the present situation regarding _____
_____. Though many might downplay its importance, we must
consider _____. It is similar to _____.
If _____, then _____. Therefore, _____
_____.

2. For summarizing a chapter: Chapter ____ is about _____. It takes place
_____. _____ is an important character in this chapter
because _____. She (he) is _____ because
_____. Another character is _____.
She (he) is _____. The action starts in this chapter when _____.
After that, _____ and _____. Finally, _____.

Remember to start with student background knowledge when introducing activities that build this skill. You can create a starter board of background knowledge topics such as friendship, family, school, music, advertising, culture, sports, television shows, movies, famous people, wars, or recent units you have studied in class.

# Activities for Developing the Skill of Communicating

## JIGSAW GROUPS (Gru)

Jigsaws provide students with a way to build summarizing skills while pushing them to authentically communicate with other students. When we communicate, we are forced to organize and clarify our thoughts into coherent sentences before we speak. This process makes an imprint on the brain, creating ownership of the information and therefore facilitating more enduring learning. The process of discussing ideas with other people also forces us to challenge our own preconceptions, to negotiate meaning, and to sharpen our thinking. In this activity, students in each group become experts on a portion of the text. These experts then teach that text to a different group.

### Procedure

1. Divide the text into three to five sections. Plan to have the same number of students in a group as there are text sections.

2. Prepare an "Expert Sheet" or study guide that will help students become experts as they summarize a section of text. The sheet may have questions (open-ended or under-the-surface), a task, or a graphic to fill in.

3. Use a pocket chart, random numbers, or another method to create home groups. Then, that expert group will study.

4. Have all students with the same letter get together and read (silently) their assigned section. Then, have them discuss their conclusions, summaries, opinions, answers, task, or graphic organizer within their expert group and decide how they will teach it to their home groups.

5. Have the experts report back to their home groups to summarize and teach the important parts of their text sections. See the graphic below for a visual representation of the entire activity.

6. Hold a class discussion, perhaps with graphic aids to organize the information.

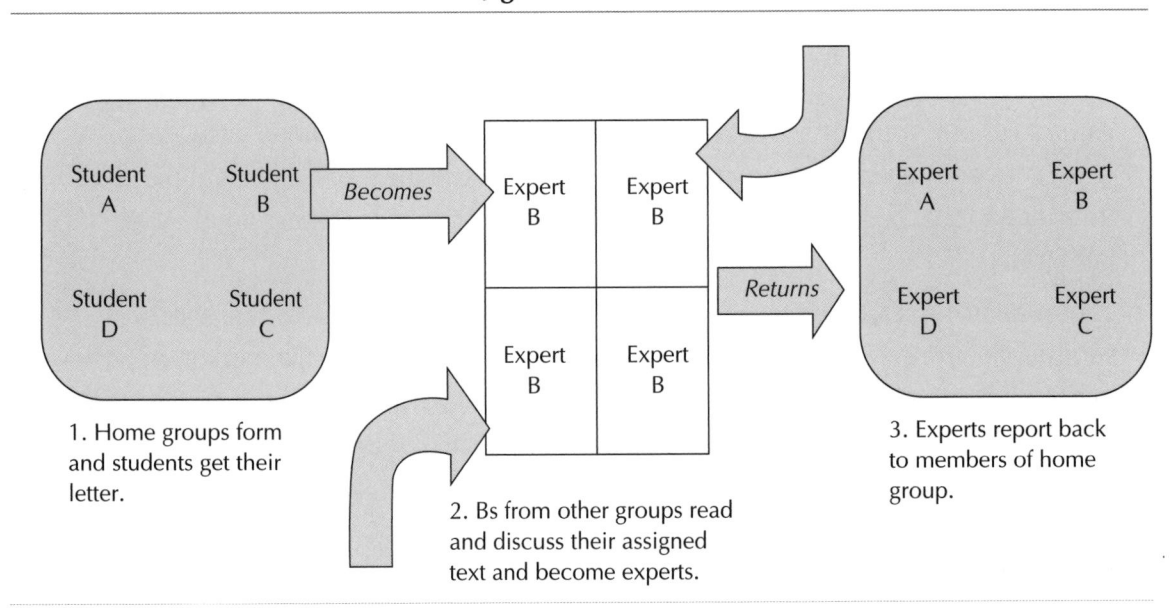

1. Home groups form and students get their letter.

2. Bs from other groups read and discuss their assigned text and become experts.

3. Experts report back to members of home group.

# LANGUAGE EXPERIENCE APPROACH PLUS (Gru)

The Language Experience Approach (LEA) (Stauffer, 1980) requires students to generate language that describes a shared learning experience. We can modify the traditional LEA, however, in order to scaffold the academic language that goes into the written product. That is, in LEA Plus, we build on students' existing language structures and vocabulary and help them to create a product that is more advanced than what they could have produced without our help. It becomes a shared, modeled, and scaffolded writing experience that helps students see how to organize thoughts into a synthesis of any type of learning.

This activity helps students to do the following:

- organize and remember content material
- identify important information to summarize
- use complete sentences and correct punctuation
- build academic language and thinking
- maximize clarity by choosing the best words
- learn minilesson concepts that they see written in their own words

## Procedure

**1.** Help students choose a topic to summarize as a class. This can be a text or other learning experience: a science procedure, math problem, story, historical event, art procedure, game rules, class opinions, video, slide show, etc. Have students individually or cooperatively take notes on the text or experience. Ask them to choose the most important pieces of information that they will share with the class when they later create a whole-class paragraph.

**2.** The students (as a whole class) should help you to create, sentence by sentence, a summary of the chosen text or process, which you write on the chalkboard or on poster paper. (Using the board allows for erasing, and the final product can later be transferred to a poster. A large poster is helpful because it can be displayed for several days.)

**3.** Allow students to modify words and phrases and to argue whether a sentence is important enough to include. Have students support their sentences with reasons for their importance. Encourage them to relate these reasons to the author's purpose or the standards for the lesson. You can give a limit for the number of sentences because it is a summary.

**4.** As students share, you should gently refine their words and sentences (i.e., give them other choices). Refer to any academic language posters on the wall. See the following example:

> Student: We find the opposite of the fraction.
> Teacher: Is there a better word than *opposite* that we have used in this class?
> Student: *Reciprocal*.
> Teacher: Do others agree? OK, let's put, "First, we find the reciprocal of the fraction."
> Teacher: Instead of using *but* again, can we use the word *however*?
> Teacher: Should we put, "We feel that since..." or "We know that because..." to begin this sentence?

**5.** Similar to a think-aloud, model aloud why you might choose certain words over others and whether to include or not include certain information—without changing the students' language too much. Offer or elicit certain key vocabulary and key academic language that students may not produce at first. This is a good way to scaffold academic language and thinking.

**6.** Read aloud the shared summary and have students make any last-minute corrections. Students can copy the paragraph if there is time.

**7.** Continue to use the LEA Plus paragraph as a text for teaching minilessons on related subjects. LEA Plus summaries can be used to teach minilessons on subjects such as academic language, main ideas, topic sentences, adjectives, adverbs, punctuation, pronunciation, persuasive writing, voice, and word choice. Remember that learning from a text is a lot more engaging if the text is yours.

# ROLE-BASED THINK TANKS (Gru)

Role-Based Think Tanks (RBTTs) are group discussions in which students take on certain roles within a group to help foster academic conversation. Popular variations of this idea include Reciprocal Teaching (Palincsar & Brown, 1984) and Complex Instruction (Cohen, 1994). RBTTs require much preparation and training before students communicate in productive and academic ways, but once they do, the activity is very effective and takes little maintenance to keep the conversations rolling.

An RBTT is essentially a scaffolded conversation in a group setting, with members taking on oscillating roles. It is powerful because students take ownership of the content and are allowed to engage in authentic reading and conversation activities. The small group allows for more talk per minute and less anxiety than speaking out in whole-class discussions. Initially, you should model what to say and how to say it by using minilessons and lots of guidance during the process.

## Procedure

1. Assign groups and roles. (Three to five students is a good group size for this activity.) You can give students a choice of roles, but you may want to choose the groups and decide which text (if there is more than one) each group will read or analyze. A pocket chart may help you to keep track of groups and assigned texts. Let students know that they are not limited to the roles given; a summarizer can share inferences, a problem finder can share comparisons, and so on. Students can also have multiple roles. Be creative with the roles you use. Following are a few of the many possible roles:

   - Facilitator
   - Word expert or word detective
   - Comparer
   - Note-taker
   - Predictor
   - Synthesizer
   - Graphic designer
   - Clarifier

   - Problem finder
   - Presenter
   - Summarizer
   - Opinion generator
   - Encourager
   - Prior knowledge connector
   - Cause and effect finder

   - Materials manager
   - Inferrer
   - Categorizer/classifier
   - Liaison
   - Questioner
   - Empathizer
   - Observer
   - Quote searcher
   - Controversy finder

2. Prereading—Build interest in the text and engage the prior knowledge of students by using anticipation guides, semantic maps, brainstorming, visual prompts, text scanning, minidramas, videos, etc. (An anticipation guide is a list of three to five statements that challenge common beliefs and provoke controversy [see Zwiers, 2004].)

3. Have each group read silently, with the group facilitator deciding on a stopping point for silent reading. This could be at the end, but it is often helpful to stop at certain points in a text to process it.

**4.** Have the summarizer give a quick summary of the section and ask for additions to the summary. Have each group discuss the main idea of the text and why the author might have written it. During this discussion, the facilitator should ask the group if there were any unclear concepts or vocabulary.

**5.** Have each group's connector offer or ask for ways in which the text connects to student life, the world at large, or current class topics. The questioners should offer or ask for explicit or implicit questions from the group. Other student(s) can also ask and answer questions. Have the groups discuss how important each question might be.

**6.** Students in other roles should share their thoughts as dictated by their roles. For example, a predictor might predict, an empathizer might share how a person in the text felt, and an opinion generator can share different sides of an issue. If you have academic language posters on the wall, have students refer to them. Train students to ask for evidence and to give evidence for any statements they make. As students respond to each other's thoughts, encourage them to follow the guidelines. You may want to post these in your classroom.

> ### Rules for Think Tank Groups
>
> Everybody helps.
>
> Give reasons and evidence for your suggestions.
>
> No one is finished until everyone is finished.
>
> You have the right to ask for help.
>
> You have the duty to offer help.
>
> You have the duty to play your role.

**7.** The students can create a final product or simply share their notes (taken by the note-taker) with other groups. They can switch roles and examine and discuss another section of text, if desired.

**8.** Optional: You can make some cards for the various roles, if desired. Include sample phrases for the student in that role to say. Laminate these cards and give them to students when you are conducting the activity. Some samples are shown below.

### Laminated Cards for Scaffolding Participation

**Facilitator**

"Let's read up to page ____."

"Can someone give a quick summary of the last section?"

"Can someone take notes on the important parts that we discuss?"

**Questioner**

"Why do you think the author wrote this part?"

"Did you find any interesting or puzzling parts?"

"Any other questions?"

**Connecter**

"How does this relate to our lives?"

"What would you have done in this situation?"

"What is your opinion about this?"

**Word Expert**

"I thought these three words were important:"

"Were there any other words that we should look at?"

"Let's look at the sentence where you found the word and its parts to try to figure it out."

# TEACHER DAY OFF (Gru)

The act of communicating a concept to another person helps us learn it better (Lyons & Pinnell, 2001). Most of us have seen how well students learn through the process of teaching other students. They learn much more in depth when they can effectively teach the target concepts to others. In this activity, they become the teachers of the moment. This gives them a more genuine goal for learning the material than simply regurgitating it on a test or in an essay. The activity works best when the other students being taught do not already know the information.

## *Procedure*

1. Briefly explain the teaching profession to the students. Explain what you think about when you prepare a lesson or when you are teaching in front of the class. Communicate the challenges of being a teacher and also the rewards. Give them a sense of how important communication is when teaching. Tell them that in this activity, they will take on the role of teachers.

2. Show students various ways to teach a concept. Brainstorm various ways in which they have learned in the past, both in your class and from other teachers. Teach them to be teachers. You can refer to chapter 2 of this book for some ideas for training the students.

3. Talk to students about multiple learning styles and (MI) multiple intelligences. Come up with some MI and GruViMoMaMu activities that they might use to teach their classmates. Tell them to think of ways that "their" students can participate, such as pair-shares, brainstorms, kinesthetics, etc. Write these on the chalkboard.

4. Explain the importance of modeling thinking and academic language as they teach.

5. Break students into teaching pairs and give each pair a section of a reading or a concept to teach. This should be new material. Have the pairs do the activities they chose in step 3 above. Monitor and support the students in their teaching efforts; you may also get some new teaching ideas from your students.

6. Lead a brief summary discussion as a whole class to solidify the main concepts learned.

# THINK-PAIR-SHARE (Gru)

A Think-Pair-Share (TPS) is a quick (two to five minutes) verbal interaction between two or three students that allows them to quickly process the academic language and content being learned. TPS can be very effective during teacher presentations for creating "breaks" that push students to organize thoughts well enough to communicate them. TPS also allows a student to hear how another person is processing the learning, which further builds communication skills.

## *Procedure*

**1.** Create a question or prompt that will get students using their background knowledge and experience to answer it. See below for tips for generating Think-Pair-Share questions or prompts.

---

### Tips for Generating Think–Pair–Share Prompts

1. Create questions/prompts that focus students on key content concepts in the text, the author's purpose, essential understandings, and ways to connect to previous learning and background knowledge. I sometimes call these FoCo prompts, for focusing and connecting. Following are some examples:

   - What was the Magna Carta, and why was it important?
   - Why do authors use metaphors to enhance a story? Give examples from our last book.
   - Draw and explain how the circulatory system interacts with the respiratory system.
   - Explain how a certain quotation proves that the character fits your description.
   - Explain how to divide fractions.
   - What does this have to do with our goal of learning the many ways in which different people helped in the war?
   - How does this relate to our objective of learning how to persuade others?

2. Create open-ended questions/prompts that connect to students' lives and allow for personalized, divergent responses:

   - If you were a colonist, would you have...? Why?
   - How does our community deal with waste and pollution?
   - Describe how acids and bases are used at your house.
   - If you found a wallet with no ID, what would you do? Why?

3. Create questions/prompts for academic skills and other skills that you want to emphasize while reading and throughout the presentation, lesson, unit, or year. These skills might include generating questions, summarizing, predicting, inferring, classifying, persuading, evaluating, analyzing, and comparing.

   - How might this war be similar to the Civil War?
   - What were the causes and effects of the Gulf War?
   - Generate two below-the-surface questions about molecular bonds.
   - Summarize how to solve equations by using the substitution method.
   - What can you infer about the character's feelings from her actions?

4. Explore the following Think–Pair–Share possibilities:

   - Content concepts
   - Problem solving
   - Summaries of text or visuals
   - Predictions and inferences
   - Connecting to background knowledge or other classes
   - Sharing part of homework
   - Comparing and contrasting
   - Opinions
   - Vocabulary

---

**2.** Have students think in silence for 30 seconds to one minute to mentally prepare what they will say. They can write down their thoughts, too.

**3.** Put students into pairs. During the pair work, students should do the following:

- Face their partner, show interest, and listen actively. They can even take notes.
- Take turns talking.
- Stay on the topic.
- Remember what their partner says in order to share it with the class later.
- Give reasons for any opinions, such as evidence from the book, class discussions, or one's own life.
- Use the vocabulary and academic language that you have modeled.
- Ask their partner questions that call for clarification and for evidence: Do you mean that...? Why do you think that? Where does it say that? Did you get that from a second grader's website? (Caution students to be polite and respectful in their questioning of one another.)

**4.** After pair time, ask students to share with the class what their partners said. This forces them to listen and also publicly validates what each partner has said.

## Variations

- **Double Prompt Pair-Share:** Create two different questions for the TPS, one for each student, so students cannot simply say things such as "ditto" or "I agree" or "you said my answer."

- **Think-Pair-Square:** After pairs are done sharing with each other, have them turn to another pair to share. This gives students a chance to share with three people instead of the entire class. It is also a good way to create groups of four for other activities.

- Insert various reading and writing components. For example, you could have TWPS (Think-Write-Pair-Share), TPWS (Think-Pair-Write-Share), RPS (Read-Pair-Share), and RWPS (Read-Write-Pair-Share).

# THREE-GENRE WRITING RESPONSES (Gru)

This activity gives students a chance to explore three or more different angles of writing about a topic. The example below is for literature, but the activity is effective in science and social studies as well. The students get to choose three genres from a list that you provide. They quickly write paragraphs for each genre to get their brains warmed up to those three types of thinking. This approximates what real-world writers do all the time: start an idea, explore it, reflect on it, and decide whether to pursue it.

## Procedure

**1.** Give the students as many genre choices as you like. Model how you write a paragraph (or just the beginning part) for any of the choices you think need modeling. You can give more choices as the year progresses, as students will have seen more genre options modeled. Some possible choices to give students include the following:

- Text connecting to one's own life
- Poetry or song
- Persuasion
- Information
- Critique

- Drama
- Screenplay
- Interview with author
- Sequel or prequel

**2.** Have students then choose which three genres they want to write about. Let them know that these are only exploratory paragraphs or beginnings that will lead to ideas and to an interest (you hope) in pursuing one of them.

### "Connect to Life" Sample Paragraph

Similar to Ana's travels through the forest, I remember when I was a child and my father let me go up into the woods alone to fish. At first I was excited, and then I was a little scared. Except I knew that if my dad let me go up there, he probably wasn't far behind, and he thought I could take care of myself.

**3.** After students write their beginnings, have them read each one again and write notes on sticky notes that they can put next to their writing in the margin. The notes should be about whether it is worth the time to build on the genre. The notes can also be ideas for expanding it. For the paragraph above, for example, a student might write the following note: "Need to describe why I was afraid and connect it better to Ana's situation."

**4.** Have students share ideas and drafts with a partner and discuss which version has the most potential or will be the most interesting (Gru).

**5.** After they decide which version has the most potential, have students write the rough draft or fill out prewriting organizers. They can use the writing process and peer revision to improve the piece.

# COLOR-CODED WRITING (Vi)

One way to highlight the key elements of different genres and their associated thinking skills is by color-coding the elements. Many people (including me) are visual learners, and color-coding helps them see the important parts. Let students know that these important elements form a foundation from which students can build their writing skills in the genre. Following are some fairly easy conventions and suggestions for quickly improving students' abilities to write the classic five-paragraph essay. They are perhaps a bit canned, but many teachers would rather be handed a clear can of thought than a murky essay written from scratch. The can is a scaffold, after all.

Color-coding can work wonders for some students. Put some visual aids on the classroom walls and give students colored pencils or highlighter pens to practice with, or have them write on colored strips of paper as they create a paragraph in pairs or groups. I have included ways for students to remember the colors even after you take down the visual aids from the walls and students are writing under less scaffolded conditions.

## *Procedure*

**1.** Model the process of coming up with a grabber or hook to begin the essay. Download sample essays from the Internet (be careful to request permission when using others' work) or district cache and analyze them for grabbers. Help students to label them as shown on the next page. Discuss which grabbers are the best and make the students want to read the essay. Copy a grabber with yellow pen onto the overhead projector, or write it on yellow paper.

**2.** Look at the background statements included in the essay that you are working with; these often lead up to the thesis statement. These tend to include the text's name and author, or they might give the time and place as a context of the thesis. Copy some background phrases or sentences in blue on the overhead, or write them on blue paper.

**3.** Find the theses of the sample essay and discuss whether they are clear enough to give the reader an idea about the body of the essay and what points of the theses the body paragraphs will support. Copy each thesis in red on the overhead. Then do the same in orange with the topic sentence of each body paragraph. Analyze whether the transitions are cohesive between paragraphs. If not, work with the students to think of ways to improve the sample essay.

**4.** Look for the *E*'s: evidence, examples, and explanations. These are the points that support the topic sentences, which in turn support the thesis. Copy these in green on the overhead. You can even use a semantic web at this point to show how the essay is organized hierarchically.

**5.** With students' input, go through steps 1–4 on the overhead to create a whole-class essay on a familiar topic, such as a recently studied unit or a current issue in the school or the world. Write each section in the appropriate color. For example, for a recent movie, students might choose to make the grabber a question, such as "What is heroism?" Write this in yellow. Write the background sentences in blue such as "In the movie *Ocean's Eleven*, the protagonists are a bunch of thieves and con artists." The thesis (written in red) might be, "We should reconsider the impact that films have on our idea of heroism and the impact on young people, in particular."

**6.** Generate appropriate topic sentences in orange with logical transitions to begin each paragraph: "First of all, heroes should be lawful and treat others with respect." The evidence and examples should then follow in each paragraph in green. "In the film *The Shawshank Redemption*, for example, the main character...."

**7.** Finally, come up with a conclusion that ties the essay together and makes the reader think about, remember, or do something in response. Write the conclusion in black. "Therefore, before we run to the theater to see the latest hot film, we should find out if its heroes are people we want our children to grow up to be."

**8.** Optional: You can color-code text on a computer and print a color transparency of it to use on the overhead. You can have students also rewrite a model essay or a piece of their own work using the color scheme.

**9.** Use the table shown here as a quick reference to help students remember the colors to use with which type of text. Mnemonics are included to help students remember as well. You may want to make a poster out of the table.

| Essay Part | Color | Examples |
|---|---|---|
| Introductory Paragraph | Yellow—The initial grabber or hook, which gets the reader interested in reading the essay. This is often a general, surprising, bold, or catchy sentence. Often this is a question, bold statement, quotation, lyric, anecdote, metaphor, single word, exclamation, vivid description, statistic, etc.<br>(Yellow = bright color, grabs attention, "**Y**eah! An interesting text!" "**Y**ikes, what's this about?") | "Do you ever wonder how wars start?" "Trials are what make us real." "To bee or not to bee: That is the question for farmers." "Life is like an onion." "Dreams." |
| | Blue—Background statement(s), which explain the context that leads up to your thesis statement.<br>(Blue = **b**ackground, **b**uildup, **b**asic information) | "In the novel...by..., the main character..." "In modern times..." |
| | Red—Thesis statement, also called the argument or main idea statement, which tells the reader what the essay is about and states your purpose. Some thesis statements include how you intend to accomplish this purpose.<br>(Red = Stop [stop signs are red] and think about this; it all **r**educes down to this.) | "Although many think that..., the text shows that..." "In order to solve this problem, we should..." |
| Body Paragraphs | Orange—Topic sentence, which usually begins with a transition and tells the reader the first main point that supports your thesis statement.<br>(Orange = "Juicy topic sentence," "**O**h, this is what this paragraph is about.") | "First...," "Then again...," "However...," "In addition...," "While...," "Although...," "On the other hand...," "Similarly...," "In contrast...," |
| | Green—The sentences that explain and support the topic sentence (main point). These have evidence and examples from the text, citations, personal experiences, and other details.<br>(Green = the E's: evidence, examples, and explanations) | "For example...," "For instance...," "She said..." |
| Conclusion | Black—Synthesis of the conclusions, and a subtle restatement of the thesis statement above. Some conclusions have clever endings that spur on the reader to think or act in some way.<br>(Black = **b**ring it all together) | "So before we...," "In conclusion...," "Ultimately...," "In summary...," |

Following is a sample essay with the appropriate color-coding indicated.

**Sample Essay: Stay Home**

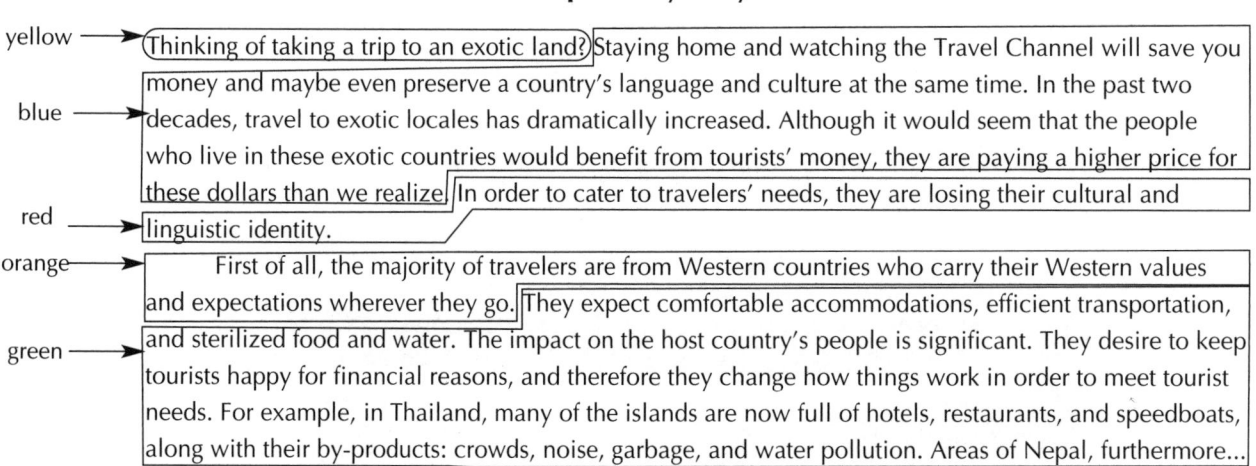

yellow — Thinking of taking a trip to an exotic land? Staying home and watching the Travel Channel will save you money and maybe even preserve a country's language and culture at the same time. In the past two

blue — decades, travel to exotic locales has dramatically increased. Although it would seem that the people who live in these exotic countries would benefit from tourists' money, they are paying a higher price for these dollars than we realize. In order to cater to travelers' needs, they are losing their cultural and

red — linguistic identity.

orange — First of all, the majority of travelers are from Western countries who carry their Western values and expectations wherever they go. They expect comfortable accommodations, efficient transportation,

green — and sterilized food and water. The impact on the host country's people is significant. They desire to keep tourists happy for financial reasons, and therefore they change how things work in order to meet tourist needs. For example, in Thailand, many of the islands are now full of hotels, restaurants, and speedboats, along with their by-products: crowds, noise, garbage, and water pollution. Areas of Nepal, furthermore...

# DEEPER DISCUSSIONS (Vi)

This activity is a product of my quest for the perfect classroom discussion. I have seen many good and many bad classroom discussions over the years, and I have found that thinking skills and academic language can play very positive roles in improving such discussions. Like teaching, sculpting a high-quality discussion is a fine art that demands much practice and dedication. It is a live performance that does not let you go back and erase the weak parts.

This particular activity for facilitating a classroom (or small-group) discussion will rely on your knowledge of the thinking skills and academic language in the other chapters of this book. You may even want to use some of the other activities' graphic organizers during the discussions. Essentially, Deeper Discussions is a way to dig beneath a simple discussion of facts and unsupported opinions, to the deeper level of understanding the essential questions and knowledge you are teaching. This is a highly malleable activity, so feel free to use it as a springboard for your own ideas for facilitating discussions. I also call this activity "Mining for Meaning."

## *Procedure*

**1.** Discuss with students the importance of having high-quality academic discussions in class. Tell them that your class can be a good training ground for future discussions in college and the world of work and that, in fact, many employers prize workers who know how, when, and *when not* to talk.

**2.** Have students generate a list of what they think would be good norms for holding discussions. Add the following to the list, if the students to do not suggest them: Listen attentively, do not interrupt, respect other opinions and comments, and respond to what speakers are saying with appropriate discussion language (some of these expressions are found at the beginning of this chapter). You can make a poster of these norms.

**3.** Show students the graphic below (or make your own version of it). Ask students what they think it means. Discuss how you hope to have classroom discussions that go deeper than just talking about facts, answering easy questions to display one's knowledge, or providing opinions without good supporting evidence. Tell them that you want to have discussions that use the thinking shown in the deeper mines of the graphic.

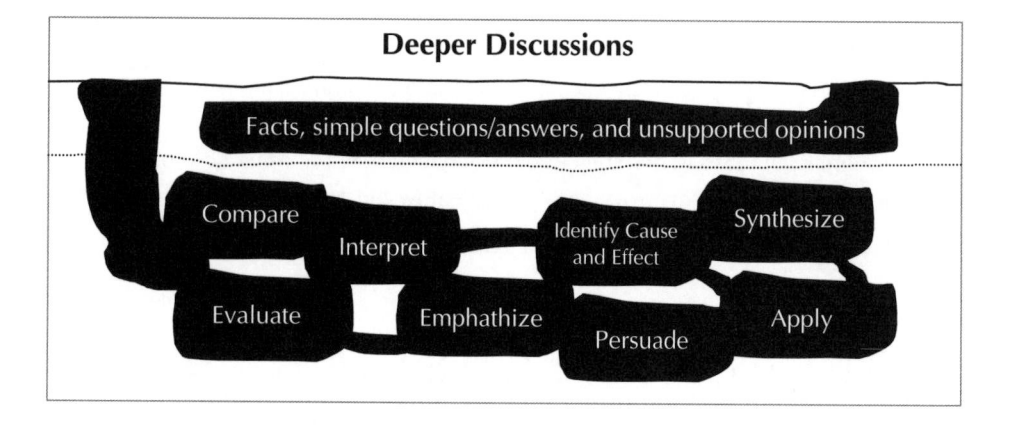

**4.** Model a shallow conversation. Take a topic from your class and, in a somewhat exaggerated manner, ask students simple, fact-based questions. Then model giving several opinions without offering supporting evidence. Then ask a student to give an opinion, and model how *not* to acknowledge his or her comment; rather, instead just come up with your own thought. (I call this "popcorn" talk.) Then, ask students what is wrong with that type of discussion. They will likely say that it jumped around, had no direction, had no depth, and so on. You can then point out that you want to have discussions with depth and direction.

**5.** Model how to have a deep discussion with students. Tell them that it is all right, and often necessary, to start with facts and simple questions, but then they need to dig deeper with questions and comments that show deeper academic thinking. Model questions that get discussion participants to think more deeply; emphasize that students should become proficient at generating such deep questions. For example, ask the following questions:

- How does that compare to modern day?
- What do you think they meant by these symbols?
- What impact did the war have on their culture?
- How did she feel?
- Was moving to a new country worth the hardships they endured?
- Why do you think the government should spend money on this?
- How can the lessons learned from World War II apply to our school?
- What do other sources have to say about this?

**6.** Have students prepare for the discussion by referring to the unit's essential question or knowledge and preparing their own questions for discussion, based on the deeper thinking skills from the list or poster made in step 2.

**7.** Before facilitating a discussion, think about the essential question or knowledge that drives the current unit of study. Then consider which "caves" of academic thinking skills in the graphic best lead students to the essential understandings of this knowledge. Cleverly guide students to use these skills as you give the discussion direction. Some tangents are to be expected, but be wary of tangents that take over your class time and lead everyone too far from the essentials.

**8.** During discussion, allow sufficient wait time after asking questions, and be sure to use a variety of strategies to encourage every student to contribute in some way. Think-Pair-Shares (see elsewhere in this chapter) work well to prime a discussion. It is also helpful for many students (and adults) to have some written information in their hands to support them as they participate in discussions, so allow the students to take and use notes during discussion. Whenever you feel that students can dig deeper, say so: "Let's dig a little deeper into...." You may then ask a student to ask a question, or you may ask your own question.

**9.** Every so often, take a meta-moment as a class to reflect on progress made toward understanding the essential question, on whether you are staying "deep," and whether the class is following the discussion norms they established.

**10.** After discussion, have students write a reflection on what they learned from the discussion.

# MI COMMUNICATION STATIONS (Mo)

MI (Multiple Intelligences) Communication Stations allows students to learn through activities that emphasize different intelligences. It gives students a chance to use their stronger academic abilities (intelligences) while at the same time developing their weaker ones. The goal of the station work, you must emphasize to students, is to communicate to you and others what they have learned in a clever way. You do not need to have students move around to various stations, but it does add a little Mo to the lesson. More ideas on using multiple intelligences to improve literacy can be found in Armstrong (2003) and in Gardner (1999).

## *Procedure*

**1.** Tell students that you are going to set up four communication stations in the four corners of the classroom. Briefly introduce students to the concept of multiple intelligences (see this book's Preface), and discuss with students which four intelligences would be good to highlight in the four corners. Ask students what they would like to work on and which intelligences help them to understand when they read. I have chosen visual, verbal, music, and kinesthetic for this example; other intelligences you may want to use are math/logic, interpersonal, intrapersonal, and naturalistic.

2. Gather some practice activities that correspond to each intelligence and place them at the stations. For example, in the visual corner, you can use graphic organizers, drawings, art projects, or posters (there are many visual ideas you can use from this handbook). The music corner might include chant writing and songwriting in response to a text or video, listening to classical music while reading, or responding to songs or poems in a journal. The kinesthetic corner might include the creation of hand motions, drama, manipulatives, or tableaux. The verbal corner might have ideas for genre transposition, categorizing vocabulary cards, brainstorming ideas, filling out prewriting organizers, looking at models of good writing, newspapers, short stories, or magazines. Refer to Appendix A for more ideas.

3. Have students start with one type of intelligence and then cycle through the communication stations. Have each student keep a notebook and a checklist for the varying types of work in each corner, and have them check off the items each time so that they do not repeat stations.

# TEACHER, YOU'VE CHANGED (Mo)

Some of the most powerful teaching comes from teachers who "make fools of themselves." This can be one such activity. But it can be fun and effective and even get you to "favorite teacher" status if you try it, because drama sticks in students' brains, especially if they are involved in some way. One teacher I know acts like a fascist dictator for a couple of days when introducing fascism. Some students figure it out quickly, and they all remember the unit. Another teacher dresses as Socrates and engages students in meaning-of-life and political discussions. Other teachers act like animals, politicians, union leaders, electrons, students, authors, artists, scientists, and so on. Creativity and a little extra energy are needed here.

## *Procedure*

1. Look at the unit or lesson and decide what you want to be. You might want to act the part of Confucius, Plato, Martin Luther King, Jr., Gandhi, Sandra Cisneros, Niels Bohr, Alice Walker, Gabriel García Márquez, a water molecule, a British soldier, Abraham Lincoln, Cesar Chavez, Albert Einstein, an extinct animal, King Tut, or the heroine of a specific novel.

2. Try to find appropriate props, such as clothes and objects, that will help you play the role.

3. Think about what you will do and say. You might be militaristic and sharp with students to imitate a dictator, ask profound questions as Socrates, pose a scientific problem as Einstein, or begin a speech as Gandhi (Mo).

4. Integrate, as much as possible, key vocabulary and academic language terms into any dialog that you present (if you talk).

**5.** Think about possible ways to get students to respond. For example, they might respond to certain questions you pose, get up and act with you in an improv situation, or meet in groups to talk about what they are going to ask you or do to you. They can also assist you in an experiment, take sides on an issue (e.g., stand on opposite sides of the room), chant a protest song along with you, take opinion polls on an issue you bring up, and so on.

**6.** Hold a brief class discussion about your role-play and how it connects to the learning you want students to do. Give them some clues about the upcoming unit and have them guess how the role-play connects to or prepares them for learning it.

**7.** Optional: Conceal your "identity" from students, and then have them guess who you are. They should support their explanations with evidence.

# SILENT SUSTAINED WRITING (Mu)

One of the biggest causes of poor writing in schools is lack of practice. Another cause is lack of confidence. This activity provides extensive practice and builds confidence in many students who, quite literally, hate writing. SSW is an extended period of writing that offers students a chance to expand their thinking as they challenge themselves to put thoughts on paper. Students have more choices, and they receive support, feedback, and minilessons in the process.

## *Procedure*

**1.** Preferably in the beginning of the year, let students know that they will be writing a lot and that they will become better writers. Hold a brainstorm session and discussion on why they think writing is important for learning and life. Emphasize that sometimes people come to new and exciting insights only through writing and that deep and creative ideas pop up that we did not know we had during the process of putting thoughts down on paper.

**2.** Let students know that you will provide prompts that will often, but not always, be optional and that they will be able to choose the prompt or a topic of their choice. Stipulate that the topic and the writing must show thinking and depth, not just be a diary account of what happened. As a quick example, write on the overhead or chalkboard, "Yesterday I woke up late. I burned the toast and missed the bus. Then I ran all the way to school and felt embarrassed when I was tardy to class." Ask students how interesting or deep this is, and you will probably get some laughs.

**3.** Have a large collection of topics ready that relate to your content area. Some possible topics and questions are found in Appendix B. Model writing that is interesting and shows academic thinking. For the first few weeks, and once per week thereafter, model your thoughts while writing on a topic (or the opposite of your thoughts) to show students how flexible they can be as they write. Model the use of academic language that relates to your content area.

**4.** A couple of times per week thereafter, hold SSW (Silent Sustained Writing) for 10 to 30 minutes. The writing that students produce during this time should be assessed mostly by quantity. This may sound odd, but quantity positively affects quality when the topic is of interest and the student desires to communicate his or her thoughts clearly on paper. Tell students to try to write a minimum number of lines (15–30) that will increase over time. Give students extra credit if they edit an entry before they turn it in to you.

**5.** Play instrumental music during SSW (Mu). Music makes most students feel more relaxed and even respected. (I have used guitar, piano, classical, and jazz.) Music can facilitate the generation of images and creative connections in the brain that might not happen in a silent room (or in a room with other students making noise). Give students some choice in the type of music played, when appropriate. Let them bring in instrumental music, too. Have a way to display the title and artist for the music currently playing.

**6.** Write the prompt on the chalkboard or overhead. The more "closed" an open-ended prompt is, the better: This means that you can help guide students' thinking if you include clear and detailed prompts. Put time into the creation of each prompt, and mix the types of prompts offered in order to meet the interests of different students. Give increasing numbers of choices throughout the year; do not give too much choice in the beginning so you can train students to think about the more academic and deep-thinking prompts. Introduce the prompt and hold a quick discussion about it to make sure students understand it, but do not let this oral segment take too much time away from writing. If desired, you can write on the board some academic language that might be useful for responding to the prompt.

**7.** During writing, be available to support the students in their efforts when needed. You can write, too, but it is most important to be available to scaffold students' thinking and writing. Think of your role as that of a sports coach during a practice session.

**8.** When the writing time is over, have students read to one another in pairs. If students have written very long pieces, have them choose one section they like best and read that to their partners. They should not be made to read if they do not wish to, however. Encourage students to suggest that their partners volunteer to read especially interesting pieces to the whole class. As each such volunteer reads to the class, break in and have students notice especially powerful word choice, sentence structure, transitions, metaphors, thinking skills, academic language, use of evidence, and so on. This is the heart of connecting to background knowledge and learning in context.

**9.** Have students self-assess their writing, using a checklist or rubric that you and your students have designed. Vary the ones you use throughout the year to emphasize different aspects of writing. Assess the quantity and quality of students' writing with the same rubric. You will want to highlight one or two areas that a student should work on over the course of several weeks.

# CHAPTER 14

# Applying

Applying is where the rubber of "what" meets the road of "how" and "why." We learn knowledge and skills in order to use them. "Why are we learning this?" and "How will we use it?" are common questions asked by students (and teachers in in-service trainings). Admittedly, some of the things we teach are simply facts that students need to know. We tend not to see their direct application in life. For example, we seldom directly use our limited school knowledge of the New Deal, literary irony, calculus, and cell mitosis in our daily lives. However, we needed to develop thinking skills to learn these and other increasingly complex concepts. These skills grew and evolved without our realizing it. These are thinking skills that we still use to learn and, when we develop our skill of applying them, use to produce products of value in society.

There are very few essays and multiple-choice tests in the daily "real world" of work, but there are endless ways that we are assessed by what we produce. Such production takes a myriad of forms, yet in most cases, we must be creative in how we apply our knowledge and skills in order to create a high-quality product or service. And because the world and its people tend to change with the tides of culture and technology, we must be ever-evolving in our practice of the skill of application.

Benjamin Bloom (Bloom et al., 1956) considered application to be a core thinking skill. He and his colleagues argued that application went beyond the knowledge that was regurgitated on worksheets and tests. Applied learning, they believed, meant that the student was able to produce knowledge that matched a new situation or problem. Bloom wrote that students must either be placed in new situations or in situations containing new elements. Likewise, Wiggins and McTighe (2000), who include application in their six facets of understanding, maintain that when students understand a concept, they can match or modify their ideas to a new context. They assert, "the problems we develop for students should be as close as possible to the situation in which a scholar, artist, engineer, or other professional attacks such problems" (2000, p. 52). With this in mind, teachers can begin to create powerful "performance-based assessments" that not only show more of what students have learned but also provide more motivation to learn in the first place. An ounce of application is worth a pound of test knowledge.

Similar to the previously discussed skill of communicating, applying plays a slightly different role than the other academic skills. This skill, in a sense, takes the other academic skills to the practical level. One might even say that applying takes the thinking out of the harbor of academia and onto the oceans of the real world. Tests, essays, and homework are only approximations of real-world thinking. They give safe (i.e., relatively risk-free) glimpses of the mind's workings, but it is in the nonsimulations that we see how well one really understands and performs—or not. I have talked to many teachers who describe an inverse relationship between test scores and being able to use knowledge in the real world: They have students who shine when the application challenges arise but who struggle on tests and essays. Other students ace the tests and five-paragraph essays but flounder when real application tasks are given.

The activities for developing this skill are the most interesting, challenging, relevant, and, of course, the most real-world in this book. They are practical because you can use them as assessments for knowledge and skills. They are interesting because they help students see the connection between learning and life and because they give students the chance to develop and use different intelligences. They are challenging because they involve multiple thinking skills and steps. They are relevant because they approximate real-world scenarios.

One of the main features of teaching application is newness. This means that the students should face unfamiliar, new versions of the issues or problems they faced while observing and practicing in the classroom setting. They should know that they must draw from the knowledge and skills they gained while learning and must synthesize and adapt that learning to the new situation.

One example of this type of newness in activities would be going out to a local stream and measuring it for pollutants. This could be done after learning about the causes and effects of pollutants in a lake from the science textbook and classroom activities. Students could measure a real stream for pollutants, then draft a persuasive letter to the local government. They send the letter and await a real response.

A rare, but powerful, strategy is to have students help you figure out ways to apply the knowledge and skills they are learning. Usually, if application is incorporated at all, we teachers are the ones who dream up ways of having students apply what they have learned. But again, when students participate and own a process, they tend to learn it better. Sometimes, students will generate surprisingly insightful and challenging ways of applying learning. The activity Performance Task Design With Student Help is one way to incorporate this type of student input.

# Academic Language, Prompts, and Frames

The following expressions, prompts, and frames are for use with the skill of applying. Get to know these terms, and point them out when you and your students use them in discussions or written tasks. Refer to chapter 1 for ideas on how to use academic language expressions, oral and writing prompts, and paragraph frames to develop academic thinking skills and academic language.

Some common expressions used when applying include the following:

- We need to apply the ideas we learned about...
- If we apply what we read about...
- What we learned about...helps us understand...
- Use these criteria to evaluate the worth of...
- In this case, we should use...
- That formula doesn't apply here because...
- We need to modify our ideas about...
- Put the theory into practice by...
- What we learned about...can help us here because...

Following are some prompts that encourage students to apply their knowledge and skills when speaking or writing:

- Write a critique of...
- Build...
- Design a...
- Judge...
- Perform...
- Role-play...
- Test...
- Adapt...
- Illustrate...

- Produce...
- Create a metaphor or analogy for...
- Solve the problem of...
- Consider the issue of...and write a letter...
- Reflect on the...and write a recommendation for...
- Imagine...
- Argue...
- Assume the role of...

Frames like those below help students to gradually pick up academic language and eventually use it to compose their own high-quality written products without help. Two frames are given here to get you started on your own subject- and student-specific frames. These two are very generic, to allow you to fine-tune them or even to start from scratch. When creating your own frames, be sure to refer to the lists of expressions and prompts given above.

### Paragraph Frames for Scaffolding Applying

1. Response to article: I recently read the article _____ by _____
_____ in _____. I became deeply concerned about
the way in which _____.
I believe that it is a violation of human rights, and I plan to take action. First, rather than simply
_____, I plan to _____
_____. This will ensure that
_____. Then I plan to _____
_____, because there will be a need to _____
_____. Finally, I think that I will _____
_____. By taking these steps, I might begin to help
solve this problem.

2. Response to story: In the story _____, by _____
_____, I was particularly struck by the main character's _____
_____. It was powerful because I have
had similar experiences. For instance, I _____.
However, I did not react the same way. Whereas I _____,
the main character _____.
I think the character handled it better than I did because _____.
In the future, I plan to _____.

Remember to start with student background knowledge when introducing activities that build this skill. You can create a starter board of background knowledge topics such as friendship, family, school, music, advertising, culture, sports, television shows, movies, famous people, wars, or recent units you have studied in class.

# Activities for Developing the Skill of Applying

## PERFORMANCE TASK DESIGN WITH STUDENT HELP (Gru)

The idea of designing real-world performance tasks might be rather radical for some teachers. But even more radical is the idea of having students help design the tasks. Much of the inspiration for this activity, which is probably the most challenging one in this handbook, came from an article I read that described how students had the right to defend their learning (Tierney, 1998). As if they were in court, students should be given some say in how they show what they know and can do; assessments provide the evidence. Almost always, teachers and other adults in far-off places (i.e., legislators, test makers, and textbook publishers) are the ones who end up deciding how students will demonstrate their learning.

It takes a large amount of serious application thinking to come up with appropriate performance tasks. Modeling this for students and then scaffolding them into designing their own tasks is powerful. And remember the buy-in factor: When students have used some thought and creativity to design what they will do, they are more likely to be interested and to perform well.

As mentioned previously, one of the most radical, yet logical, components of this activity is the involvement of students. In effect, you are saying, "This is what you need to learn. Now let's work together to decide the best ways to show that you have learned it." This process, interestingly enough, can give as much (or more) thinking practice as the actual performance task being created. In other words, the performance task is the process of designing the performance task. But the process can also be chaos without sufficient modeling, parameters, and discussion. Hence, the following steps outline how to design performance tasks, with suggestions for involving students in the process.

### Procedure

1. You and your students need to arrive at a crystal-clear understanding of what the target standards for the learning unit mean and how they relate to the big idea or central question(s), problems, challenges, and themes. Before sharing as a whole class, students can work in groups to discuss their interpretations of the standards and questions.

2. Design a rough sketch of the rubric that you will use to assess learning. This rubric also should be used for student self-assessment during the learning process. Consider the content (what students will need to *know* at both deep and surface levels), performance and skills (what students will need to *do*), the academic thinking skills (how students will need to *think*), and the academic language (what students will need to *say*) for the rubric. Also, emphasize that you want students to reflect on how well they will be able answer the big idea or central question(s). You may have to hold a discussion on what "deep understanding" means. Have students help you with the language of the rubric so that they understand it clearly when they use it for self-assessment.

**3.** Think of possible roles or professions in which students need to use the target standards and academic thinking skills to answer the big idea or central question(s). Ask questions such as these:

- Who might use this knowledge and for what purposes?
- How is this knowledge or set of skills used to solve problems or resolve issues outside of school?
- What couldn't people do if they didn't have this knowledge or set of skills?

For example, students may take on the role of an accountant for a small business, an environmental engineer, a veterinarian, a doctor, a historian, a news reporter in the future, two brothers on opposite sides of the Civil War, an attorney, a farmer in the Middle Ages, a politician in the 1950s, a marine biologist, a novelist, a character from a play, a music expert, a cultural anthropologist, or a museum curator. Have students help come up with roles.

**4.** Come up with a problem to solve, a product, or a performance that someone in the chosen role(s) would need to accomplish. This becomes the performance task. Keep in mind that the task needs to be more than just entertaining or time-consuming. It must show that the students understand the concepts and standards that underlie the ability to answer the big idea or central questions of the unit. It is very helpful to quickly go down the list of thinking skills in this book and see how they might be used in the task (see Table 5 for ideas; note that some of these ideas can apply to more than one skill). Sample tasks might include these:

- A doctor might need to isolate a bacterial infection by comparing symptoms and treatments.
- A museum curator may need to design an exhibit by interpreting an artist's works, synthesizing background documents, and communicating with patrons.
- An author may need to research the topic about which he or she will write by analyzing primary documents, classifying the information, synthesizing it, and empathizing with the people in the research to create characters.
- A marine biologist might analyze plankton levels to predict whale migrations and then use a cause and effect argument to persuade other scientists to change their minds about whale behaviors.
- An attorney might analyze student's rights to free speech at school, interpreting current laws and evaluating the extent to which the school rules conflict with them.
- A reporter during the Civil War may need to empathize with people on both sides, interpret their words and actions, and synthesize it all into an article.

**5.** Have students, in pairs, brainstorm possible scenarios, problems, products, or performances to use that will be engaging and will also show they have learned the

**Table 5. Performance Task Ideas**

| | Social Studies | English | Science |
|---|---|---|---|
| **Analyzing** | Prepare a newspaper article that informs the public of the advantages of studying history | Analyze several high-quality essays and prepare a one-page "cheat sheet" for future students in the class on how to write essays | Create a poster that shows the process of generating nuclear power and highlights areas where potential dangers exist |
| **Comparing** | As advisors for the current president, create a visual that clearly and quickly shows the president the differences between two opposing approaches for economic growth | Write a letter to an author showing and questioning the incongruities between two of the author's works (or between a book and its corresponding movie) | Create a nutrition log that records a weekly diet and then compares it to the recommendations for calorie and nutrient intake |
| **Classifying** | Design the perfect society and include descriptions of economics, jobs, education, law enforcement, art, etc. | Devise a way to classify the importance of characters and events in a story | Generate a new taxonomy to classify animals |
| **Identifying Cause/Effect** | Design a simulation that will teach younger students about supply and demand forces in the economy | Role-play an interview with an author who tells about the life factors that influenced his or her themes and choices in a story | Create a dramatic presentation that teaches younger students about the causes and effects of earthquakes |
| **Solving Problems** | Write a proposition that helps homeless people, and work for voter approval on it | Create a list of suggestions to give to an author who is having trouble coming up with a sequel to her novel; say why you think your ideas will touch the hearts and minds of readers | Clarify the evidence on global warming, and propose further studies and possible solutions in a letter to the EPA |
| **Persuading** | Write a letter to the school board that asks for money to buy primary documents to supplement the biased textbook | Take on the role of an author, and persuade listeners to use a certain literary device | Write an article for the entire school that persuades them to consider being astronauts for a trip to Mars |

| | Social Studies | English | Science |
|---|---|---|---|
| Empathizing | Create a journal entry from the perspective of a WWII soldier | Create a monologue to act out in front of the class or a small group on the thoughts you have as a main character (e.g., Hamlet) after the story ends | Write a first person story from the point of view of a blood cell in the human body |
| Synthesizing | Analyze several songs written during the Civil War, and synthesize their contents into a letter to President Lincoln | Read several poems or songs by one author, and create a television advertisement to sell the author's work | Create a dialog between an anthropology student and a scientist who is explaining the process and accuracy of radiocarbon dating |
| Interpreting | Create a master list of the 10 biggest mysteries of history, and explain why they are important | Take on the persona of an author, and create a speech that explains the underlying meaning of a book | Observe an insect, and interpret its actions and physical features with respect to adaptation principles |
| Evaluating | As the Commissioner for Historical Accuracy, evaluate Christopher Columbus's actions and decide how he should be described in history texts | Create a literary critique talk show (like Ebert & Roeper) that promotes or criticizes a novel | Take on the role of a scientist who has just discovered a new form of energy that is clean and cheap, but could be turned into a bomb; write a journal entry describing your feelings about announcing it |
| Communicating | Design a training manual for WWI troops that outlines the enemy's weapons and tactics | Read several poems or songs by one author, and create a television advertisement to sell the author's work | Create a dramatic presentation that teaches younger students about the causes and effects of earthquakes |
| Applying | Design a museum exhibit on the roles of nonmilitary people in the American Revolution | Write a short story that teaches readers about an important human theme or struggle | Measure the pollution levels in a local stream and prepare a report for local authorities |

material at deep levels. Have pairs share their ideas with another pair, and then have all the pairs share with the whole class.

6. After designing a performance task(s), revise the rubric to include any other "know, do, think, or say" standards.

7. Have students help you draft a written copy of the assignment and features of the performance task, which you will polish and hand out the next day. Go over various requirements that students will need to accomplish before starting the task, such as research and materials. Remind students that they are to be, in a sense, lawyers who must prove by doing the performance task that they know the standards at deep and enduring levels.

8. Have students prepare for the task and then execute it. Have them assess themselves in the process by using the rubric that they helped to create.

# REAL-WORLD PROJECT
## (Gru, Vi, Mo, Ma, Mu)

Just as the name implies, this is the ultimate in application. It is a project that students work on to improve the world in some way, often with real, out-of-school people. The rationale for this activity is straightforward: Students are more motivated to do something well and thoroughly when it is authentic. Students also, although it may not seem so at times, thrive on making a positive difference in the world when given the chance. Of course, from a thinking skills development perspective, it takes some planning to maximize students' learning from this experience.

## Procedure

1. Brainstorm with your students what the class might do to improve the community or world with a project that is related to your current unit. Many schools have service learning programs with excellent ideas for projects and with resources to help you design such a project for your students; if your school has such a program, see what assistance it can give you with this activity. Possible projects might include the following:

   • Writing poetry and songs to share with hospital patients (Mu)
   • Story/poetry share day with younger students
   • Entering a writing contest
   • Creating a newsletter or newspaper for the school or community
   • Volunteering to design a museum exhibit (Ma)
   • Creating a mural on local history (Vi)
   • Awareness days at school (multicultural, AIDS, environment, careers) (Mo)
   • Studying, and preparing a report on local pollution (Ma)
   • Creating a nonprofit relief organization that helps developing communities (Gru)

**2.** Make sure the suggested projects require academic thinking skills. For example, many projects have a persuasive nature to them, in which participants gather data and try to change an existing problem in the school, community, country, or world. Most also will involve analyzing, problem solving, comparing, evaluating, and communicating in some way. Keep these skills in mind when you create the project parameters, reports, or documents to send outside the school, and any type of final report that is to be turned in to you at the end of the project.

**3.** Allow students to work in pairs, groups, individually, and in a whole-class format (Gru). You might give out a checklist of the various parts of the project that are to be done in each of these modes. For example, for a report to a textbook publisher, students might gather pieces of research evidence individually, synthesize the information in pairs, create recommendations to the editor in groups of four, then craft the final report as a whole class.

**4.** Have students carry out the activity and then write a final report or letter that describes what they learned and future steps that are needed. This creates some individual accountability and allows students to show you what they have learned. Students will be much more interested in writing a report about meaningful experiences that they have actually had. Encourage them to use academic language in the crafting of their letters or reports.

# CHILDREN'S BOOK FOR ACADEMIC THINKING (Vi, Ma)

This activity gives middle school and high school students a chance to teach the thinking skills that they are learning by way of writing for younger students. Much of human thinking and language is used to solve problems and make decisions. Problems and decisions also happen to be the main ingredients of many children's books. In fact, it is tough to find a good story or movie without a main problem that must be overcome, often through bravery and/or cleverness. This activity requires students to know thoroughly the type of thinking they are teaching, and yet it allows them to be creative in the process for an authentic purpose. This activity can be especially powerful in content area classes, where students can teach not only the thinking skill but also a content concept at the same time.

## *Procedure*

**1.** Choose an academic thinking skill from this book. Brainstorm possible problems that a person or animal might have that would need to be solved by using the thinking skill that you chose. For example, empathy might be needed to solve a problem of discrimination; interpretation might be needed to find a treasure using a map; evaluation might be needed to decide whether or not to steal; or persuasion might be needed to convince a parent to go back to school. You can work with the students to come up with ideas for each thinking skill and make a chart of them.

2. Create a rubric that has the elements that you will want to see in the story that students create. This rubric will help guide students in their writing of the story. Elements might include sensory language, character development and internal change, figurative language, and effective illustrations.

3. Think aloud as you model the process of creating a story. You can use a story map for extra organizing (use the Story Map blackline master in Part III of this book, page 216).

4. Model how to go from the story map to a storyboard, where you must now think about what text goes on each page and what kind of illustration will best depict it (Vi).

5. Optional: Students can turn the storyboard directly into a comic book with dialog bubbles and explanation boxes.

6. Model how to transfer the storyboard story onto binder paper and write the text at the bottom of each page. Then create a quick sketch of each illustration. There should be around 8–20 pages.

7. Have students go through steps 1–4 to create their own rough drafts on binder paper for their stories.

8. Have students pair up and review each other's stories. They can use sticky notes for revision areas, questions, parts that need clarification, and positive remarks. They can go over the rubric as they read and make comments.

9. Have students create their final drafts on white paper or on the computer. They should then illustrate the pages and bind the pages together (Ma). They can then create appropriate covers, either on the computer or with markers and paints.

10. Tell students they will be reading their books to students in lower grades, and train students to be teachers when they do this. That is, teach them to read extra-expressively, to stop and think aloud to model their thoughts, and to stop and prompt the younger pupils to react, predict, infer, empathize, compare, evaluate, etc. Let your students do a practice run-through in groups of four or in pairs before going to visit other classes.

11. Arrange for students to share their books with younger siblings or with students in lower grades.

## INTERRUPTED IMPROV ROLE-PLAY (Mo, Ma)

This activity helps students develop language in the context of its use, rather than just learning its grammar. If you have second-language learners in your class, you and they will find this activity to be especially effective. This activity "feeds two birds with one crumb" because you can develop academic language and content at the same time, without taking extensive time away from the lesson schedule. The interruption is a "surprise" situation or information that forces students to apply what they have learned in new ways. Rather than filling in blanks, memorizing dialogs, or answering questions, students get to be in conversations that approximate the unknowns of real-world discourse. You can also call this activity "Throw-a-Wrench-in Role-Plays."

## *Procedure*

**1.** Quickly explain the expression "throwing a wrench into." Explain that as students do a role-play (a process with which most students are already familiar), you will interrupt with an unexpected situation or issue to which they will have to respond as they talk and act.

**2.** Start off with some fun and easy practice. Put students in pairs and give them an easy or fun situation, such as talking about a teacher, planning a party, complaining about food, discussing a movie, or gossiping. Let them begin, and then interrupt with a situation or problem that they were not expecting and see how they react. You can ask the class for other responses that might have worked, too. Once the idea of a role-play that gets interrupted is learned, you can move on to the academic application of this idea.

**3.** Work with the students to pick a concept from the essential standards of a unit or text. For example, you might choose photosynthesis, a novel's climax, an important battle, or a famous person. Try to find a concept that can have two to five participants in a role-play. Following are some situations and interruptions (improv wrenches) you can use; you will want to come up with your own. You can also have students submit ideas on separate slips of paper.

| Situations | Interruptions (Improv Wrenches) |
|---|---|
| Two brothers on opposing sides of U.S. Civil War | Their mother enters and says that they must choose one side. |
| Romeo and Juliet in the afterlife, discussing what happened | Shakespeare enters and asks them how he could have changed the story. |
| Howard Carter discussing King Tut's treasure with Cairo authorities | King Tut enters and tells them what they should do. |
| An environmental engineer discussing acid rain with a senator to draft a bill that limits air pollution | A representative from the main factory producing the pollution enters and explains the costs and loss of jobs that would be caused by their proposal. |
| Harriet Tubman and Harriet Beecher Stowe discussing the joint creation of a poem about freedom | Diego Rivera enters and says he would like to paint a mural that goes with the poem. |
| Ponyboy from *The Outsiders* talking with his brother at home about the future | A social worker comes to ask about recent events to decide if Ponyboy should be in a foster home. |
| Galileo discussing his theories with a judge who is about to put him in jail | Einstein shows up to set the record straight. |

**4.** Write a quick narrative of the general sequence of events that will happen in the role-play (Mo). These are simply notes for your own use. Jot down a few vocabulary words that you want to include. Visualize where you want the students to go, what they will do, and what they will say. Much of the dialog will be ad-libbed when students are doing the role-play;

later, you can have students write and direct the role-plays themselves. For example, you might write the following exchange:

> Montezuma: But he is the plumed serpent of the legend. This was the designated year of his return. We must obey him.
> Cortés: (enters and demands gold)

**5.** Decide what types of props would be helpful and convenient (Ma). You may have items already in the classroom or readily available from home that you can use, such as hats, brooms, cardboard, old clothes, and blankets. Put them on a table to use during the role-play.

**6.** Choose students for the role-play who will be animated, but not too animated. Tell them what their roles are and give them a bit of background, in front of the entire class. They can wear name tags, if needed.

**7.** Guide the students in the role-play, similar to conducting a rehearsal. Remember that much of it can be improvisation on your part and the students', but continue to guide where students will go and what they will do and say. You will be doing much of the modeling, and some joking is all right. Every so often, ask the performers how they feel or what they think they should say right then. Or, ask students in the audience what the actors should do or say.

**8.** Toward the end of the role-play, you should become a character, join the role-play, and add the interruption. The actors must now respond without your help. From this point, carry out the role-play as long as you desire. Remember that it does not have to be historically accurate if you are going to later study the true account(s) in the unit. Referring back to a role-play like this and comparing the research evidence to it can be powerful.

**9.** Have the students in the audience respond to questions that you give them when you stop at times, similar to when you stop and ask questions during a read-aloud.

**10.** After the role-play, have all students do a written recap of the role-play and why they think this event was important. They can then share their recaps in pairs and then with the whole class.

**11.** Have students (individually, in pairs, or in group) design ways to redo the drama they just saw but with a different ending, or have them prepare their own role-plays with other events or concepts. Have each student or group describe their proposed new role-play to you or give you a rough draft, and with each one, think about how you can interrupt with an "improv wrench" when they eventually present the role-play.

**12.** Have students present their role-plays, during which you interrupt as explained above. You can also whisper instructions to a student from the audience, who will then interrupt and become part of the role-play.

**13.** Have students assess themselves and the other students who perform, and ask everyone to try to maintain a level of acting professionalism and seriousness. Create a rubric or checklist for assessing this.

# PART III

# Reproducibles

This section contains the reproducible blackline masters you can use for classroom activities. Sample reproducible forms and worksheets for this book can also be found at the International Reading Association website, www.reading.org, in the Books area of the Publications section. Of course, you should adapt these forms to meet your specific needs and use them as idea springboards for further development of thinking skills, academic language, and content learning within your curriculum.

# THINK-ALOUD NOTE TABLES

# Notes on

_____'s Thoughts

# Notes on

_____'s Thoughts

# BEST PRACTICES COLLECTION TABLE

| Lesson Mode | Activity<br>(Teacher with students or students only) | Gru<br>Vi<br>Mo<br>Ma<br>Mu |
|---|---|---|
| **Stage Setting and Concept Introduction** | | |
| | | |
| | | |
| **Practice**<br>(oral, aural, visual, etc.) | | |
| | | |
| | | |
| **Prereading** | | |
| | | |
| | | |
| **Reading** | | |
| | | |
| | | |
| **Prewriting** | | |
| | | |
| | | |
| **Writing** | | |
| | | |
| | | |
| **Formative Assessment and Feedback** | | |
| | | |
| | | |
| **Summative Assessment** | | |
| | | |
| | | |

# STORY MAP

Title: _____

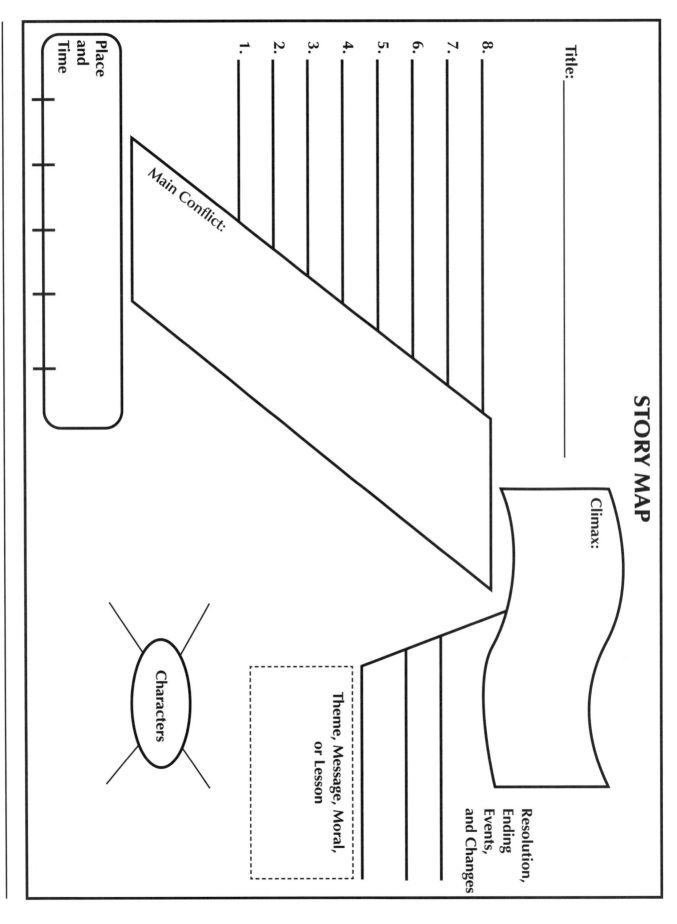

Climax:

Main Conflict:

1.
2.
3.
4.
5.
6.
7.
8.

Resolution,
Ending
Events,
and Changes

Theme, Message, Moral,
or Lesson

Characters

Place
and
Time

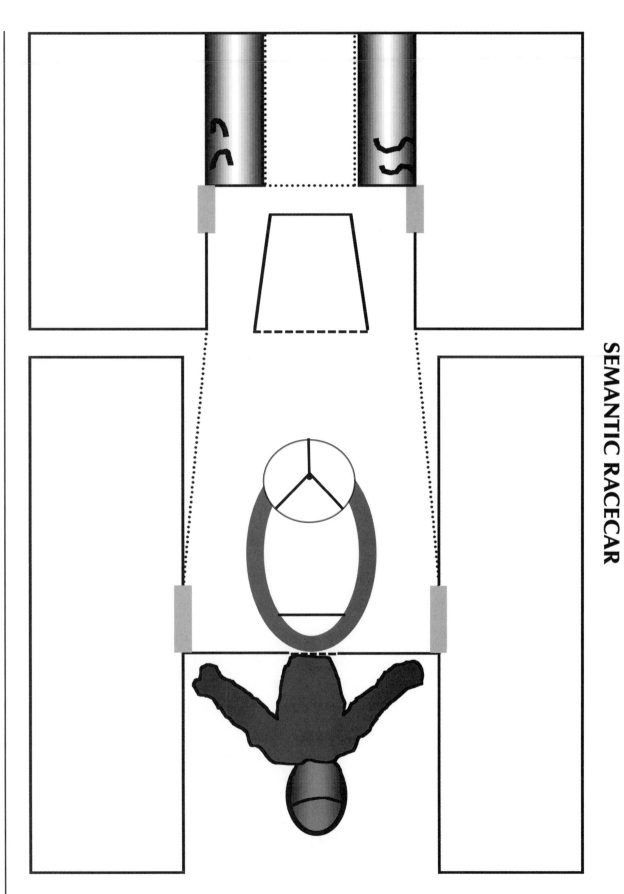

**SEMANTIC RACECAR**

# COMPARISON ROAD

# MAIN IDEA MEMORY STORAGE

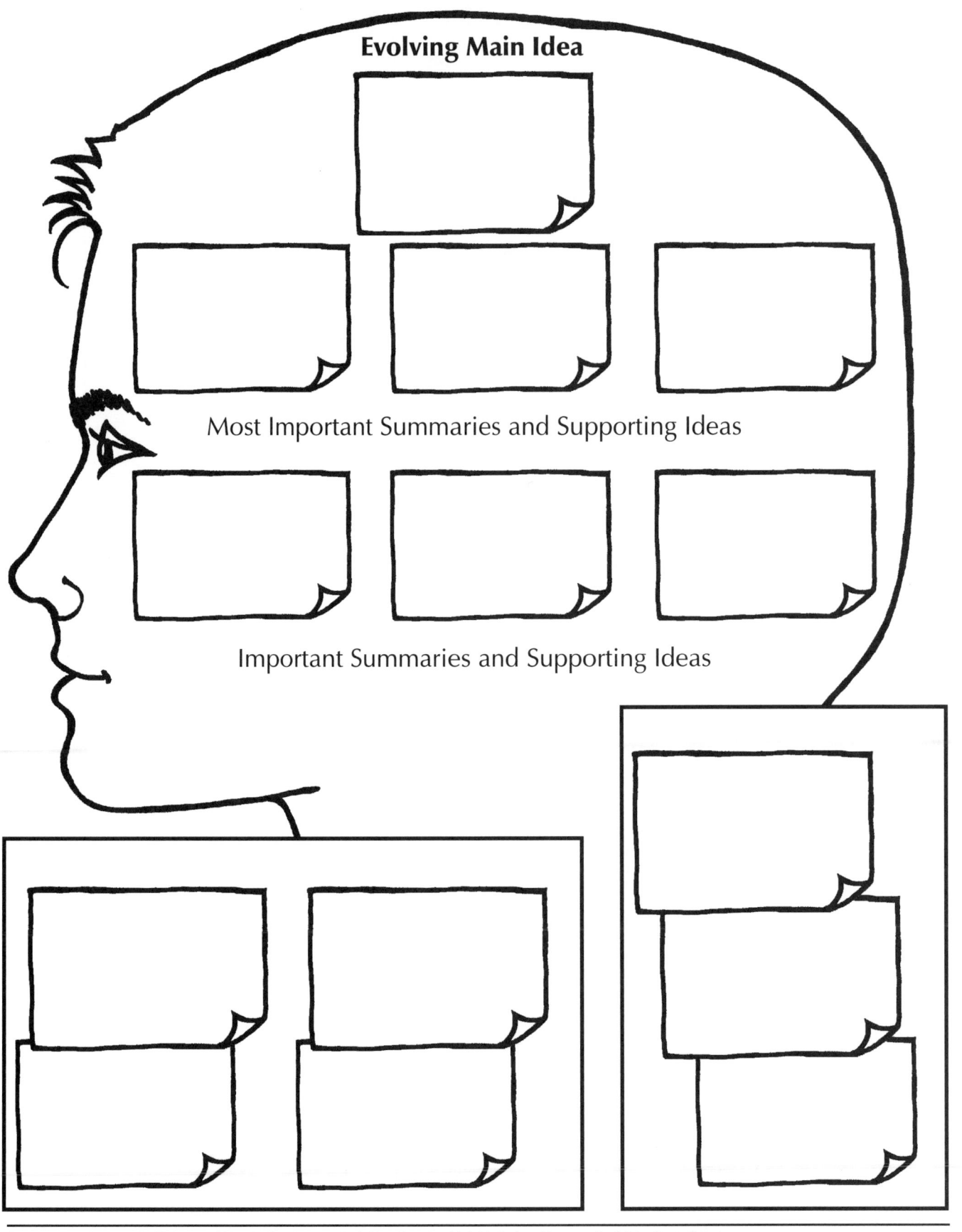

**Evolving Main Idea**

Most Important Summaries and Supporting Ideas

Important Summaries and Supporting Ideas

# CAUSE AND EFFECT DIAGRAM

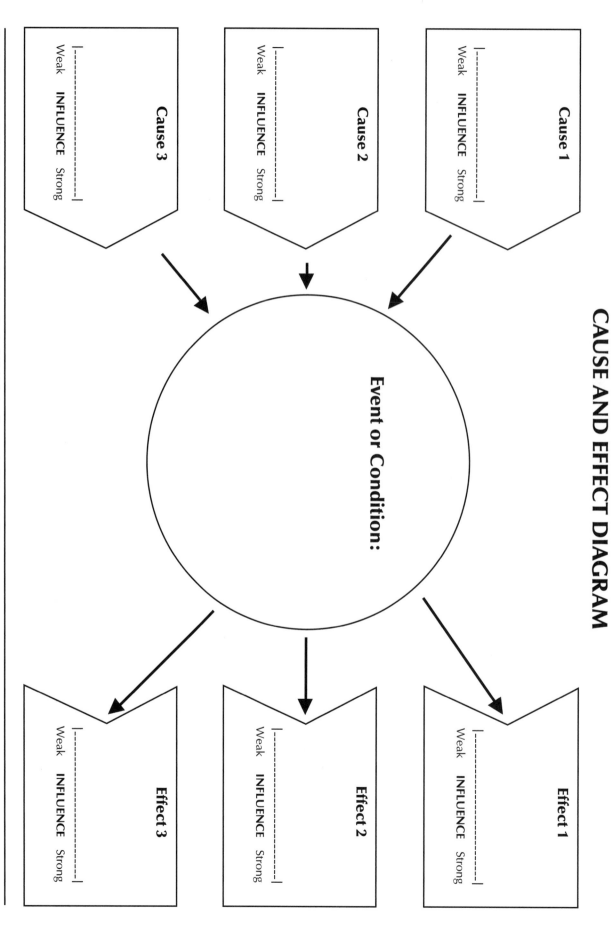

Cause 1

Weak **INFLUENCE** Strong

Cause 2

Weak **INFLUENCE** Strong

Cause 3

Weak **INFLUENCE** Strong

Event or Condition:

Effect 1

Weak **INFLUENCE** Strong

Effect 2

Weak **INFLUENCE** Strong

Effect 3

Weak **INFLUENCE** Strong

# CAUSE AND EFFECT TREE

**Branches and Fruit =**
Visible Signs and Effects

**Roots =**
Underlying Causes and Influences

# CAUSE AND EFFECT TIMELINE

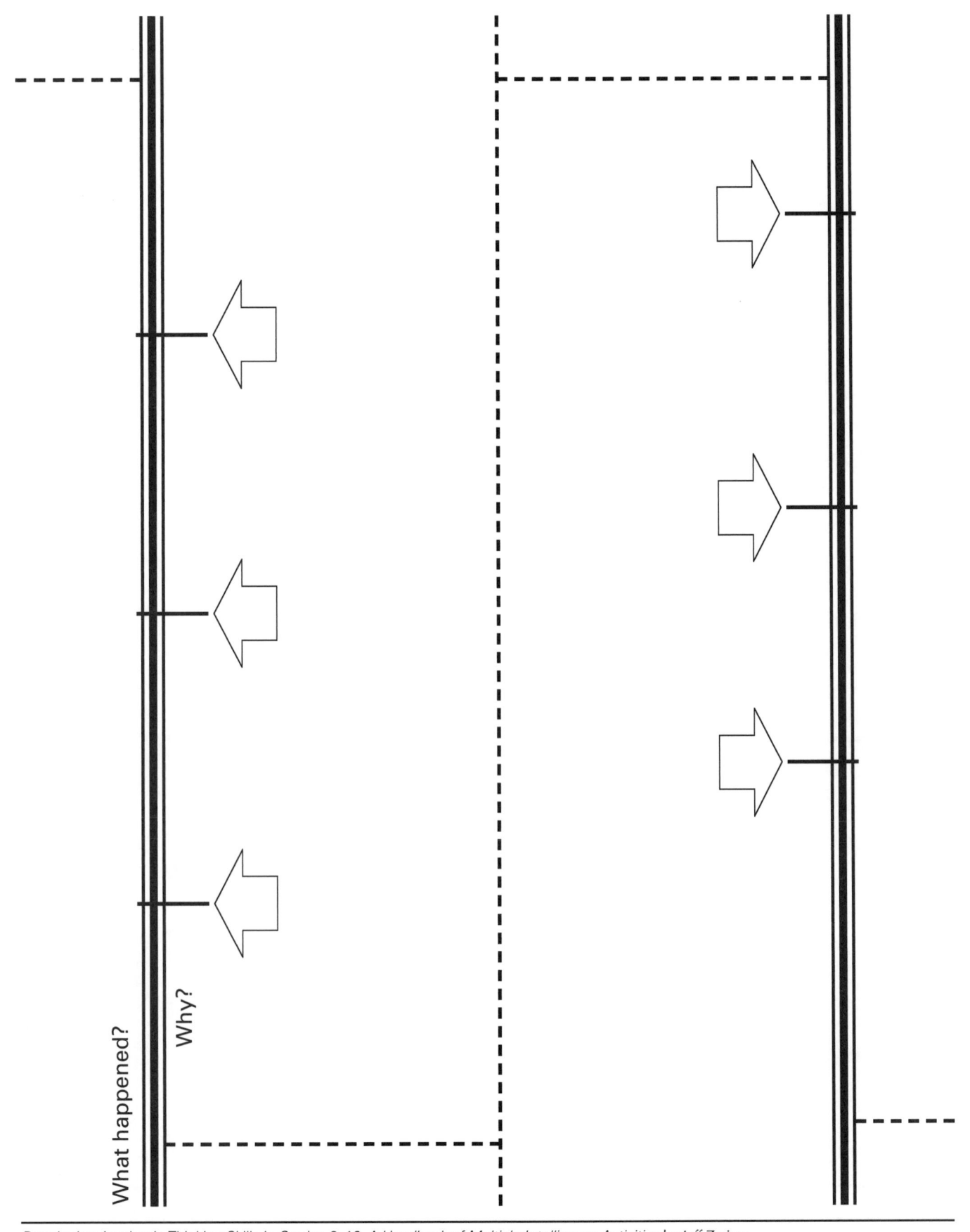

What happened?

Why?

# RIGHT AND LEFT BRAIN PROBLEM PAIRS

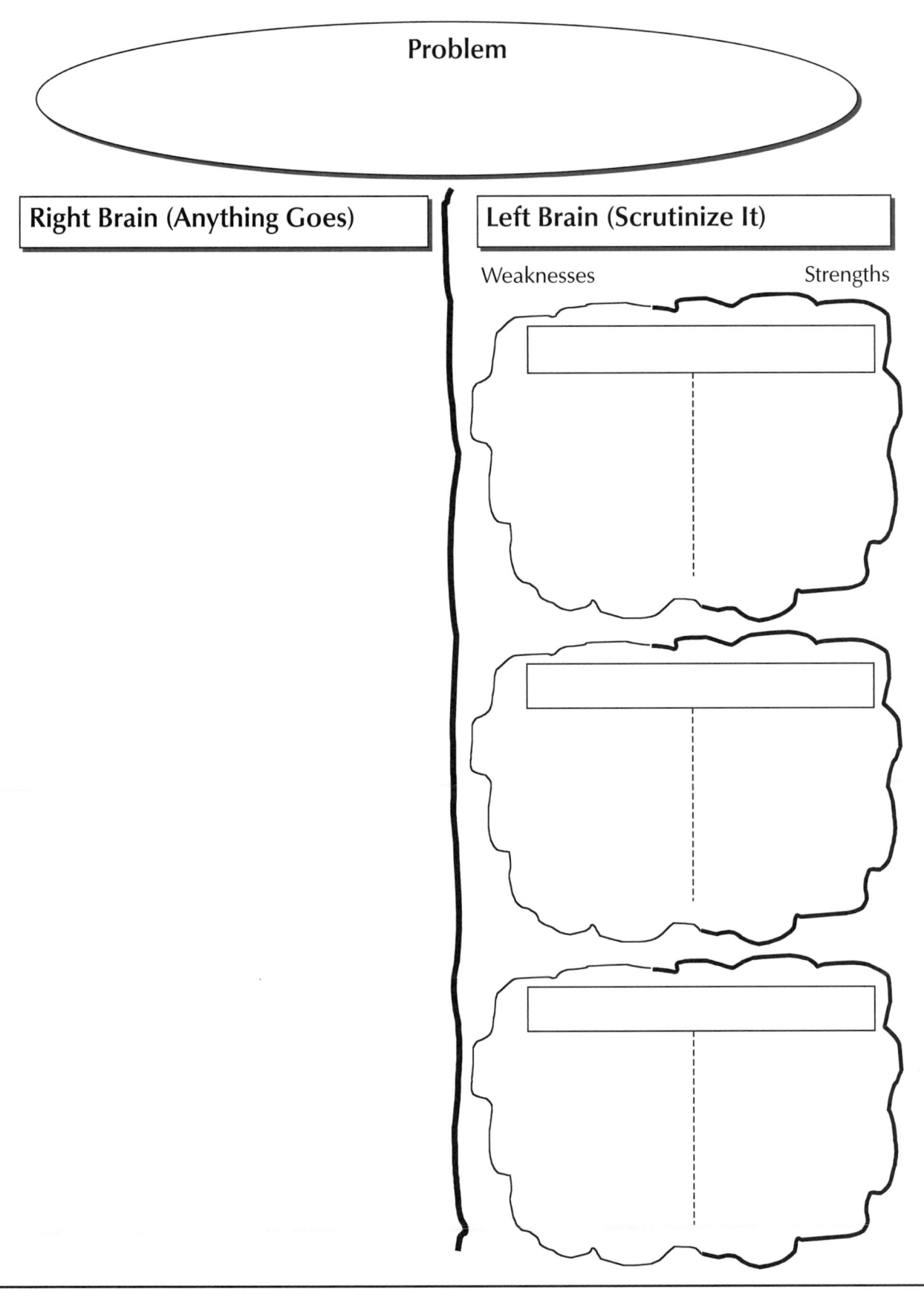

Problem

Right Brain (Anything Goes)

Left Brain (Scrutinize It)

Weaknesses                    Strengths

# HOT AIR BALLOON

# RATE THE REASONS

**Opinion Statement:**

Reason =

Evidence =

Reason =

Evidence =

Reason =

Evidence =

Reason =

Evidence =

Garbage

# PERSUADE PROCESS CHART 1

| PERSUADE Process | Notes |
|---|---|
| **P**ick a side<br>Figure out what is happening, which sides exist, and which side you think will bring about the better solution or decision. | |
| **E**xcite the reader to read your whole piece with a good hook (short shocker, question, quotation, poetic description, statistic) at the beginning, and then give some background information that explains the problem and leads to your thesis statement. | |
| **R**educe all the ideas into one thesis statement that you will argue and support—your point (usually fits best at the end of the introductory paragraph). | |
| **S**tack up statistics, reasons, and evidence for your side (in the body of the paper). | |
| **U**nderstand (recognize) counterarguments, and admit that they have some good points (in the body of the paper). | |
| **A**nswer (address) counterarguments; explain how opposing points are not strong enough (in the body of the paper). | |
| **D**escribe how your arguments are stronger. Use measures such as loss of life, harm to environment, cost, time, morals, respect for nature and humans, religious grounds, law, health, historical trends, or freedom of choice. | |
| **E**nd with a conclusion that sums up your main points and describes how and why the reader should act or change—or not. Edit for punctuation and "persuasion language." | |

# PERSUADE PROCESS CHART 2

| PERSUADE Process | Motion | Visual Reminder |
|---|---|---|
| **P**ick a side<br>Figure out what is happening, which sides exist, and which side you think will bring about the better solution or decision. | Pretend to pick fruit with one hand | |
| **E**xcite the reader to read your whole piece with a good hook (short shocker, question, quotation, poetic description, statistic) at the beginning, and then give some background information that explains the problem and leads to your thesis statement. | Make a hooking or grabbing motion with finger | |
| **R**educe all the ideas into one thesis statement that you will argue and support—your point (usually fits best at the end of the introductory paragraph). | Squeeze an imaginary tube from top to bottom | |
| **S**tack up statistics, reasons, and evidence for your side (in the body of the paper). | Pretend that one hand gets heavier and leans way over | |
| **U**nderstand (recognize) counterarguments, and admit that they have some good points (in the body of the paper). | Use one hand to balance the other and stand it up straight | |
| **A**nswer (address) counterarguments; explain how opposing points are not strong enough (in the body of the paper). | Pretend that one hand gets heavier and leans back over to the side | |
| **D**escribe how your arguments are stronger. Use measures such as loss of life, harm to environment, cost, time, morals, respect for nature and humans, religious grounds, law, health, historical trends, or freedom of choice. | | |
| **E**nd with a conclusion that sums up your main points and describes how and why the reader should act or change—or not. Edit for punctuation and "persuasion language." | Use an imaginary magnifying glass; connect two cords together | |

# PURSE OF PERSUASION

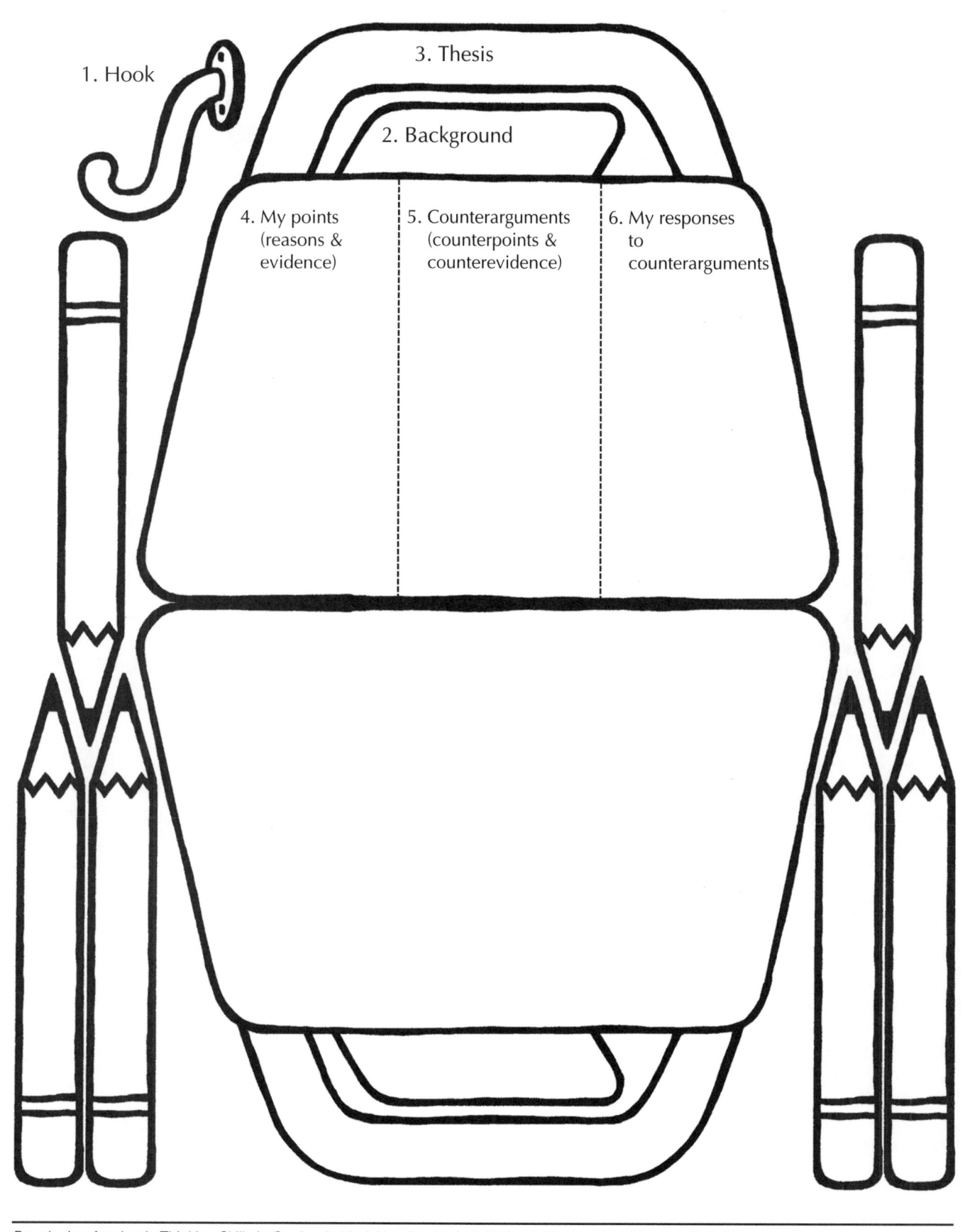

1. Hook

3. Thesis

2. Background

4. My points (reasons & evidence)

5. Counterarguments (counterpoints & counterevidence)

6. My responses to counterarguments

# EXPERT POINT OF VIEW

## As a _____, this is how I think...

# LATEST CARD GAME CRAZE CARDS

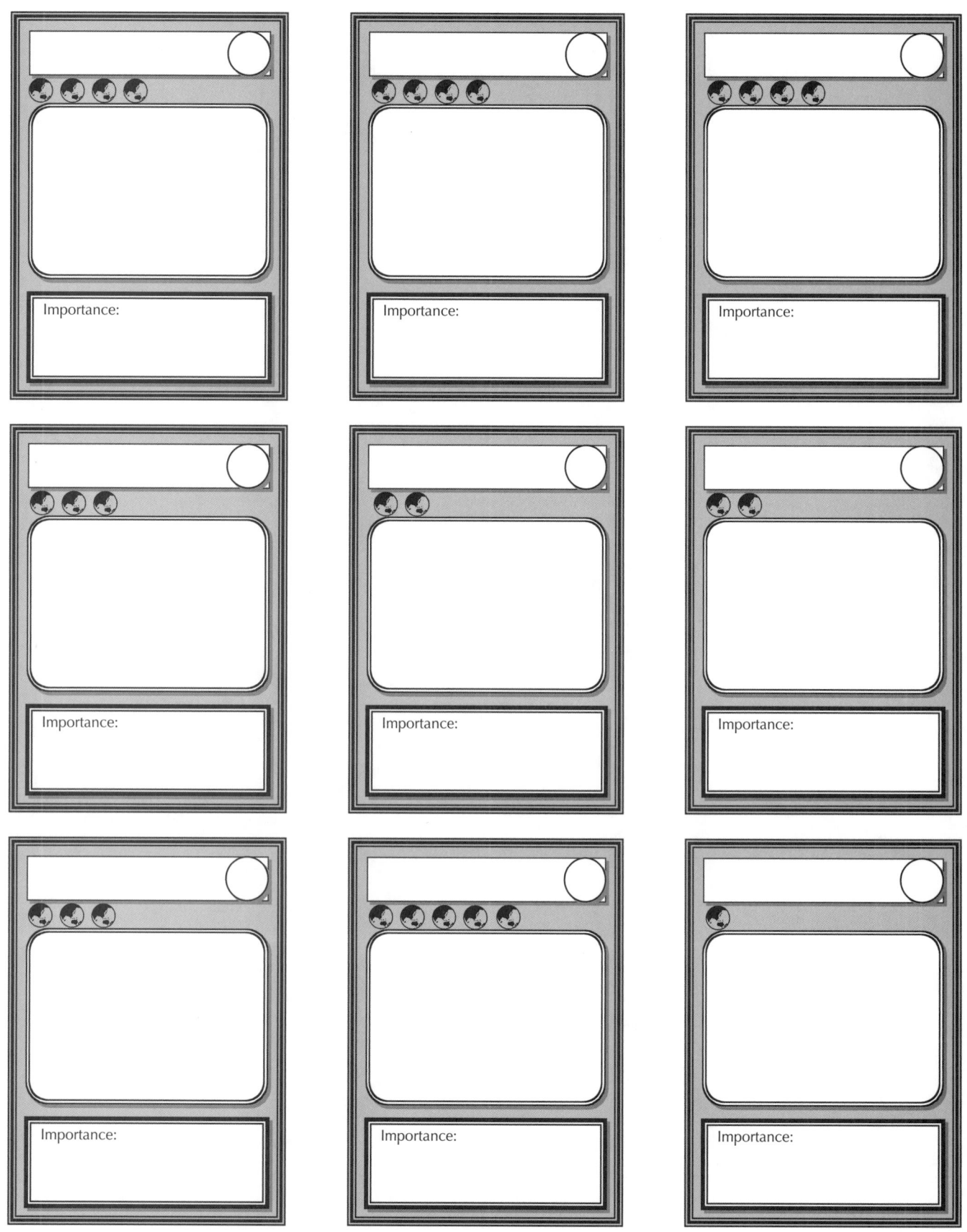

The nine cards each contain the label "Importance:"

# ADMIT AND EXIT TICKETS

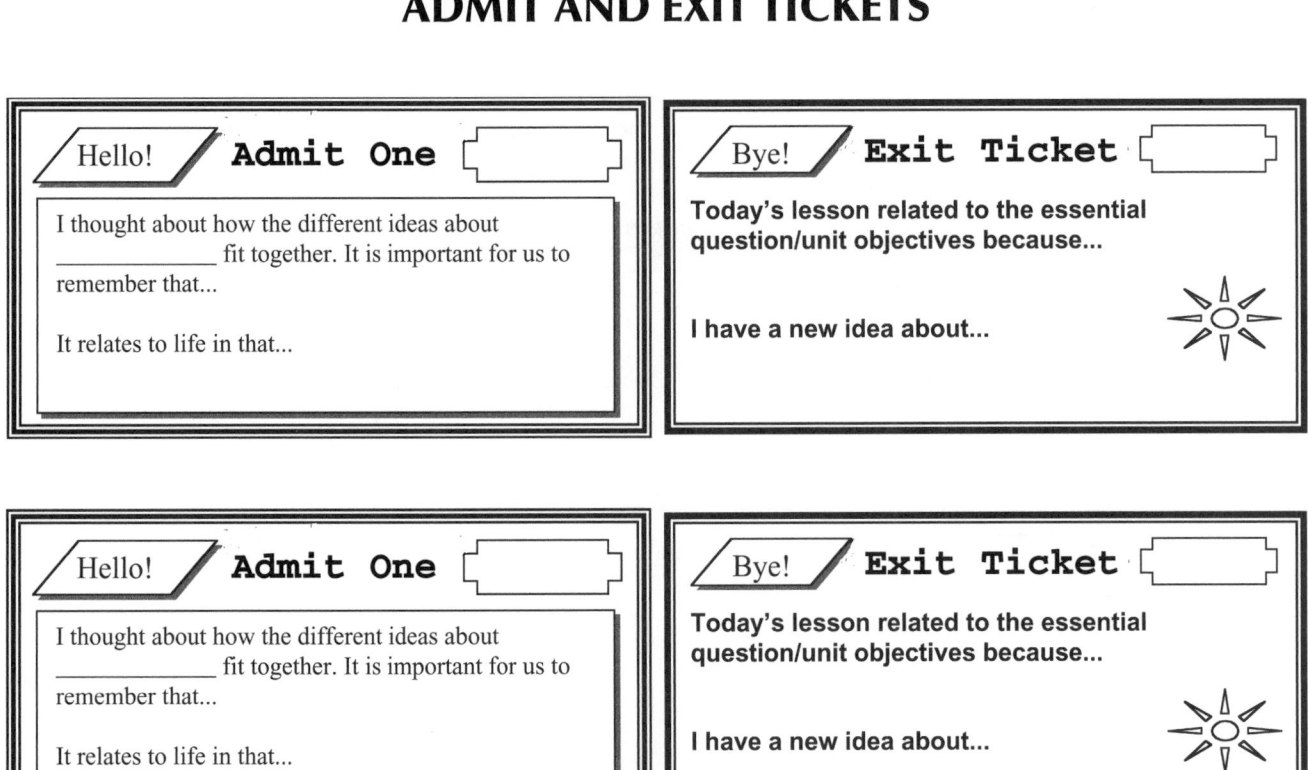

| Hello! / **Admit One** [ ] | Bye! / **Exit Ticket** [ ] |
|---|---|
| I thought about how the different ideas about _____ fit together. It is important for us to remember that...  It relates to life in that... | Today's lesson related to the essential question/unit objectives because...  I have a new idea about... |

| Hello! / **Admit One** [ ] | Bye! / **Exit Ticket** [ ] |
|---|---|
| I thought about how the different ideas about _____ fit together. It is important for us to remember that...  It relates to life in that... | Today's lesson related to the essential question/unit objectives because...  I have a new idea about... |

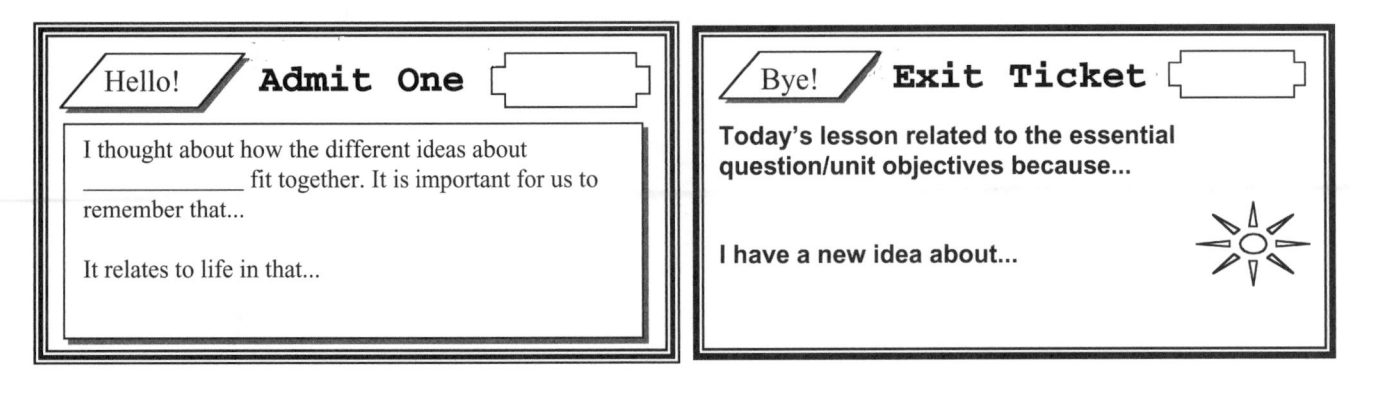

| Hello! / **Admit One** [ ] | Bye! / **Exit Ticket** [ ] |
|---|---|
| I thought about how the different ideas about _____ fit together. It is important for us to remember that...  It relates to life in that... | Today's lesson related to the essential question/unit objectives because...  I have a new idea about... |

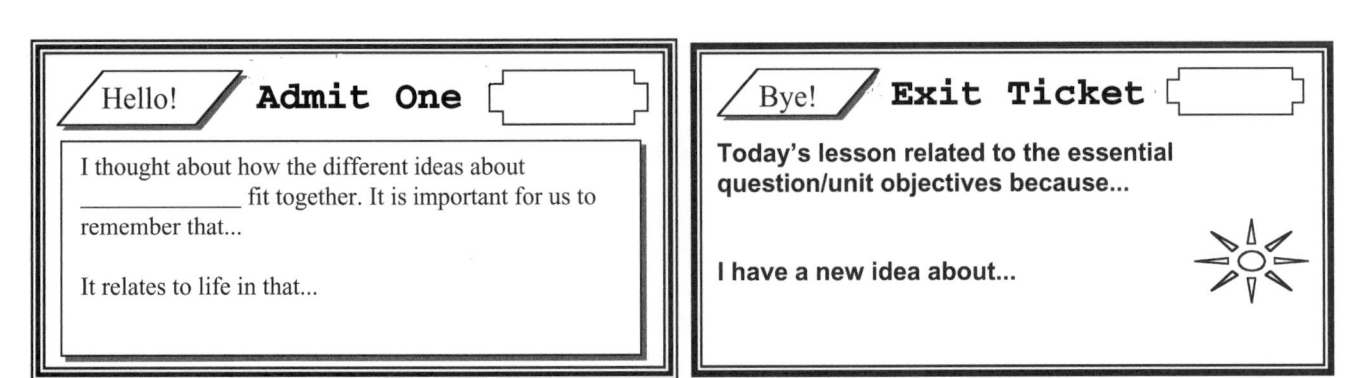

| Hello! / **Admit One** [ ] | Bye! / **Exit Ticket** [ ] |
|---|---|
| I thought about how the different ideas about _____ fit together. It is important for us to remember that...  It relates to life in that... | Today's lesson related to the essential question/unit objectives because...  I have a new idea about... |

# ACADEMIC LANGUAGE INTERPRETATION CHART

**2. What it describes**
(Literal)

*3. Explain...*
*What the author is trying*
*to emphasize*
*How the two are similar*
*Why I think they relate*

**1. Academic language in text**
(Figurative)

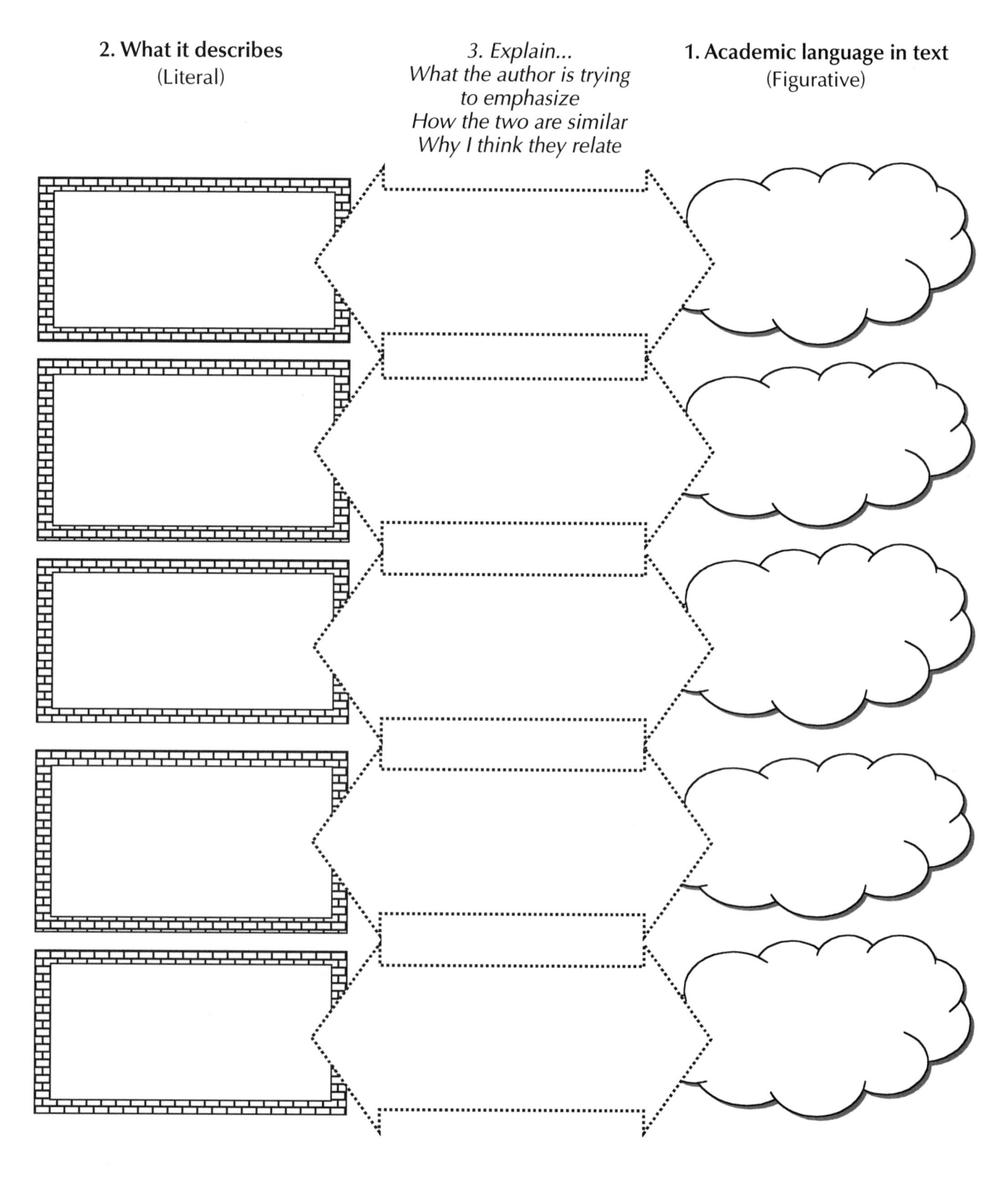

# RESPONSE TO LITERATURE RAP ORGANIZER

| Lines From the Lit Response Rap | Notes and Thoughts |
|---|---|
| First, I reflect on the title, plot, and scene | |
| And what I learn about the characters, flat or deep, <br> I empathize with them, I "walk in their shoes" <br> I infer how they feel by what they say and do | |
| I look for the main challenge or problem to solve | |
| And watch how the characters change and evolve | |
| And all throughout the story I keep one eye <br> on the underlying purpose the author had in mind | |
| The plot on the surface is interesting | |
| But gold nuggets of wisdom are found beneath | |
| I use the other eye to search for universal themes <br> like love, faith, commitment, culture, justice, hope, <br> and greed | |
| And I relate them to my own experience in life <br> I let it teach me how to think about what's wrong <br> and right | |
| I reflect on how the book touched my heart and head | |
| And compare the piece to other works I've read | |
| I look for key quotations and text for support | |
| I interpret figurative language such as metaphors | |
| I become a tough book critic for a moment <br> I evaluate the plot and character development | |
| Finally, I organize it all so it flows like a stream | |

# CENTRAL QUESTION DIAGRAM

## Question with Should..., Could..., Would..., or Do you think that....

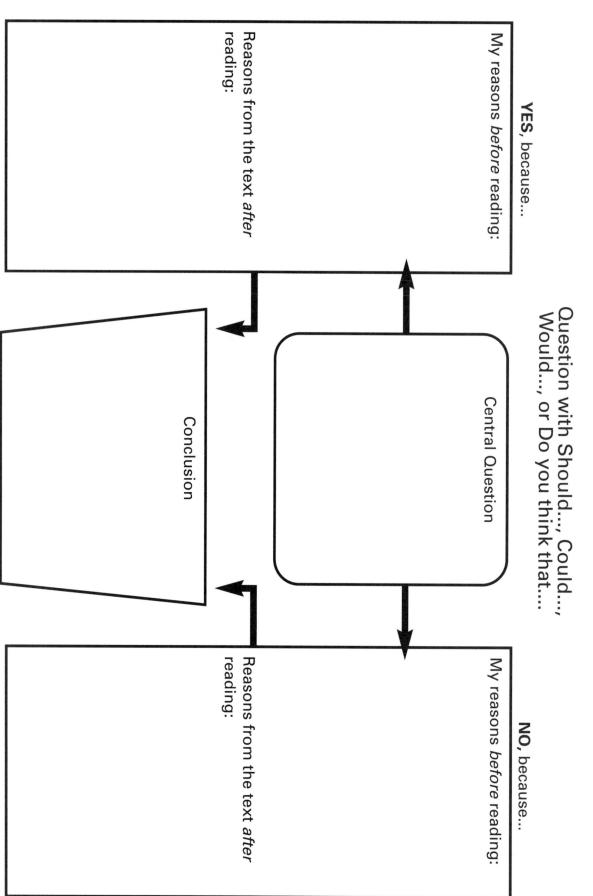

**YES**, because...

My reasons *before* reading:

Reasons from the text *after* reading:

Central Question

Conclusion

**NO**, because...

My reasons *before* reading:

Reasons from the text *after* reading:

# CRITERIA BAR GRAPH

**Main Issue or Question:**

| Criterion 1: | Criterion 2: | Criterion 3: |

## Meets Criteria

**Completely**

**Very Well**

**Well**

**Somewhat**

**Not at all**

Why? How? Evidence?　　　Why? How? Evidence?　　　Why? How? Evidence?

# 3-D BALANCE SCALE

| Criterion: | Criterion: | Criterion: | Criterion: | MVP Criterion: |
|---|---|---|---|---|
| Reason | Reason | Reason | Reason | Reason |
| Evidence | Evidence | Evidence | Evidence | Evidence |

*Fulcrum*

**MVP Criterion:**

This Position: [box]

**Issue/Question Being Evaluated:**

This Position: [box]

# APPENDIX A

# Activities for Multiple Intelligences

## *Artistic–Visual–Spatial Intelligence*

- Draw a world map or timeline that shows and explains important historical events.

- Design an exhibit for a museum on a social theme, scientific concept, or famous person (artist, historical figure, author). Choose what to show and where to present it in the building, then create the explanation signs for each part of the exhibit. Create a poster or television commercial for the exhibit that shows why it is important.

- Close your eyes and visualize a text as it is read aloud by the teacher.

- Draw events, people, and symbols from a story or text as the teacher reads aloud.

- Create an advertisement for a time travel company that can take you back to a certain time period. Explain the positives and negatives and the impact that period had on the future.

- Build or draw a three-dimensional object that symbolizes a concept from the class.

- Explain a piece of abstract art to the class in a short presentation.

- Choose an artist and describe why he or she is popular.

- Give a presentation entitled "What Is Art?" and give some unexpected examples.

- Create a collage on a topic from science, social studies, or English and give a detailed explanation of the pieces.

- Make a brochure or postcard for a travel destination.

- Write a journal from the perspective of a blood cell that travels through the body.

- Make a mobile, sculpture, or puppet show about a topic or story.

- Illustrate a math or science problem.

- Make a map of a story and its events.

- Create your own version of a famous painting (e.g., modernize it), and explain the differences between yours and the original.

- Create a mural about the history of a group of people.

- Design a park or playground for a certain group of people (design it as though money were no object).

- Make a book cover for a story you are reading.

- Design innovative graphic organizers (with some modeling by the teacher) for learning a complex topic.

## Musical Intelligence

- Learn to play a song, and perform it in front of the class.
- Make a presentation on sound waves and how they make up music and all the other sounds in life.
- Make a recording of various types of sounds found in nature or in the community.
- Make a presentation on how to read musical notes.
- Do a research project on a musical instrument or a famous musician and present it to the class.
- Add sound effects to a story or poem to bring out certain characteristics and liven it up; the class can then make the sounds when each part is read in class.
- Listen to various songs, then brainstorm on what makes a song or piece of music good.
- Present a favorite song and say why it is important.
- Design the artwork for a music CD cover.
- Create a song or chant to remember facts from math, science, social studies, or English.
- Interpret the symbols and metaphors in some song lyrics.
- Create a chant that includes the dialogue of characters in a story.
- Create a chant from the perspective of a story character or historical figure.

## Kinesthetic–Bodily Intelligence

- Research an interesting sport from another country and teach the class how to play it.
- Play charades, using characters and concepts as the clues.
- Do math with small items, hands-on objects, and other manipulatives.
- Take apart and put together appliances and machines.
- Create a human body with Popsicle sticks as bones and rubber bands as muscles.
- Design tools to solve a problem of your choice.
- Learn gestures and facial expressions used in other cultures.
- Put together a puzzle.
- Act out various major concepts of science (e.g., planet orbits, cell respiration, etc.).
- Create a drama that shows how a group of people lived in the past.
- Design an experiment that will test a hypothesis.
- Show the class why exercise and healthful diet are good for the body.
- Act out a story or part of a story and explain its significance.
- Invent a dance that helps to illustrate the ideas of a story or poem.
- Create a puppet show and perform it for younger students.
- Learn some sign language and teach it to the class.

- Create a videotaped advertisement for a helpful product or service.
- Come up with hand motions and gestures for important vocabulary words.

## *Social–Interpersonal Intelligence*

- Create a recipe for friendship.
- Develop a script of dialog from a story and dramatically present it to the class.
- Create a group picture book and share it with another group.
- Take one side of a current issue and debate it with another student who takes the other side.
- Create interviews with important characters or personages from the subject you are studying.
- Discuss a text in a group setting with each student having a defined role (e.g., reciprocal teaching).
- Solve problems in a group or in pairs.
- Use checklists and rubrics to self-assess and to improve constructive criticism, active listening, compromising, reaching agreement, and other group norms.
- Use role-play to learn how to see the world through the eyes of another person.
- Plan a major event with other students, such as a fair, car wash, art show, play, museum exhibit, convention, etc.
- In a group, take on the roles of different leaders and discuss a current controversy.
- Do a jigsaw reading in which you and other students become experts on a certain part of a text; share your expertise with your group.
- Role-play a conversation with an important historical figure.
- Work as a class to create class rules and assessment rubrics.

## *Self–Intrapersonal Intelligence*

- Write and illustrate an autobiography.
- Make a personal shield with important areas of your life portrayed by symbols (and a written explanation).
- Describe the three animals that best embody who you are or want to be.
- Make a Venn diagram that compares yourself as you are now with the younger you, one that compares how others see you with who you really are, or one that compares you with how you want to be in the future.
- Keep a journal of thoughts, feelings, and important events of your life.
- Make a compilation of songs that are important to you and say why they are important.

- Write a song or poem that illustrates who you are and discusses the people and events that have formed you.

- Write two columns on a paper listing your strengths and weaknesses.

- Set some short-term and long-term goals for life.

- Make a scrapbook of your life: pictures, sayings, poems, ticket stubs, etc.

- Write an allegory or narrative song about your life.

- Create a To Do list for all of your life, and prioritize the items.

- Relate the content of reading and lessons to personal experiences and future plans.

- React and respond to hypothetical ethical dilemmas.

## Math–Logic Intelligence

- Make a graph or chart of something you do or observe.

- Conduct a survey and describe the results in a graph or table.

- Create a poem or song that describes what you are learning in math.

- Learn how to play chess and teach it to other students.

- Decipher codes (e.g., Egyptian hieroglyphs) and then use them to communicate.

- Use both inductive and deductive reasoning to understand a concept.

- Use spreadsheet software to organize data and design real-world scenarios.

- Draw an accurate scale model of your classroom, house, or school.

- Design ways to measure difficult-to-measure things (e.g., diameter of the moon, distance to Alpha Centauri, etc.).

- Create a poster that explains a complicated math concept to younger students.

- Create a company that makes music CDs, and figure out the minimum cost per CD to make a profit.

- Invent word problems relating current events to current math concepts.

## Scientific–Natural Intelligence

- Keep a journal that gets you to keep asking, "Why?" and searching for answers.

- Refer to the science section of the newspaper and either report on it or do a related experiment.

- Take field trips to aquariums, zoos, forests, tide pools, lakes, etc.

- Watch nature videos in class, and stop to comment on the concepts being learned.

- Take photographs that cover a specific theme; then analyze them and categorize them.

- Cultivate a terrarium or aquarium.

- Make posters on how to respect flora and fauna.

- Grow flowers and vegetables in a classroom garden.
- Use a matrix to classify plants and animals.
- Learn the scientific names of plants and animals.
- Draw a complex diagram or create a 3-D model of food chains from different ecosystems.
- Contemplate the size of the universe, discuss light-years, and design methods for space travel.
- Summarize and synthesize an article of interest from *National Geographic* magazine.
- Use pictures of strange animals to discuss their adaptations, and compare these with human adaptations.
- Research the current state of the environment in different areas of the world, and discuss how to prevent problems.
- Create models, diagrams, and computer images of the greenhouse effect, the water cycle, photosynthesis, plate tectonics, tides, the solar system, the circulatory system, etc.
- Create a way to move around to act out the complex concepts of science.
- Research an extinct or endangered species and report on it to the class.

## *Verbal Intelligence*

- Explain a poem using illustrations or artwork.
- Make up a way to memorize facts, such as a poem or mnemonic device.
- Make up a code language that serves a certain purpose.
- Write a song or poem that describes a story or important grammatical concept.
- Write a letter to a famous person from the past, present, or future.
- Make a picture book to share with younger students.
- Write a persuasive letter to a politician about an important issue.
- Write a letter or poem from the point of view of a famous person, politician, story character, animal, object, Martian, teacher, family member, singer, etc.
- Rewrite a fairy tale from the point of view of a minor character.
- Become an expert on a certain topic and give an oral report to the class.
- Write a journal entry(s) from the point of view of a character in a story.
- Compare two or more different stories that have similar plots; find connections between two very different stories.
- Before you read a text, write a short brainstorm on all that you know about a topic, and share the list with a partner.
- Generate an oral story from experience as the teacher writes it on the board.
- While reading, stop and use sticky notes to write down important thoughts (predictions, summaries, questions, highlights, connections, purposes, etc.).

- Create a newspaper about events in a story or current topic of study (e.g., *Civil War Times, Solar System Gazette*).

- Learn other languages.

- Study the origins of words.

- Choose a song that depicts the tone or mood of a story.

- Debate the decisions made by characters in a story.

- Rewrite the end of a story.

- Write a prequel or sequel to a story.

- Work with classmates to do a Readers Theatre presentation, in which students read parts of a script aloud.

- Make a character chart that outlines the major traits and actions of the characters from a story.

- Assess your own strengths and weaknesses during reading.

# Deep Questions and Controversial Topics

This appendix contains a large number of possible questions and controversial topics for use in discussion and in several of this handbook's activities. In particular, refer to the Persuade Process Charts in chapter 8 and the Deep Questions activity in chapter 12.

## *Philosophical and Reflective Questions*

(These tend to be good "Questions of the Day" for journal entries.)

- If you had $1 million to give to a humanitarian cause, what would the cause be, and why?

- What would you like to have written on your tombstone about how you lived life?

- With which person from the past or present would you like to have dinner? What would you ask him or her?

- What abilities or qualities do you desire? Why?

- If you could choose only one, would you choose to be intelligent or rich? Why?

- Would you take 10 years off your life to give 10 years to another person? Whom?

- What do (might) you want to be in the future and why? (You have to choose something; you are not allowed to say you do not know.)

- What past action would you do differently if you had the chance? Why?

- What personality traits do you think you need to work on to be a perfect person?

- If a Martian landed and only had time to read one book or see one movie, what would you recommend and why?

- If you were invisible, what would you do?

- What is a big risk you have taken? What is a big risk you think you will take someday?

- What items are sentimental to you? Why are they meaningful?

- If you knew you could take a pill to live 1,000 years, would you take it? What would you do during your millennium of life?

- If you won a one-month trip to anywhere, where would you go? What would you do?

- Would you accept $5 million to never see or talk to your best friend again?

- Do you influence others, or do they influence you? Should this change?

- Which historical event would you like to have witnessed? Why?

- Is a doctor's job more important than a teacher's? Than a bus driver's?

- What have you learned from a difficult time in your life?
- Which scientific discovery has been the worst? The best? Why?
- If you could take one object with you after death, what would that be? Why?
- Whom would you take with you after death, if a person could be with you?
- If you could live the life of someone else for one day, who would it be?
- What one or two things would you like never to have known?
- If you had to change your identity completely, what would the new you be like?
- Which of your character traits are you proud of and not proud of?
- Which human accomplishments, past or present, large or small, make you proud to be human? Ashamed?
- If you were told that you were born for a great purpose, what do you think it would be? Or what would you want it to be?
- Describe a moment that changed the world.
- If you could know one thing about the future, what would it be?
- How would you finish the phrase "We were put here on the Earth to..."?
- What is an example of true trust?
- Should we always forgive? Why or why not?
- If you had three wishes, what would they be?
- What do you think about when you look at the stars?
- If you were offered the gift of knowing what will happen 10 years into the future, would you accept it?
- What are three big questions you have about life?
- What is your definition of love?
- If you had 10 minutes to write down your advice for your children, what would it be?
- If you could be the main character in any movie, whom would you be and why?
- If you could say anything to all the people in the world, what would it be?
- If you were old and dying, and doctors could put your brain in another person's body, would you do it? What if the other person's body was of the opposite sex?
- Describe the perfect teacher, parent, or friend.
- Which deceased person would you like to have living again?
- If they were to name a holiday after you, what would it be, and what accomplishment would you like to have honored?
- What event in history would you change, and why? How would things be different now?
- What is you favorite song, movie, or television show, and why?
- Do you think humans are becoming better or worse overall?

- Would you go with aliens to another planet if you had to be gone for two years?
- If you could talk to an animal, which one would it be, and what would you ask?
- What would you do if you could fly?
- What are you afraid of?
- In what ways will you raise your children differently than you were raised?
- What are the three greatest achievements of humankind?
- Is it all right at times to tell lies? To steal?
- What personality traits do you like in the opposite sex?
- What is romance?
- If men had babies instead of women, how would the world be different?
- If you could become an instant expert at something, what would it be, and why?
- If you had to leave the country forever and could take only five things, what would they be?
- If you were paid $1,000 for each A you made, would you study harder?
- Describe yourself to a person in whom you are romantically interested.
- What traditions are important to you or your family?
- What or whom do you miss?
- What are three nouns and three adjectives that describe you? Why?
- If you could be famous for something, what would it be? Why?
- How are you similar to your mother? Father? Grandparents? Siblings?
- What makes you happy?
- Describe the most peaceful and relaxing scene in the world to you.
- What would you miss if you were stranded on a desert island?
- With which three famous living people would you like to be friends?
- If you had to live in the past, when and where would it be? What would you bring with you?
- If you were the first person to step onto the surface of Mars, what would you say?
- Do you think there is life on other planets? Why?
- What is your worst quality? How can you change it?
- If you could do anything you wanted for a year, what would you do?
- What is a happy memory from your childhood?
- What would be your list of 10 Rules for Being a Good Human Being?
- What are some goals you have for your life?
- List 10 things (either abstract or concrete) that you would eliminate to make the world a better place.
- How much money is enough to have a happy life?

- Who are the three greatest people in history?

- What changes would you make in our school system?

- If you could turn yourself into a superhero, what powers would you have and what would you do? What name would you have?

- What are the three greatest inventions of all time? Why?

- How does television affect our society? Children? You?

- If God does not exist, is everything permissible?

- What is happiness?

## Controversial Topics and Questions

### Culture and Society

- Why is it important for people and cultures to create stories?

- What purposes does religion have in a culture?

- What makes someone a hero in a culture?

- What are the advantages of friendship?

- Why is music so important to so many people? To you?

- Why are so few people truly happy?

- What sport (video game, card game, outdoor activity) would you like to invent?

- What can we learn from older and younger generations?

- Will there be too many people in the future? If so, what should we do?

- Should we redistribute wealth to poor people?

- Is money the root of all evil? Why or why not?

- Is capital punishment wrong?

- Should pornography be illegal?

- Is home-schooling more effective than traditional schooling?

- Should parents receive federal vouchers to be used at the school of their choice?

- Should the school curriculum be standardized for all students?

- Are humans evolving as a species? How?

- Does religion improve mental health? Physical health?

- Why are pets so important to people? Why are they used to help sick people feel better?

- Is criminal behavior biologically inherited?

- Are boys and girls treated differently by teachers at school?

- Do gender differences come primarily from nature or nurture?

- Do television talk shows have negative effects on society?

- Are gangs created by a need for family?
- Do certain types of music contribute to crime?
- Should there be a separation of church and state in our schools? How should this be accomplished or maintained?
- What is the biggest problem facing education today?
- Should tracking and ability grouping be eliminated in schools?

**Language, Literature, and Art**

- What is the purpose of art?
- Can a picture paint a thousand words?
- Why do writers write?
- How do the actions and words of story characters reveal their personalities?
- How is language used to control and manipulate us?
- Can we think without using language?
- How is literature like real life? How is it not?
- What can we learn by studying literature?
- How can writing help us understand the world and share our thoughts with others?
- What are some enduring questions and conflicts that authors dealt with centuries ago that are still relevant today?
- Are there universal themes in literature that all cultures possess to some degree?
- What helps a piece of literature to become a classic?
- Can literature serve as a means for social change?

**History and Politics**

- How does the study of history help modern people?
- How do prejudice and bias originate, and how are they overcome?
- What are the most effective ways to stand up to injustice?
- What is a utopian society? Is it attainable?
- Why does the United States sometimes intervene in foreign wars? Should it?
- Does the world need nuclear weapons?
- Should the United States have dropped the atomic bomb on Japan?
- Do people have a right to choose not to go to war, even if they are drafted?
- What is or are the main cause(s) of war?
- Do political campaigns tend more to inform voters or to deceive them?
- Would you change the number of years and terms a U.S. president can serve? In what way, and why?

- Should a society have a right to censor its artists?
- Should the United States be the world's police?
- What is freedom? Is it open to all in U.S. society?
- Which freedoms should we sacrifice in the interest of security?

## Science and Business

- Should doctors be allowed to assist in patient suicides?
- Should politically motivated murders be forgiven for the purposes of reconciliation?
- Should tobacco advertising be banned?
- Can people really own land?
- Should smoking in public be banned?
- Should racist groups be allowed to exist?
- Should cloning be banned?
- Should health insurance companies have access to genetic testing results?
- Should animal experimentation be allowed?
- Should there be stricter laws for controlling pollution? What if it costs more?
- Should the United States end welfare?
- How can we effectively stem global warming?
- Is alcoholism hereditary?
- Should athletes be allowed to use steroids?
- Should genetic engineering be banned?
- Is the Internet a good thing for society?
- Are video games good or bad for children and adolescents?

# List of Familiar Tunes for Making Up Songs

- Are You Sleeping, Brother John?
- Bad to the Bone
- Ballad of Jed Clampett
- Camptown Races
- Cielito Lindo
- Daylight Come and I Want to Go Home
- *Gilligan's Island* theme
- Guantanamera
- Head, Shoulders, Knees, and Toes
- Heard It Through the Grapevine
- Heartbreak Hotel
- Here Comes the Sun
- The Hokey Pokey
- Home on the Range
- If You're Happy and You Know It
- I'm Looking Over a Four-Leaf Clover
- Inch by Inch, Row by Row
- Jingle Bells
- La Bamba
- Lean on Me
- Lime in the Coconut
- London Bridge

- Louie, Louie
- Old Lady Swallowed a Fly
- Old MacDonald Had a Farm
- On Top of Old Smokey
- Pop! Goes the Weasel
- Rapper's Delight
- Rock Around the Clock
- Row, Row, Row Your Boat
- She'll Be Coming 'Round the Mountain
- Skip to My Lou
- Ten Little Piggies
- This Little Light of Mine
- This Old Man
- Three Blind Mice
- Twinkle, Twinkle, Little Star
- We Will Rock You
- What I Like About You
- The Wheels on the Bus Go Round and Round
- Yankee Doodle
- Yellow Submarine
- You've Lost That Loving Feeling

# REFERENCES AND SUGGESTED RESOURCES

## References

Ackerman, D., & Perkins, D.J. (1989). Integrating thinking and learning skills across the curriculum. In H. Jacobs (Ed.), *Interdisciplinary curriculum: Design and implementation* (pp. 77–95). Alexandria, VA: Association for Supervision and Curriculum Development.

Alvermann, D.E. (1991). The discussion web: A graphic aid for learning across the curriculum. *The Reading Teacher, 45*, 92–99.

Alvermann, D.E., & Phelps, S.F. (2002). *Content reading and literacy* (3rd ed.). Boston: Allyn & Bacon.

Armstrong, T. (2003). *The multiple intelligences of reading and writing: Making the words come alive*. Alexandria, VA: Association for Supervision and Curriculum Development.

Baumann, J.F. (1986). *Teaching main idea comprehension*. Newark, DE: International Reading Association.

Bean, T., Singer, H., & Cowan, S. (1985). Analogical study guides: Improving comprehension in science. *Journal of Reading, 29*, 246–250.

Benjamin, A. (2002). *Differentiated instruction: A guide for middle and high school teachers*. Larchmont, NY: Eye on Education.

Berman, S. (2001). Thinking in context: Teaching for open-mindedness and critical understanding. In A.L. Costa (Ed.), *Developing minds: A resource book for teaching thinking* (3rd ed., pp. 11–17). Alexandria, VA: Association for Supervision and Curriculum Development.

Beyer, B.K. (1987). *Practical strategies for the teaching of thinking*. Boston: Allyn & Bacon.

Beyer, B.K. (2001a). Infusing thinking in history and social studies. In A.L. Costa (Ed.), *Developing minds: A resource book for teaching thinking* (3rd ed., pp. 317–325). Alexandria, VA: Association for Supervision and Curriculum Development.

Beyer, B.K. (2001b). Practical strategies for direct instruction thinking skills. In A.L. Costa (Ed.), *Developing minds: A resource book for teaching thinking* (3rd ed., pp. 393–400). Alexandria, VA: Association for Supervision and Curriculum Development.

Beyer, B.K. (2001c). Developing a scope and sequence for thinking skills instruction. In A.L. Costa (Ed.), *Developing minds: A resource book for teaching thinking* (3rd ed., pp. 248–252). Alexandria, VA: Association for Supervision and Curriculum Development.

Bloom, B.S., Engelhar, M.D., Furst, E.J., Hill, W.H., & Krathwohl, D.R. (Eds.). (1956). *Taxonomy of educational objectives: The classification of educational goals (Handbook I: Cognitive domain)*. New York: Longman.

Bruner, J. (1985). Models of the learner. *Educational Researcher, 14*(6), 5–8.

Buehl, D. (2001). *Classroom strategies for interactive learning* (2nd ed.). Newark, DE: International Reading Association.

Carr, J. (2001). *A map for teaching and assessing California's English language development (ELD) and English language arts (ELA) standards for English learners*. San Francisco: WestEd.

Chamot, A.U., & O'Malley, J.M. (1993). *The CALLA handbook: Implementing the Cognitive Academic Language Learning Approach*. Upper Saddle River, NJ: Pearson.

Cohen, E.G. (1994). *Designing groupwork*. New York: Teachers College Press.

Costa, A.L. (2001). *Developing minds: A resource book for teaching thinking* (3rd ed.). Alexandria, VA: Association for Supervision and Curriculum Development.

Cunningham, P.M. (1995). Phonics they use: Words for reading and writing. New York: Addison-Wesley/Longman.

Davey, B. (1983). Think-aloud: Modeling the cognitive processes of reading comprehension. *Journal of Reading, 27*, 44–47.

Dennis, J.M., Griffin, S.M., & Wills, R.D. (1981). *English through drama: An introduction to language-learning activities developed by Mark Rittenberg and Penelope Kreitzer*. San Francisco: Alemany.

Dequine, L. (2003). *Strategies for persuasive writing*. Unpublished notes.

Dewey, J. (1938). *Experience and education*. New York: Macmillan.

Druyan, S. (1997). Effect of the kinesthetic conflict on promoting scientific reasoning. *Journal of Research in Science Teaching, 34*(10), 1083–1099.

Dutro, S., & Moran, C. (2003). Rethinking English language instruction: An architectural approach. In G.G. García (Ed.), *English learners: Reaching the highest level of English literacy* (pp. 227–258). Newark, DE: International Reading Association.

Farr, R. (2001). Think-along/think-alouds and comprehending lead to better comprehension. *California Reader, 34*(2), 29–33.

Freire, P., & Macedo, D. (1987). *Literacy: Reading the word and the world.* Westport, CT: Bergin & Garvey.

Gagnon, P. (Ed.). (1989). *Historical literacy: The case for history in American education.* New York: Macmillan.

Gardner, H. (1999). *Frames of mind: The theory of multiple intelligences.* New York: Basic.

Gee, J.P. (2003). *What video games have to teach us about learning and literacy.* New York: Palgrave Macmillan.

Genesee, F., & Upshur, J.A. (1996). *Classroom-based evaluation in second language education.* Cambridge, UK: Cambridge University Press.

Gregory, G.H., & Chapman, C. (2002). *Differentiated instructional strategies: One size doesn't fit all.* Thousand Oaks, CA: Corwin.

Hall, L.E. (1989). The effects of cooperative learning on achievement: A meta-analysis. *Dissertation Abstracts International, 50,* 343A.

Heacox, D. (2001). *Differentiating instruction in the regular classroom: How to reach and teach all learners, grades 3–12.* Minneapolis, MN: Free Spirit.

Hyerle, D. (1996). *Visual tools for constructing knowledge.* Alexandria, VA: Association for Supervision and Curriculum Development.

Ivie, S. (1998). Ausubel's learning theory: An approach to teaching higher order thinking skills. *High School Journal, 82*(1), 35–42.

Jaworski, A., & Coupland, N. (Eds.). (1999). *The discourse reader.* London: Routledge.

Johns, J.L., & Berglund, R.L. (2001). *Strategies for content area learning: Vocabulary comprehension response.* Dubuque, IA: Kendall/Hunt.

Johnson, D.W., Maruyama, G., Johnson, R., Nelson, D., & Skon, L. (1981). Effects of cooperative, competitive, and individualistic goal structures on achievement: A meta-analysis. *Psychological Bulletin, 89*(1), 47–62.

Knight, J.E. (1990). Coding journal entries. *Journal of Reading, 34,* 42–47.

Kolb, G.R. (1996). Read with a beat: Developing literacy through music and song. *The Reading Teacher, 50,* 76–77.

Lowry, L. (1993). *The giver.* Boston: Houghton Mifflin.

Lyman, F.T. (1987). Think trix: A classroom tool for thinking in response to reading. *Reading Issues and Practices, 4,* 15–18.

Lyons, C., & Pinnell, G. (2001). *Systems for change in literacy education: A guide to professional development.* Portsmouth, NH: Heinemann.

Marzano, R.J. (1988). *Dimensions of thinking: A framework for curriculum and instruction.* Alexandria, VA: Association for Supervision and Curriculum Development.

Marzano, R.J. (2000). *Designing a new taxonomy of educational objectives.* Thousand Oaks, CA: Corwin.

Marzano, R.J., Pickering, D.J., & Arredondo, D.E. (1997). *Dimensions of learning: Teacher's manual* (2nd ed.). Alexandria, VA: Association for Supervision and Curriculum Development.

Marzano, R.J., Pickering, D.J., & Pollock, J.E. (2001). *Classroom instruction that works: Research-based strategies for increasing student achievement.* Alexandria, VA: Association for Supervision and Curriculum Development.

Merkley, D., & Jefferies, D. (2001). Guidelines for implementing a graphic organizer. *The Reading Teacher, 54,* 350–357.

Miller, A., & Coen, D. (1994). The case for music in the schools. *Phi Delta Kappan, 75*(6), 459–461.

Mooney, M., Hoyt, L., & Parkes, B. (2003). *Exploring informational texts: From theory to practice.* Portsmouth, NH: Heinemann.

Pace, D., Pugh, S.L., & Smith, B.J. (1997). *Studying for history.* Upper Saddle River, NJ: Pearson.

Palincsar, A.S., & Brown, A.L. (1984). Reciprocal teaching of comprehension-fostering and comprehension-monitoring activities. *Cognition and Instruction, 2,* 117–175.

Peregoy, S., & Boyle, O. (2000). *Reading, writing, & learning in ESL: A resource book for K–12 teachers* (3rd ed.). Reading, MA: Pearson Addison Wesley.

Pugh, S., Hicks, J., & Davis, M. (1997). *Metaphorical ways of knowing: The imaginative nature of thought and expression.* Urbana, IL: National Council of Teachers of English.

Readence, J.E., Bean, T.W., & Baldwin, R.S. (2001). *Content area literacy: An integrated approach* (7th ed.). Dubuque, IA: Kendall-Hunt.

Rivard, J.D., & Bieske, G.B. (1993). Open to suggestion. *Journal of Reading, 36,* 492–493.

Rosenblatt, L.M. (1996). *Literature as exploration*. New York: Modern Language Association of America.

Rosenshine, B., & Meister, C. (1992). The use of scaffolds for teaching higher-level cognitive strategies. *Educational Leadership, 49*(7), 26–33.

Ruggiero, V.R. (2000). *The art of thinking: A guide to critical and creative thought* (6th ed.). New York: Pearson Longman.

Slavin, R. (1994). *Cooperative learning: Theory, research and practice* (2nd ed.). Boston: Pearson Allyn & Bacon.

Snow, M.A., & Brinton, D.M. (1997). *The content-based classroom: Perspectives on integrating language and content*. Upper Saddle River, NJ: Pearson Higher Education.

Stauffer, R. (1980). *The language experience approach to the teaching of reading*. New York: HarperCollins.

Sternberg, R.J. (1997). *Thinking styles*. New York: Cambridge University Press.

Stipek, D.J. (2001). *Motivation to learn: Integrating theory and practice* (4th ed.). Boston: Pearson Allyn & Bacon.

Tierney, R.J. (1998). Literacy assessment reform: Shifting beliefs, principled possibilities, and emerging practices. *The Reading Teacher, 51*, 374–390.

van den Broek, P., & Kremer, K. (2000). The mind in action: What it means to comprehend during reading. In B.M. Taylor, M.F. Graves, & P. van den Broek (Eds.), *Reading for meaning: Fostering comprehension in the middle grades* (pp. 1–31). New York: Teachers College Press; Newark, DE: International Reading Association.

Vygotsky, L.S. (1962). *Thought and language*. Cambridge: MIT Press.

Vygotsky, L.S. (1978). *Mind in society: The development of higher psychological processes*. (M. Cole, V. John-Steiner, S. Scribner, & E. Souberman, Eds. & Trans.). Cambridge, MA: Harvard University Press. (Original work published 1934)

Vygotsky, L.S. (1981). The genesis of higher mental functions. In J.V. Wertsch (Ed.), *The concept of activity in Soviet psychology* (pp. 144–188). Armonk, NY: M.E. Sharpe.

Wiggins, G., & McTighe, J. (2000). *Understanding by design*. Englewood Cliffs, NJ: Prentice Hall.

Wineburg, S. (2001). *Historical thinking and other unnatural acts: Charting the future of teaching the past*. Philadelphia: Temple University Press.

Wolfe, P. (2001). *Brain matters: Translating research into classroom practice*. Alexandria, VA: Association for Supervision and Curriculum Development.

Zwiers, J. (2004). *Building reading comprehension habits in grades 6–12: A toolkit of classroom activities*. Newark, DE: International Reading Association.

## Literature Cited

Golding, W. (1997). *Lord of the flies*. New York: Riverhead.

Hinton, S.E. (1997). *The outsiders*, New York: Puffin.

Hughes, L. (1994). *Collected poems*. New York: Knopf.

Lee, H. (1988). *To kill a mockingbird*. Boston: Little Brown.

Sachar, L. (1998). *Holes*. New York: Dell.

## Suggested Resources

Cummins, J. (1989). *Empowering minority students*. Sacramento: California Association for Bilingual Education.

Delpit, L.D. (1993). The silenced dialogue: Power and pedagogy in educating other people's children. In L. Weis & M. Fine (Eds.), *Beyond silenced voices: Class, race, and gender in United States schools* (pp. 119–142). Albany: State University of New York Press.

Delpit, L.D. (1995). *Other people's children: Cultural conflict in the classroom*. New York: New Press.

Duffala, J. (1987). *The teacher as artist*. Santa Rosa, CA: Author.

Eberle, B. (1997). *Scamper on*. Waco, TX: Prufrock.

Freed, C., & Peña, R. (2001). Minority education and analytical thinking skills: Traditionalizing disempowerment. *High School Journal, 85*(2), 24–32.

Heath, S.B. (1983). *Ways with words: Language, life, and work in communities and classrooms*. New York: Cambridge University Press.

Marzano, R.J. (2003). *What works in schools: Translating research into action*. Alexandria, VA: Association for Supervision and Curriculum Development.

O'Malley, J.M., & Pierce, L.V. (1996). *Authentic assessment for English language learners: Practical approaches for teachers*. Upper Saddle River, NJ: Pearson Higher Education.

Pressley, M., Burkell, J., Cariglia-Bull, T., Lysynchuk, L., McGoldrick, J.A., Schneider, B., et al. (1990). *Cognitive strategy instruction*. Cambridge, MA: Brookline.

Rillero, P., Zambo, R., Cleland, J., & Ryan, J. (1996). Write from the start: Writing to learn science. *Science Scope, 19*(7), 30–32.

Rogoff, B. (1990). *Apprenticeship in thinking: Cognitive development in social context*. New York: Oxford University Press.

Urquhart, A.H., & Weir, C.J. (1998). *Reading in a second language: Process, product, and practice*. New York: Longman.

U.S. Bureau of Census. (1993). *Current population reports, P25-1104: Population projections of the United States, by age, sex, race, and Hispanic origin: 1993 to 2050*. Washington DC: U.S. Government Printing Office.

# INDEX

*Note:* Page numbers followed by *f* and *r* indicate figures and reproducibles, respectively.